Stockholm
day BY day™

1st Edition

by Mary Anne Evans

WILEY

A John Wiley and Sons, Ltd, Publication

Contents

UK Publisher: Sally Smith
Executive Project Editor: Daniel Mersey
Commissioning Editor: Fiona Quinn
Project Editor: Hannah Clement
Cartographer: Tim Lohnes
Photo Research: Jill Emeny

Wiley also publishes its books in a variety of electronic formats. Some
content that appears in print may not be available in electronic books.

British Library Cataloguing in Publication Data

A catalogue record for this book is available from the British Library

ISBN: 978-0-470-69974-4

Typeset by Wiley Indianapolis Composition Services

Printed and bound in China by RR Donnelley

5 4 3 2 1

Organizing your time. That's what this guide is all about.

Other guides give you long lists of things to see and do and then expect you to fit the pieces together. The Day by Day guides are different. These guides tell you the best of everything, and then they show you how to see it *in the smartest, most time-efficient way*. Our authors have designed detailed itineraries organized by time, neighborhood, or special interest. And each tour comes with a bulleted map that takes you from stop to stop.

Looking forward to the taste of salt air as you take a Baltic boat trip, walking the winding medieval streets of Gamla Stan or shopping for modern design pieces? Thinking about savouring Swedish tastes or drinking an acquavit at midnight looking over the waters? Whatever your interest or schedule, the Day by Days give you the smartest routes to follow. Not only do we take you to the top attractions, hotels, and restaurants, but we also help you access those special moments that locals get to experience—those "finds" that turn tourists into travelers.

The Day by Days are also your top choice if you're looking for one complete guide for all your travel needs. The best hotels and restaurants for every budget, the greatest shopping values, the wildest nightlife—it's all here.

Why should you trust our judgment? Because our authors personally visit each place they write about. They're an independent lot who say what they think and would never include places they wouldn't recommend to their best friends. They're also open to suggestions from readers. If you'd like to contact them, please send your comments our way at feedback@frommers.com, and we'll pass them on.

Enjoy your Day by Day guide—the most helpful travel companion you can buy. And have the trip of a lifetime.

Warm regards,

Kelly Regan

Kelly Regan, Editorial Director
Frommer's Travel Guides

About the Author

After co-writing learned volumes on Japanese prints and guitars, Mary Anne Evans turned to her more immediate surroundings and became one of the leading travel writers on London and Britain, particularly on restaurants. Several guide books and many magazine articles later, Europe beckoned. Stockholm has always been close to her heart as she is married to a Finn and has spent many happy holidays in Stockholm and Finland.

Acknowledgments

My special thanks to photographer Ossi Laurila for his wonderful pictures, and to Sylvie Kjellin at the Stockholm Visitors Board and Philippa Sutton at Visit Sweden for all their sound advice and help. And finally to Camilla Zedendahl who showed me so much of Sigtuna, the Viking town that makes such a great start or finish to a Stockholm visit.

An Additional Note

Please be advised that travel information is subject to change at any time—and this is especially true of prices. We therefore suggest that you write or call ahead for confirmation when making your travel plans. The authors, editors, and publisher cannot be held responsible for the experiences of readers while traveling. Your safety is important to us, however, so we encourage you to stay alert and be aware of your surroundings.

Star Ratings, Icons & Abbreviations

Every hotel, restaurant, and attraction listing in this guide has been ranked for quality, value, service, amenities, and special features using a **star-rating system.** Hotels, restaurants, attractions, shopping, and nightlife are rated on a scale of zero stars (recommended) to three stars (exceptional). In addition to the star-rating system, we also use a **kids icon** to point out the best bets for families. Within each tour, we recommend cafes, bars or restaurants where you can take a break. Each of these stops appears in a shaded box marked with a coffee cup–shaped bullet **☕**.

The following **abbreviations** are used for credit cards:

AE	American Express	DISC	Discover	V	Visa
DC	Diners Club	MC	MasterCard		

Frommers.com

Now that you have this guidebook to help you plan a great trip, visit our website at **www.frommers.com** for additional travel information on more than 4,000 destinations. We update features regularly to give you instant access to the most current trip-planning information available. At Frommers. com, you'll find scoops on the best airfares, lodging rates, and car rental bargains. You can even book your travel online through our reliable travel booking partners.

A Note on Prices

In the "Take a Break" and "Best Bets" sections of this book, we have used a system of dollar signs to show a range of costs for 1 night in a hotel (the price of a double-occupancy room) or the cost of an entree (main meal) at a restaurant. Use the following table to decipher the dollar signs:

Cost	Hotels	Restaurants
$	under $100	under $10
$$	$100–$200	$10–$20
$$$	$200–$300	$20–$30
$$$$	$300–$400	$30–$40
$$$$$	over $400	over $40

An Invitation to the Reader

In researching this book, we discovered many wonderful places—hotels, restaurants, shops, and more. We're sure you'll find others. Please tell us about them, so we can share the information with your fellow travelers in upcoming editions. If you were disappointed with a recommendation, we'd love to know that, too. Please write to:

Frommer's Stockholm Day by Day, 1st Edition
Wiley Publishing, Inc. • 111 River St. • Hoboken, NJ 07030-577

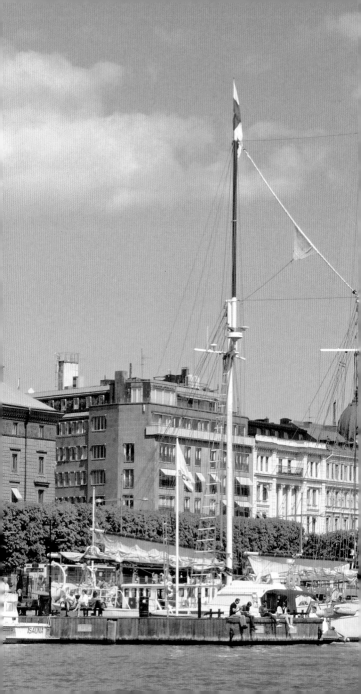

12 Favorite
Moments

12 Favorite **Moments**

1 Boat trips
2 Hiring a boat
3 Vasamuseet
4 Wandering through Gamla Stan
5 Shopping for Swedish design
6 New Swedish cooking at Leijontornet
7 Centralbadet
8 Skating in winter
9 The Nationalmuseum
10 Partying the night away
11 Looking from on high
12 Östermalms Saluhall

Ⓜ	Metro Stop
+	Church
ⓘ	Information
⊠	Post Office
✡	Synagogue

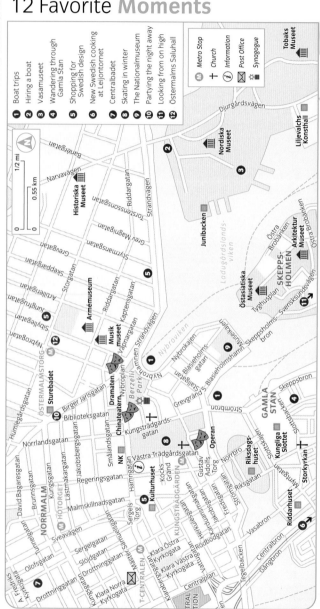

ou can just sit back and look at the views over one of the world's most beautiful cities. Alternatively, you can go back to the Middle Ages on a stroll through Gamla Stan, discover Stockholm's exciting new cooking, row a boat along a tree-lined canal in summer, or skate on the sea in winter. Stockholm is a city for all seasons and for all pleasures. Here are some of my favorite things to do in Sweden's beautiful and elegant capital.

❶ Slipping through Stockholm on a boat. Stockholm is a city where the water is never far away. Getting on a boat and going almost anywhere—sightseeing around the main islands, out to the Baltic Sea Archipelago, or through the sheltered waterways onto Lake Mälaren—is the first thing I always do every time I arrive in Stockholm. If you do the trip in winter, the sound of ice breaking replaces the cries of seagulls. See p 25.

❷ Hiring a boat and taking to the waters. The sea and Lake Mälaren are full of all kinds of boats in the summer. You can canoe, sail, zip up and down in a motorboat, or just paddle. I love getting together with friends, hiring a rowboat from Djurgårdsbrons Sjocafé, and putting together a picnic and rowing along the canal that separates Ladugårdsgärdet from Djurgården. We find somewhere to park the boat and have an *al fresco* feast. See p 26.

❸ Walking into the Vasa Museum. No matter how many times I visit this museum, the hairs on the back of my neck always rise when I walk in from the bright sunlight to be confronted by this huge 17th-century wooden warship, raised from the dead and now permanently moored in its own building. Go when the crowds are few and you can feel the ghosts of the dead sailors walking along with you as you pass the gun decks and gaze up at the ornately carved prow. See p 9.

❹ Wandering through the medieval streets of Gamla Stan. This may be Stockholm's most visited area, but catch it early in the morning when the light filters through the narrow alleyways and the shutters on the houses are still closed—you feel you've stepped back four centuries. Then walk down narrow Mårten Trotzigs Gränd, the 90cm (less than 3 feet) wide street where the drainpipes cling crazily to the peeling, damp walls. See p 59.

❺ Shopping for a new look. There's something about the strong shapes of furniture conceived by the Scandinavian icons of modern design that makes me want to transform my house. So I always spend time in Jacksons and Modernity. But they stock mainly collectors pieces; for something I can afford (and take home),

The medieval streets of Gamla Stan.

I go along to Design Torget and 10 Swedish Designers. And I always leave plenty of room in my luggage for textiles and those small items that are distinctly Scandinavian. *See p 97*.

6 Sampling the new Swedish cooking. Many of Stockholm's young chefs might have had a French culinary training, but they've taken the classics and reinvented them. They use native ingredients such as Arctic char, lingonberries, mousse, and elk and put the tastes together in a unique way. Try the 'new Swedish cooking' of the likes of Gustav Otterberg at Leijontornet and you'll see why Stockholm is rapidly becoming the hot destination for serious gastronomy. *See chapter 6*.

7 Spending the evening in Centralbadet. The Jugendstil Centralbadet spa is a wonderful place to round off the day. I don't book any of the treatments; I just get steamy in the sauna, swim in the outdoor pool, and sit in the leafy garden with a cup of coffee and let the world's troubles fade away. *See p 100*.

8 Joining the skaters in winter. I think that Scandinavians must be born with skates on; everybody, young and old, seems to take expertly to the ice in winter. You can join them on the little Kungsträdgården rink, or

Centralbadet.

hire or buy your own skates and take to Lake Mälaren—and the sea if the temperature really plummets below zero. You can skate all the way to Sigtuna from Stockholm, but you may have to be Scandinavian to achieve that. *See p 46*.

9 Discovering northern art at the Nationalmuseum. A visit to the Nationalmuseum is a bit like taking an external art history degree. I come away ashamed at my ignorance of northern European artists and excited by the amount of great and unknown art that I've seen. *See p 14*.

10 Partying the night away. It's true that Stockholm is a clubber's paradise, but if you feel either too old, or not well dressed enough, ignore the crowds outside the hippest places and pick either a couple of bars or a jazz club for your evening's entertainment. There's something about emerging at 3am into the light of day that seems to keep you going. *See chapter 7*.

11 Looking at the view from on high. Of all the magnificent views you get in Stockholm, I love sitting on Mosebacke Terrass with a glass of wine, invariably surrounded by musicians who are going to play there that evening, looking out towards Skeppsholmen and down towards the Södermalm shoreline. This is where you can see the huge ferries that go between Stockholm and Helsinki, making a real mix of old and new. *See p 75*.

12 Shopping in Östermalms Saluhall. This is one of the great indoor food markets of Europe. It's relatively small, but packed full of infinite types of salmon and herring, moose and elk, sourdough and rye bread, conserves, preserves, and pastries. And when you've done looking or shopping, settle down for the freshest sole or salted salmon with warm dill potatoes in Lisa Elmqvist. *See p 16*. ●

1

The Best
Full-Day Tours

The Best **in One Day**

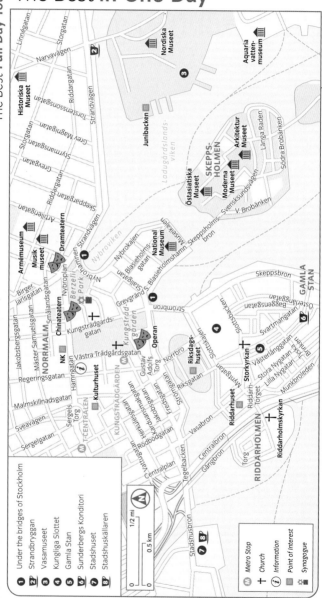

1 Under the bridges of Stockholm
2 Strandbryggan
3 Vasamuseet
4 Kungliga Slottet
5 Gamla Stan
6 Sunderbergs Konditori
7 Stadshuset
8 Stadshuskällaren

1/2 mi
0.5 km

Metro Stop
Church
Information
Point of Interest
Synagogue

Historiska Museet
Nordiska Museet
Aquaria vatten-museum
Junibacken
Ladugårdslands-viken
SKEPPS-HOLMEN
Arkitektur Museet
Långa Raden
Östasiatiska Museet
Moderna Museet
V. Brobänken
Södra Brobänken
Armémuseum
Musik museet
Dramteatern
National Museum
Svensksundsvägen
Nybroviken
Chinateatern
Berzelii Park
Nybroplan
Strandvägen
Greygrand S. Blasieholmshamn
Nybrokajen
Blasieholms-gatan
Stallgatan
Skeppsholms-bron
Kungsträdgårds-gatan
Kungsträd-gården
Operan
Strömbron
Slottsbacken
GAMLA STAN
Skeppsbron
Österlånggatan
Bagnegatan
Svartmangatan
NK
Västra Trädgårdsgatan
Gustav Adolfs Torg
Norrbro
Riksdags-huset
Myntgatan
Storkyrkan
Stora Nygatan
Lilla Nygatan
Västerlånggatan
Kulturhuset
KUNGSTRÄDGÅRDEN
Riksgatan
Riddarhuset
Riddarholms-Torget
Munkbroleden
T-CENTRALEN
Sergels Torg
Vasabron
Centralbron
RIDDARHOLMEN
Riddarholmskyrkan
Centralplan
Tegelbacken
Gångbron
Stadshusbron
NORRMALM
Birger Jarlsgatan
Jakobsbergsgatan
Mäster Samuelsgatan
Regeringsgatan
Malmskillnadsgatan
Sveavägen
Sergelgatan
Hamngatan
Herkulesgatan
Drottninggatan
Klara V. Kyrkogata
Klarabergsgatan
Rödbodgatan
Fredsgatan
Strömgatan
Vattugatan
Lindngatan
Storgatan
Narvavägen
Riddargatan
Torstensonsgatan
Grev Magnigatan
Styrmansgatan
Grevgatan
Artillerigatan
Skeppargatan

Stockholm's capital stretches out over 14 islands so you're never far from the water. Start with a boat tour before visiting the blockbusters of Stockholm's past: the Kungliga Slottet (Royal Palace) in Gamla Stan and the impressive Vasamuseet. As you walk around on this first day, you come across beautiful and different views over the water, which is the main attraction of this historic city.
START: **T-bana Gamla Stan.**

❶ ★★★ kids Under the bridges of Stockholm. With the sun, or the wind, in your face, take to the boats on a trip that shows you the city as people have seen it for centuries. You begin on the Baltic Sea side and then pass through the Slussen Lock into the shelter of Lake Mälaren, the third largest lake in Europe. As you slip under 15 bridges, your journey takes you past grand buildings and once-gritty, working-class areas. The commentary is full of information, both useful and delightfully useless. You'll come away knowing that performers at the amusement park, Gröna Lund, have included the Beatles and Jimi Hendrix, who was enjoying himself so much the organizers had to unplug his guitar to get him to stop. It's great fun. ⏱ *1 hr 50 mins. Nybroplan.* ☎ *1200 40 00. www.stockholmsightseeing.com.*

Tickets 190 SEK adults, 95 SEK children 6–11 years. Boats leave Strömkajen on the hour, from Nybroplan 45 minutes later. Daily May 1–31, Aug 31–Sep 20 10am–4pm, Jun 1–21 10am–6pm, Jun 22–Aug 30 10am–7pm. Check on website for out-of-season dates and times. Tickets in advance from website or the departure point booth. T-bana Kungsträdgården.

❷ ★ Strandbryggan. It's a short walk along Strandvägen past the moored boats to this café. Order a coffee, meal, or drink at this all-day eatery that floats on two boats, and look towards the Bridge to leafy Djurgården. The smug feeling of being a local and watching the tourists is irresistible (so what's wrong in pretending?). *Strandvägskajen 2.* ☎ *660 37 14. $$.*

A different view of the capital.

❸ ★★★ kids Vasamuseet.
Nothing prepares you for the drama of Stockholm's blockbuster of a museum and the massive 17th-century Vasa ship it contains. Walking into the darkened museum specially built to house the vessel, you get a very real impression of the might of the battleships that brought glory to the winners and horror to those who lost. Even the most blasé teenager is stunned into silence. *See mini tour, p 9.*

❹ ★★★ kids Kungliga Slottet.
Arrive early or late to miss the crowds. Built on the site of the Tre Kronor (Three Crowns) fortress, the Royal Palace was destroyed by fire in 1697. The huge building (with a whopping 608 rooms), designed by the royal architect Nicodemus Tessin the Younger (1654–1728) and completed in 1754, is imposing rather than beautiful so it's not surprising that the Royal Family prefers to live at Drottningholm (p 41) and use this palace for offices and state occasions only. Decorated by the main artists of the day and added to over the centuries, it gives an idea of Sweden's huge wealth and importance since the 18th century. There are four different parts to visit (see the **Kungliga Slottet** tour, p 29). If you only have limited time, I suggest just visiting the State Apartments.

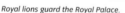

Royal lions guard the Royal Palace.

🕐 *3 hrs. Slottsbacken.* ☎ *402 61 30. www.royalcourt.se. For details see p 29. T-bana Gamla Stan/ Kungsträdgården.*

❺ ★★★ kids Gamla Stan. With the story of Stockholm in your mind, go back to the beginnings of the city on Gamla Stan. This tiny island once commanded the strategic entrance to Lake Mälaren from the Baltic Sea, protected by the Tre Kronor (Three Crowns) fortress. The crowded, medieval sprawl of houses largely burnt down in 1625 and a new city emerged with impressive waterfront stone buildings. Tourists choke the main streets in the summer but I'm amazed at how the herd instinct leaves many of the narrow alleyways and streets that criss-cross this timewarp of a quarter so undisturbed. *See p 59.*

❻ ★ kids Sundbergs Konditori.
You'll have to compete with locals *and* tourists to grab an outside table at Stockholm's oldest pâtisserie. Opened in 1785, Sundbergs Konditori remains totally traditional—cakes, coffee, and history are all served here. *Järntorget 83.* ☎ *10 67 35. $.*

❼ ★★★ Stadshuset. Finish at the nerve center of the city. The tower of Stockholm's City Hall, at 106m (348 feet) high, dominates the skyline from all over the city. Even on a dull day, you can pick out the extravagantly gilded Tre Kronor—

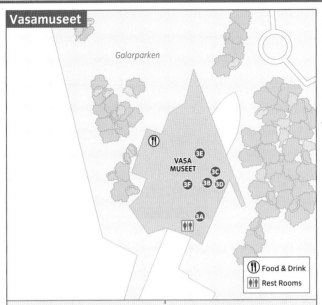

Vasamuseet

Galarparken

VASA MUSEET
3E
3C
3B 3D
3F
3A

🍴 Food & Drink
🚻 Rest Rooms

Start with the 25-minute **film** of the discovery and raising of the Vasa, which sank in Stockholm's harbor on August 10 1628 on its maiden voyage **3A**. Rediscovered in 1956 by wreck specialist, Anders Franzén, it took five years before the ship was lifted. A **slide show** in English illustrates why the ship sank **3B**: one of the major reasons was the two gundecks laden with heavy cannons. A full-size model of the **upper gun deck 3C** shows the conditions in which the sailors operated. Life on board for the ordinary seaman was nasty, brutal, and short, seen through **artifacts** such as their simple wooden utensils **3D**. Written records show particularly nasty and invariably fatal punishments such as keelhauling—the condemned man was dropped over the side head first into the water and pulled with a rope under the keel to the other side of the ship. The **stern 3E** was wonderfully decorated with the Swedish national emblem; the ship was built to impress and its wooden sculptures symbolized Sweden's power. You can walk around the entire ship, ending with a close look at the **gun ports 3F** and the **lion figurehead** of the King who commissioned the ship, Gustav II Adolf (1594–1632), known as the Lion of the North (6G). ⏱ *2 hrs. Galärvarvsvägen 14.* 📞 *519 548 00. Admission 95 SEK adults, students 50 SEK, under-19s free. Free with Stockholm Card (see p 11). June 1–Aug 31 8.30am–6pm; Sep 1–May 31 10am–5pm (Wed to 8pm). Closed Dec 23–25, Jan 1. Bus 47. Ferry to Djurgården (summer).*

The mighty Vasa warship.

the three crowns that has been Sweden's heraldic symbol since the 14th century—atop the tower. The huge redbrick building, designed by the leading architect of the Swedish National Romantic style, Ragnar Öst-berg (1866–1945), and completed in 1923, stands at the southeastern tip of Kungsholmen on the bay of Rid-darfjärden. City Hall is best known for the annual Nobel Prize banquet, held on December 10 for some 1,300 guests in the Renaissance palace-style Blue Hall. You can only see the building on a guided tour; however, you can climb the 365 steps in the tower on your own (with an elevator taking you halfway if needed). It's worth it for the fantastic view. ⏱ *1½ hrs. Hantverkar-gatan 1.* ☎ *50 82 90 59. www.stockholm.se/stadshuset. Tour 60 SEK adults, 30 SEK accompanied 12–18 year olds, under-12s free. Free*

Abba

It began in June 1966 when Björn Ulvaeus of the Hootenanny Singers met Benny Andersson, then with the Hep Stars. They teamed up, recorded with Stig 'Stikkan' Anderson on his Polar label, met Agnetha Fältskog and Norwegian Anni-Frid Lyngstad and got married (Björn to Agnetha in 1971 and Benny to Anni-Frid in 1978). They became Abba, and in Brighton, UK in 1974, won the Eurovision Song Contest with the song 'Waterloo'. The rest, as they say, is history. One of the most successful groups ever (along with the Beatles), they last performed together way back in 1982—but the music goes on. Unfortunately the museum, which was due to open in 2009, doesn't. It's been put on indefinite hold while a suitable building is found. Fans will have to be content with endless visits to either the film or stage version of Mamma Mia!

The Stockholm Card

The Stockholm Card is worth investing in. The Card gives free admission to 75 museums and attractions; free travel by public transport on the T-bana, buses, commuter trains, and trams; free sightseeing by boat on the Royal Canal Tour and Historical Canal Tour, free trips on the Nybroplan ferry to Djurgården and on the M/S Emelie to Hammarby Sjöstad, and special offers on boat trips to Drottningholm; bus tours on Stockholm Panorama and Open Top Tours and a guidebook. Adults: 24 hours 330 SEK, 48 hours 460 SEK, 72 hours 580 SEK. Children 7–17 years old: 24 hours 160 SEK, 48 hours 190 SEK, 72 hours 220 SEK. It is validated from the time and date you first use it. Buy it in advance on the Internet (www.stockholmtown. com/stockholmcard), or at the Stockholm Tourist Center in Sweden House (Sverigehuset, Hamnagatan 27, Norrmalm. ☎ 50 82 85 08. www.stockholmtown.com. Mon–Fri 9am–7pm, Sat 10am–5pm, Sun 10am–4pm).

with Stockholm Card (see p 11). 45 min tours in English on the hour. Jun–Sep 10am–4pm, Oct–May 10am, noon daily. Tower Jul–Aug 10am– 5pm, Sep 10am–4pm. Closed Oct– May. Admission 20 SEK. Free with Stockholm Card (see p 11). T-bana T-Centralen. Bus 3, 62.

🍴 ★★ **Stadshuskällaren.** Underneath the splendors of the Stadshuset are some culinary delights. The Nobel banquet for 1,400 takes place every year in the Blue Hall,

but mere mortals who are not invited can, from January the following year, order the previous year's Nobel banquet for dinner in the cellar restaurant. If you're a group, you can select a menu from any banquet dating back to 1901. Otherwise choose from an excellent salad buffet with soup, bread and butter, coffee, and a main dish for around 80 SEK or just go à la carte. *Stadshuset, Hantverkargatan 1.* ☎ *506 322 00. $$$.*

Stadshuset from the water.

The Best in Two Days

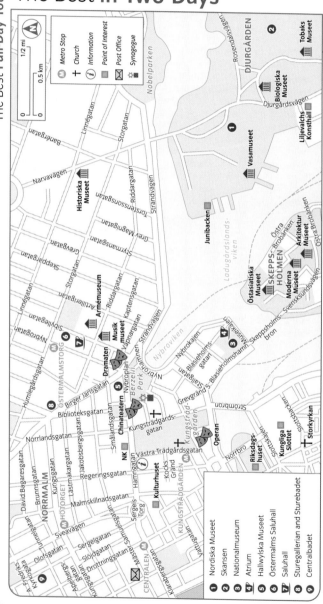

- **1** Nordiska Museet
- **2** Skansen
- **3** Nationalmuseum
- **4** Atrium
- **5** Hallwylska Museet
- **6** Östermalms Saluhall
- **7** Saluhall
- **8** Sturegallerian and Sturebadet
- **9** Centralbadet

Map legend:
- Ⓜ Metro Stop
- ✝ Church
- ⓘ Information
- ■ Point of Interest
- ⊠ Post Office
- ☼ Synagogue

Scale: 1/2 mi / 0.5 km

Labels on map: DJURGÅRDEN, Tobaks Museet, Biologiska Museet, Djurgårdsvägen, Liljevalchs Konsthall, Vasamuseet, Nobelparken, Rosendalsvägen, Arkitektur Museet, Östra Brobänken, SKEPPS-HOLMEN, Moderna Museet, Östasiatiska Museet, Skeppsholmsbron, Svensksundsvägen, Junibacken, Ladugårdslands-viken, Museivägen, Nybroviken, Historiska Museet, Narvavägen, Linnégatan, Banérgatan, Storgatan, Riddargatan, Strandvägen, Torstenssonsgatan, Grev Magnigatan, Styrmansgatan, Skeppargatan, Grevgatan, Storgatan, Artillerigatan, Kaptensgatan, Valhallavägen, Armémuseum, Musik museet, Dramaten, Sibyllegatan, Linnégatan, Nybrogatan, ÖSTERMALMSTORG, Humlegårdsgatan, Birger Jarlsgatan, Biblioteksgatan, Nybroplan, Berzelii Park, Chinateatern, Kungsträdgårds-gatan, Operan, NORRMALM, Norrlandsgatan, Smålandsgatan, Jakobsbergsgatan, Västra Trädgårdsgatan, Strömbron, Strömgatan, Grevgränd, Blasieholms-gatan, S. Blasieholmshamn, Skeppsbron, S-Blasieholmshamnen, Nybrokajen, Riksdags-huset, Kungliga Slottet, Storkyrkan, Norrbro, Slottsbacken, Slottskajen, David Bagaresgatan, Brunnsgatan, Kungsgatan, Lästmakargatan, Regeringsgatan, Hamngatan, NK, Kulturhuset, Kocks Gränd, KUNGSTRÄDGÅRDEN, Malmskillnadsgatan, Sveavägen, Olofsgatan, Sergelgatan, Sergels Torg, HÖTORGET, Mäster Samuelsgatan, Drottninggatan, CENTRALEN, Klarabergsgatan, Vasagatan, A. Fredriks Kyrkogata, Adelbergs-gatan, Tunnelgatan, Karlbergsvägen, Sjöldgatan, Kungsbron, NORRMALM

By now, you'll have your bearings, so that on this second day you should find the districts of Norrmalm and Östermalm easy to navigate. Start with a rare treat, a dip into Scandinavian art at the Nationalmuseum. START: **T-bana to Kungsträdgården.**

1 ★★ kids **Nordiska Museet.** I love museums that show how people lived and the Nordic Museum gives a vivid picture of Sweden from the Middle Ages to today. The museum was created by teacher and folklorist, Artur Hazelius (1833–1901), who also founded the open-air museum, Skansen (p 49). Designed by architect Isak Clason (1856–1930) in truly monumental style, it was opened in 1907. You're greeted in the Great Hall by an enormous statue by Carl Milles (1875–1955) of Gustav Vasa (1523–60), the heroic King who won Swedish independence from the Danes. The 1.5 million objects encompass everything from 18th-century shoes that could come from today's creative designers to some quite remarkable headgear. It's like walking through a giant Nordic dolls' house with folk art and Viking-style revival furniture from the 1860s when famine and fear of a Russian invasion sent the Swedes back to their supposedly strong, invincible ancestors. 1½ hrs. Djurgårdsvägen 6–16. ☎ 51 95 46 00. www.nordiskamuseet.se. Admission 60 SEK adults, under-19s free. Free Wed 4pm–8pm (off season). Free with Stockholm Card (see p 11). Jun 1–Aug 31 daily 10am–5pm; Sep 1–May 31 Mon–Fri 10am–4pm (Wed to 8pm), Sat, Sun 11am–5pm. Bus 47. Tram 7. Ferry to Djurgården (summer).

2 ★★★ kids **Skansen.** In 1891, Artur Hazelius (1833–1901) opened the world's first open-air museum. 150 old buildings, farms, houses, shops, churches, and workshops were brought from all over Sweden to show countryside traditions. This was a time when, according to 19th-century Romantics, the old way of life was rapidly disappearing. Now, it's a place to wander around, from the town quarter where you can see old crafts such as glass-blowing, to the turf shelters of the Sami camp.

The Nordiska Museum was opened in 1907.

Turf-rooved houses at Skansen.

Nordic animals such as bears, wolves, and elk wander around enclosures planted with native flora and fauna. There's plenty to see and various cafés and restaurants to keep you going. In the summer, costumed guides show you around. You can either spend a few hours here or all day on a separate tour. ⏱ *2 hrs. Djurgårdsslätten 49-51.* ☎ *442 80 00. www.skansen.se. Admission from 90-120 SEK for adults; 30-50 SEK for children (6-15 years), depending on time of year. Free with Stockholm Card (see p 11). May 1–Jun 19 & Sep,*

Nationalmuseum.

10am–8pm; Jun 20–Aug 31 10am–10pm. For other times, telephone or check the website. Bus 47. Tram 7. Ferry to Djurgården (summer)

❸ ★★★ Nationalmuseum.
Designed by the German architect, August Stüler (1800–1865) and finished in 1866, the National Museum houses Sweden's largest art collection. The staircase itself is a work of art with its series of frescoes painted by Carl Larsson (1853–1919) in 1896. The warm pink façade of the museum resembles an Italian Renaissance palazzo and so you expect to see the familiar masterpieces by the likes of Watteau, Rembrandt, and Renoir that the museum holds. What is not so familiar and is more exciting for the first-time visitor, are the relatively unknown north European painters such as David Klöcker von Ehrenstrahl (1628–1698) who worked in Sweden under Gustavus Adolphus (reigned 1611–1632) and the great Queen Christiana (reigned 1632–1654). After a feast of these paintings, head to the first floor for the impressive applied art and design section. Here the collection is arranged into different periods and concepts. For a mini tour, see p 15.

Nationalmuseum

FIRST FLOOR

SECOND FLOOR

Stairs

Rest Rooms

The top floor has paintings and sculptures from France, Holland, Flanders, and Sweden and a Renaissance section. Among the best works to look out for is *The Ill-Matched couple* of 1532 by Lucas Cranach the Elder (1472–1553), which was captured by Swedish troops from Emperor Maximilian in Munich in 1632 ③A. The best-known picture by the leading 18th-century Swedish painter, Alexander Roslin (1718–1798), is a portrait of his wife looking seductively out from behind her veil. Johan Tobias Sergel (1740–1814), the Swedish 18th-century neo-classical sculptor, worked in Rome from 1767–1778 but most of his work, such as his *Cupid and Psyche* ③B, is in Stockholm.

The applied art and design section is overwhelmingly Swedish. Monumental pieces such as the chest of drawers by **Georg Haupt** (1741–1784), who became King Gustav III's cabinet maker (you can see many of his pieces in the Kungliga Slottet (see p 29)), show how

European influences spread to Sweden ③C. Move onto the 20th century for pieces such as **Swedish Art Nouveau glass** from the Kosta Glassworks in 1900 ③D. The international importance of native designers really emerges here—look out for the coffeepot of **Naum Slutzky** (1894–1965) ③E, Maria Elmquist's 1993 necklace inspired by the shapes of the sea, and the extraordinary Chandelier of Anders Jakobsen (b. 1972) ③F. There are also sections on the **Scandinavian Design Movement of the 1950s** ③G and **Swedish New Simplicity** from the 1990s ③H. ⏱ *2 hrs. Södra Blasieholmshamnen.* ☎ *519 543 00 100. www.nationalmuseum.se. Admission 100 SEK adults, under-19s free. Free admission to ground floor. Free with Stockholm Card (see p 11). Tues 11am–8pm, Wed–Sun 11am–5pm (September–June to 8pm on Thurs). Closed public holidays. T-bana Kungsträdgården. Bus 65.*

Östermalms Saluhall.

★★ **Atrium.** The restaurant in the National Museum is a cut above your average. It's a light, airy space, with granite floors and limestone walls (which make it quite noisy). The cooking is good with a daily lunch special at 95–100 SEK. Otherwise, relax over coffee and cakes. ☎ 611 34 30. www. restaurang atrium.se. $$.

⑤ ★★★ kids Hallwylska Museet. It was a typical 19th-century marriage. Wilhelmina was the daughter of an extremely wealthy Swedish timber merchant; Walter van Hallwyl had the breeding—his Swiss family was one of Europe's oldest. But money won over family and he moved to Sweden. The Countess Wilhelmina had a passion for collecting, so the couple commissioned Isak Clason (1856–1930)—who designed the Nordiska Museet (see p 13, bullet ❶)—to create a winter home, the likes of which Stockholm had not seen before, to house all her art. The entrance is well-concealed from the street, but behind the façade, you step into a Mediterranean palace. Finished in 1898, the house was a model of the modern age kitted out with the latest central heating, electricity, elevators, bathrooms, and telephones. At the same time the ornately decorated rooms were filled with the vast, valuable, and idiosyncratic collection of treasures, art, furniture, and silverware the Countess had amassed. Her idea was always to leave the house as a museum to the state; it opened to the public in 1938. Visiting it is a wonderful experience because the house is preserved exactly as she left it. A costumed guide helps you step back into the gilded past as you tour the whole house. Otherwise, on your own, be content only to wander around on the first floor. ⏱ 1 hr. Hamngatan 4. ☎ 519 555 99. www. hallwylskamuseet.se. Admission 70 SEK adults with guided tour; 50 SEK adults first floor reception rooms only, under-19s free. Free with Stockholm Card (see p 11). Jan 2–Jun 30, Sep 1–Dec 31 Mon–Fri 11.45am–4pm (Wed tour 5.45pm–7pm), Sat, Sun 11.30am–4pm; Jul 1–Aug 31 Mon–Fri 1.45am–5pm, Sat, Sun, 10.30am–5pm. Guided tours in English telephone/check website for details. T-bana Östermalmstorg.

⑥ ★★★ Östermalms Saluhall. Östermalms food market is gourmet Stockholm at its finest. The gastronomic temple, built in eight months and opened by King Oscar II in 1888, has been supplying the capital's inhabitants with fresh bread, cakes, fish and seafood, vegetables, smoked, cured and fresh meat, and more ever since. ⏱ 1 hr. Östermalmstorg. www.ostermalmshallen.se. Mon–Thurs 9.30am–6pm, Fri 9.30am–6.30pm, Sat 9.30am–4pm. Jun–Aug Sat 9.30am–2pm. T-bana Östermalmstorg.

★★★ **Saluhall.** Once you've done the rounds of the market, lunch with the ladies who do just that at **Lisa Elmqvist** for a simple plate of gravadlax or a whole sea bass. You may have to share your table, but it's worth it. ☎ 553 40 40, *www.lisaelmqvist.se*. **$$**. **Gerda's** is great for seafood and the two work together so you can be sure of lunch at one or the other. ☎ 553 404 40, *www.saluhall.se*. **$$**. Or try **Nyroe Smørrebrød** for open sandwiches piled high with whatever takes your fancy. ☎ 662 37 20. **$**.

8 ★★ **Sturegallerian and Sturebadet.** Sturegallerian is where wealthy, upper-crust Stockholmers come to shop for international and Swedish names, and lunch in cafés and restaurants. The shopping complex was built around the original Sturebadet art nouveau swimming pool, opened in 1885 and restored in 1989 to also provide a swish spa and gym. ⏱ 1 hr. Stureplan 4. T-bana Östermalmstorg.

9 ★★★ **Centralbadet.** Go on, after all that culture and exercise— pamper yourself. And where better than in the restored 1904 Jugendstil-style Centralbadet? On offer are all the treatments you expect, from facials to Swedish massage; otherwise the entrance fee gives you

Eat at Lisa Elmquist in Östermalms Saluhall.

access to the swimming pool, gym with free weights, warm water baths, bubble and thermal pools, and the sauna. You enter through a charming shaded garden where people sit and chat over cups of coffee and cakes at little tables under the shady trees. In summer there's a roof terrace and outdoor gym. *Drottninggatan 88.* ☎ 545 213 00. *www.centralbadet.se. Mon–Fri 6am–8pm, Sat 8am–8pm, Sun 8am–5pm. Entrance 120 SEK adults except Fri and Sat after 3pm: 170 SEK. Age restriction 18 unless with an adult. Tel for prices and facilities. T-bana Hötorget. Bus 52.*

Centralbadet.

The Best **in Three Days**

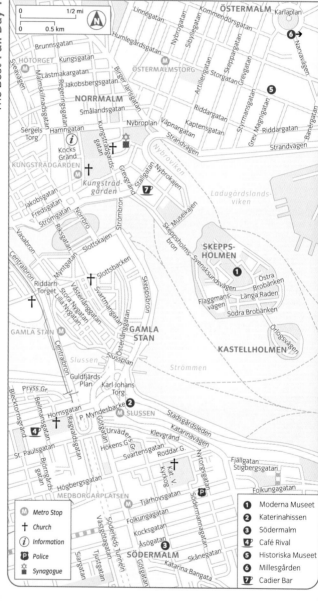

0 — 1/2 mi
0 — 0.5 km

Linnégatan
Kommendörsgatan
ÖSTERMALM
Karlaplan

Humlegårdsgatan
Nybrogatan
Sibyllegatan
Skeppargatan
Grevgatan
Narvavägen

Brunnsgatan
Kungsgatan
HÖTORGET
Mästersamuelsgatan
Lästmakargatan
Regeringsgatan
Jakobsbergsgatan
ÖSTERMALMSTORG
Artillerigatan
Storgatan

Sveavägen
Malmskillnadsgatan
NORRMALM
Birger Jarlsgatan
Smålandsgatan

Styrmansgatan
Grev Magnigatan
Banérgatan

Riddargatan
Nybroplan
Kaptensgatan
Vapnargatan

Sergels Torg
Hamngatan
Kungsträdgårds-gatan
Strandvägen
Riddargatan
Strandvägen

Kocks Grand
KUNGSTRÄDGÅRDEN
Grevgrand
Stallgatan
Nybroviken

Jakobsgatan
Fredsgatan
Strömgatan
Kungsträd-gården
Norrbro
Strömbron
Museikajen
Nybrokajen
Ladugårdslands-viken

Vasabron
Centralbron
Riksgatan
Myntgatan
Slottskajen
Slottsbacken
Skeppsholms-Svensksundsvägen
SKEPPS-HOLMEN
Östra Brobänken

Riddarh-Torget
Västerlånggatan
Stora Nygatan
Lilla Nygatan
Svartmangatan
Skeppsbron
Österlånggatan
Flaggmans-vägen
Länga Raden
Södra Brobänken

GAMLA STAN
GAMLA STAN
KASTELLHOLMEN
Örlogsvägen

Centralbron
Slussen
Slussplan
Strömmen

Pryss Gr.
Guldfjärds-Plan
Karl Johans Torg
Fjällgatan
Stigbergsgatan

Bleckornsgrand
Belmansgatan
Hornsgatan
Ragvaldsgatan
Götgatan
P. Myndesbacke
SLUSSEN
Stadsgårdsleden
Katarinavägen
Nytorgsgatan
Folkungagatan

St. Paulsgatan
Blomgårds-gatan
Urväders Gr.
Hökens G.
Svartensgatan
Klevgränd
Roddar G.
Kat. V. Kyrkog.

Högbergsgatan
MEDBORGARPLATSEN
Tjärhovsgatan
Södermannagatan
Folkungagatan

Söderleds Tunneln
Vasagötagatan
Kocksgatan
Åsögatan
Skånegatan

Slargatan
Tjulsgatan
SÖDERMALM
Götgatan
Katarina Bangata

Ⓜ	Metro Stop
†	Church
ⓘ	Information
Ⓟ	Police
✡	Synagogue

❶ Moderna Museet
❷ Katerinahissen
❸ Södermalm
❹ Café Rival
❺ Historiska Museet
❻ Millesgården
❼ Cadier Bar

Today you try something different. Begin at the Modern Art Museum café looking over the water before taking in one of Europe's great contemporary art collections. Finish the day with a trip out to see the stunning sculptures in Carl Milles' former home. It shows you how pleasantly rural living outside the center could be.

START: **Moderna Museum on Skeppsholmen.**

Moderna Museet.

1 ★★★ kids Moderna Museet. You know this is the Modern Art Museum by the crazy colored Yves Tingueley sculptures outside. The light modern building by Catalan architect Rafael Moneo (b. 1937) opened in 2004 after the previous one closed due to structural problems. This fabulous museum is large enough to display superb examples of every major modern artist and yet compact enough to keep your attention. Groundbreaking when it opened in 1958, this is now one of Europe's best contemporary art collections. It's arranged in reverse order, so walk to the farthest point of the museum and start with early 20th-century art. Picasso, de Chirico, Dali, Rauschenberg, Brancusi, and Chagall are all here as well as videos and contemporary installations. You come across pieces such as Picasso's *Déjeuner sur l'Herbe*, Andy Warhol's *Mao* of 1973, and the most

famous piece in the museum, the bizarre Robert Rauschenberg's *Monogram*, known as 'The Goat'. Take the guided tour for an in-depth visit. I became so absorbed that a glance through a big picture window into the outside world came as a shock. *1½ hrs. Skeppsholmen. 519 552 00. www.moderna museet.se. Admission 80 SEK adults, under-18s free. Guided tour in English is included with admission July, Aug Tues, Thurs, Sun at 1pm. Tues 10am–8pm, Wed–Sun to 6pm. T-bana Kungsträdgården. Bus 65. Ferries from Djurgården and Nybroplan in summer.*

2 ★ kids Katarinahissen. Walk back over the Stadshuset bridge and catch the 53 bus to Slussen. The steam-driven Katarinahissen elevator opened in 1883 and was replaced in the 1930s with an electric one to join the lower part of the town with the upper. From the 38m (125 feet) high tower, the view is

View to Riddarholmen and Stadshuset from Katarinahissen.

predictably grand. To prolong the experience, try an evening drink at Gondolen (p 127) hanging under the bridge and look down at the lights sparkling in the city below. In high summer you may have to wait in line for a while. 🕐 *1 min (15 mins wait at lift in summer). Stradsgården 6.* ☎ *642 47 86. Lift 10 SEK. Free with Stockholm Card (see p 11). Jan–mid-May, Sep–Dec 10am–6pm; mid-May–Aug 8am–10pm. T-bana Slussen.*

❸ **Södermalm.** The laidback atmosphere of 'Söder' as it is locally known, contrasts with the hustle and

Café Rival.

bustle of the center of the city. Södermalm is a large island, a surprising mix of small parks, steep hills with great views, 18th-century cottages, gardens and allotments, plus an uninhibited nightlife and two of the more unconventional entertainment venues, the Folk Opera (p 139) and the Södra Theater. Traditionally working-class, it's now vaunted as Stockholm's hippest area, revitalized by an influx of the young who come here for the new shops, cafés, and bars. The area that most typifies the change is SoFo (south of Folkungagaten and east of Gogatan). Check out one of the two Södermalm walks to discover the best parts of the island (p 71 and 75). 🕐 *2 hrs. T-bana Slussen.*

🕎★ **Café Rival** Join the young and fashionable at the café that belongs to the Hotel Rival, owned by Benny Andersson—yes, he of colossal Abba fame. You get good coffee, cakes, and sandwiches supplied by the hotel's own Rival Bakery, served on a summer terrace that is the perfect spot for people-watching. Who knows? You may even spot Benny himself. *Mariatorget 3.* ☎ *545 789 00. www.rival.se. $.*

⑤ ★★ kids Historiska Museet.

The Museum of National Antiquities was once a rather fusty place with old-fashioned displays. Now the pre-history section is about as cutting-edge as you can get, causing a certain frisson of disapproval among Sweden's conservatives. But like the children around me, I found it fascinating, with the exhibits grouped together to tell human stories from the Stone, Bronze, and Iron Ages. A question and answer approach carries on into other sections. In the Textile gallery, questions such as how people sewed before sewing machines and who could afford gold thread in their clothes are answered. It's done in such a way to show that our ancestors had very much the same concerns, fears, and hopes as we do today. The fearsome reputation of the Vikings is also dealt with; in fact most were farmers and traders going about their daily business. The Gold Room houses a spectacular collection of Sweden's gold and silver treasures from collars to crowns—it's helped by the law that any finds made from gold, silver, or copper alloys are

Religious antiquities adorn the walls in the Historiska Museet.

bought by the state. ⏱ 1½ hrs. *Narvavägen 13–17.* ☎ *51 95 56 00. www.historiska.se. Admission 50 SEK adults; under-19s free. Free with Stockholm Card (see p 11). Guided tour in English daily, 1pm. May–Sep 10am–5pm, Oct–Apr Tues–Sun 11am–5pm, Thurs 11am–8pm. T-bana Karlaplan.*

Carl Milles

Carl Milles (1875–1955) studied under Rodin in Paris before returning to Stockholm in 1906 and buying a plot of land in Lidingo to build his house and garden. In 1931 he left for the USA and an international career. He became artist-in-residence at Cranbrook Educational Community in Bloomfield Hills, Michigan, and was commissioned to produce statues throughout the US—in Detroit, Virginia, and St. Louis. All was not plain sailing, however; his playful, sometimes erotic sculptures, proved too much for some audiences and he employed a fig leaf maker on a retainer. He returned home in 1951 and spent every summer in Millesgården until his death in 1955. His burial here was courtesy of King Gustaf VI Adolf, who authorized it, overturning Swedish law that requires burial in sacred ground. The King, a keen gardener and friend, helped plant the garden at the site.

Milles Garden is inspirational.

6 ★★★ **Millesgården.** Take the train out to Torsvik, and a 10-minute walk uphill brings you to the former house and studio of sculptor Carl Milles, now the Milles Garden Museum. The modest approach doesn't prepare you for the hilltop garden full of sculptures overlooking the waters of Lilla Värtan. Some of the sculptures stand on high plinths; others are set in pools of water; some are massive; others delicate. From the garden, steps take you up to the house and studio. Milles was a collector as well as an artist and on his travels he built up the largest private collection in Sweden of Greek and Roman statuary. It's a beautiful, tranquil place with a serenity you don't find in most museums. The house is delightful, with his wife Olga's paintings on the cupboards in the breakfast room, and classical details such as marble walls and mosaic floors in the gallery and the Red Room. When the couple returned here in 1950, Milles' half-brother Evert, an architect, designed a second house on the lower terrace. Anne's House is so-named after Milles' assistant Anne Hedmark who lived here after his death. If you want a small replica of one of the sculptures, the shop can oblige. In Stockholm, you can see any of the 26 sculptures including the *Orpheus* fountain in front of Konserthuset and the arching *Gud på himmelsbågen* (God on the Rainbow) at Nacka Strand. ⏱ *1½ hrs. Herserudsvägen 30.* ☎ *446 75 90. www.millesgarden.se. Admission 80 SEK adults, under-18s free. Free with Stockholm Card (see p 11). Mid-May–Sep 11am–5pm, Oct 1–mid May Tues–Sun noon–5pm. Train to Torsvik then walk.*

7 ★★ **Cadier Bar** You deserve it, so enjoy a posh drink. Named after King Oscar II's (1829–1907) head chef, Regis Cadier, who cannily founded the Grand Hotel in 1874, the Cadier Bar is great for a break. The high prices are worth it for the view and a glimpse of conservative Swedish society. Anyway, the Grand Hotel is an institution, and institutions should always be treasured. *Södra Blasieholmshamnen 8.* ☎ *679 35 00. www.grandhotel.se. $$.* ●

MUSIK

Stockholm & the Sea

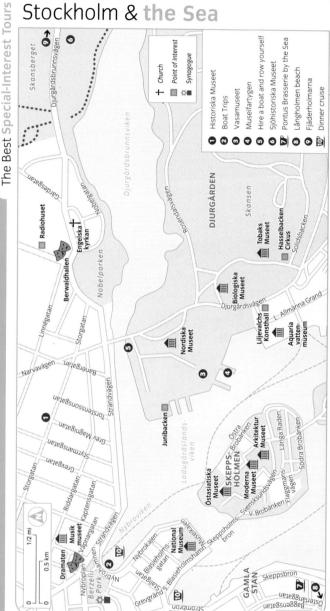

Legend

- ✝ Church
- ▪ Point of Interest
- ✡ Synagogue

1. Historiska Museet
2. Boat Trips
3. Vasamuseet
4. Museifartygen
5. Hire a boat and row yourself
6. Sjöhistoriska Museet
7. Pontus Brasserie by the Sea
8. Långholmen beach
9. Fjäderholmarna
10. Dinner cruise

S tockholm life has always been tied to the sea and it's this maritime love affair that makes the capital such an attractive city. The sea today is as important as ever to the inhabitants, but it's a rather more peaceful relationship than in the past. In summer, the city empties as locals leave for their summer cottages in the archipelago islands, leaving the place for visitors. START: **T-bana Karlaplan.**

❶ ★★ kids Historiska Museet. We all grew up knowing about the fearsome Vikings; to us they may have been villains, but to the Swedes, Danes, and Norwegians, they were heroes and settlers; only 1% of the population were those feared, rape-and-pillage Vikings, while 90% were thoroughly peaceful farmers and 9% were traders. Although the Vikings who raided Britain came mainly from Denmark, the Old Norsemen were united by a common culture. This museum has a good section on Viking life, with models of their settlements, weaponry, and jewelry plus a special summer program for would-be Vikings. ⏱ *1½ hrs. See p 21, bullet* **❺**.

❷ ★★★ kids Boat trips. During the summer I love taking the hop-on, hop-off sightseeing boat that chugs between various islands. The 2½ hour Archipelago tour goes past some of Stockholm's great buildings before heading out to give you a glimpse of just a few of the 24,000 islands that make up this beautiful part of the world. Sit back and imagine what it's like to be Swedish, to own a summer cottage, and spend a whole month in the midnight sun. ⏱ *2½ hrs. Nybroplan. www.stromma kanalbolaget.se. Ticket 220 SEK. Jun 6–Aug 16 10.30am, noon, 1.30pm, 3pm; Aug 17–Sep 27 10.30am, noon, 1.30pm. Check first as some sailings are only at weekends on certain dates and out of season times. T-bana Kungsträdgården/Östermalmstorg.*

❸ ★★★ kids Vasamuseet. It took three years to build the Swedish Navy's most expensive, powerful, and ornate ship. She was constructed on the island of Blasieholmen, and brought to the quay just below the Kungliga Slottet. News of the great warship traveled the length and breadth of an apprehensive Europe; she was, it seemed, invincible. On August 10, 1628, watched by countless spectators in the harbor, she unfurled her sails and set off. After just 1,300m the wind increased, the ship capsized, and the Vasa sank. The brackish waters preserved the ship until she was rediscovered and lifted from her watery grave 333 years later. For a tour, see p 9. ⏱ *2 hrs.*

❹ kids Museifartygen. More stories of Sweden's seafaring

Vasa's stern reconstructed in bold colors.

tradition are found on two nearby ships. The lightship **Finngrundet** (1903) was kept on the Finngrund banks in the Gulf of Bothnia until lighthouses took over in the 1960s, and she was retired to a small berth here. Next door is the **St Erik**, a seagoing icebreaker built in 1915. The technique is simple: the boat climbs onto the ice and crushes it as it moves slowly but noisily forward. ⏲ 40 mins. Galärvarvet. ☎ 51 95 48 91. Admission included with Vasamuseet ticket. Mid-Jun–mid-Aug noon–5pm. Bus 47. Tram 7. Ferry to Djurgården (summer only).

⑤ ★★★ kids Hire a boat and row yourself. There's nothing more enjoyable and, until you have the hang of it, challenging than doing as the locals do and taking to the waters. Hire your own boat at Djurgårdsbrons Sjocafé over the bridge on Djurgården and set off across the peaceful waters that lead onto the delightful canal and beyond. Stop here, or you'll find yourself all at sea! Galärvarvsvägen 2. ☎ 660 57 57. Hire rates vary according to the boat. A rowboat is

85 SEK for the 1st hour, 75 SEK 2nd hour, and 400 SEK for the whole day. ID or passport required. Bus 47.

⑥ ★★ kids Sjohistoriska Museet. This is a dream for all those who love ships and the sea. The National Maritime Museum has more than 100,000 exhibits and an impressive 1,500 accurate model ships, all beautifully and painstakingly made. Get an idea of life on board in interiors such as the cabin and stern of the royal schooner *Amphion* built at the Djurgården shipyard in 1778, and Gustav III's flagship during the 1788–1790 war with Russia. There are films on destroyers, a Pirates exhibition, and splendid maritime art, all housed in a building by Ragnar Östberg (architect of the Stadshuset, 1866–1945) overlooking the water towards Stockholm. ⏲ 1 ½ hrs. Djurgårdsbrunnsvägen 24. ☎ 519 549 00. www.sjohistoriska.nu. Admission 50 SEK adults, under-18s free. June–Aug 10am–5pm, Sep–May Tues–Sun 10am–5pm. Guided tours daily 1pm (pre-book for the English tour). Bus 69.

Model ships sail endlessly in the Sjohistoriska Museet.

The outside terrace of Pontus Brassiere by the sea.

7 ★★★ **Pontus' Brasserie by the Sea.** This exquisite summer bar and restaurant draws in the crowds for its position on the waterfront, elegant but casual ambience, and comfortable wicker chairs. Less formal than the second restaurant of chef Pontus Frithiof (Pontus! p 119), it's ideal for a freshly caught seafood lunch and gets particularly popular after work. *Tullhus 2, Skeppsbrokajen* ☎ *20 20 95. www.pontusfrithiof.com. $$$.*

8 ★★ **Långholmen beach.** I find it amazing that you can swim in Lake Mälaren while remaining right in the heart of the city. How many other capitals offer such a treat? There are good beaches on Långholmen, both sandy and rocky. The water is pure, the beaches safe; perfect for families. See p 73. 2 hrs.

9 ★★**Fjäderholmarna.** I'd recommend a trip out to the Fjäderholmarna islands with all the atmosphere of a small seaside town. The boat trip is only 25 minutes and so it's particularly popular on summer weekends. Depending on how you feel, you can spend a few hours or a whole day and take in the small museum of old wooden boats. See p 158.

10 ★★ **Dinner cruise.** Finish the day with a dinner cruise on a Stockholm summer 'white night'. In the late summer or autumn, you slip out into the Archipelago to see the sunset. There are various options from a dinner of traditional prawns to a 3-course dinner. *From Stadshusbron or Strandvägen. Various departures 5.30pm, 6pm, 7pm, depending on destination. Ticket 575 SEK. Drinks not included. Book in advance on www.strommakanalbolaget.se.*

The Fjäderholmarna islands make a perfect day out.

Kungliga Slottet

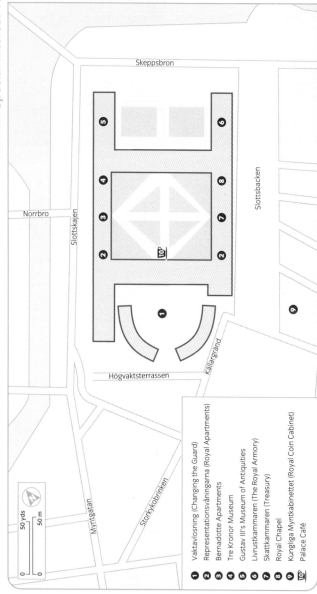

Skeppsbron

Slottsbacken

Norrbro

Slottskajen

Källargränd

Högvaktsterrassen

Storkyrkobrinken

Myntgatan

50 yds

50 m

1 Vaktavlosning (Changing the Guard)
2 Representationsvåningarna (Royal Apartments)
3 Bernadotte Apartments
4 Tre Kronor Museum
5 Gustav III's Museum of Antiquities
6 Livrustkammaren (The Royal Armory)
7 Skattkammaren (Treasury)
8 Royal Chapel
9 Kungliga Myntkabinettet (Royal Coin Cabinet)
10 Palace Café

The Royal Palace stands high above Gamla Stan, on a site that has defended access to Lake Mälaren since the 11th century. The present building with its 608 rooms was designed by the Royal architect, Nicodemus Tessin the Younger in 1754. START: **T-bana Gamla Stan. Bus 2, 43, 55, 76.**

1 ★★ **Vaktavlosning.** The Changing of the Guard takes place daily at the Royal Palace. The Guard leaves from the Army museum and marches through the city along Slottsbacken to the Outer Courtyard of the Palace. It's a low-key affair with a bit of marching and flag twirling and is fun rather than impressive, although if you're lucky you might catch the mounted guards on one of their parades. 30 mins. Mon–Sat 12.15pm, Sun and holidays 1.15pm.

2 ★★★ **kids Representationsvåningarna (Royal Apartments)** Climb the entrance staircase to the rooms that make up the State Apartments and the Guest Apartments used for visiting Heads of State. The splendid Hall of State where the king opened Parliament every year until 1975 is an opulent ceremonial room built to impress. In the State Apartment you go from the Council Chamber, where the King meets several times a year with the Government, to the theatrical State Bedchamber where Gustav III died after being shot at the nearby Opera House in 1792. Karl XI's Gallery, modeled on Versailles and used for the annual honoring of the Nobel laureates, is magnificent; the saloon known poetically as 'The White Sea' is used at State banquets. Take the guided tour in English (included with the ticket) for a more detailed look at royal life. 1 hr. Guided tours mid-May–mid-Sep daily

The Royal Palace's magnificent 'White Sea'.

The Royal Treasury at the Palace.

11am, 1pm, 3pm; mid-Sep–mid-May, Wed, Fri–Sun 2pm.

3 ★★ kids Bernadotte Apartments. Recently restored, this fabulous suite of rooms includes the Pillar Hall and the Rococo magnificence of the East Octagonal Cabinet. Named after the gallery of Bernadotte portraits, it's the place for receiving foreign ambassadors and ceremonial events. ⏲ *20 mins.*

4 ★ kids Tre Kronor Museum
For a good impression of the massive original 12th-century defensive architecture of the old Tre Kronor palace, go down into the dimly lit 16th- and 17th-century brick vaults. Two models and a short film tell you the story of the palace, along with artifacts that survived the fatal fire of 1697. ⏲ *30 mins.*

5 ★★ Gustav III's Museum of Antiquities. Don't dismiss this gallery by thinking it's going to be boring; it's a wonderful collection housed in the Greater and Lesser Stone Galleries. The black-and-white marble floor and classical columns make a suitably stark setting for the King's collection of classical statuary. It's easy to imagine the monarch in this esoteric collection,

walking slowly through his rogue's gallery of the antique world. Here are names to conjure with: the goddess Minerva, Lucrium Verus, Marcus Agrippa, Tiberius, Gaius Caligula, the child Britannicus, a suitably sensual Nero, Marcus Aurelius, Jupiter, and a particularly evil-looking Pan. ⏲ *30 mins.*

6 ★★★ kids Livrustkammaren. The Royal Armory, started in 1633, is a fascinating, gigantic toy box of a museum, which takes you through 500-odd years of Swedish regalia, weaponry, and even clothing. Here you'll see ornate, heavily embroidered wedding dresses and the masked costume worn by King Gustav III when he was assassinated in 1792. Royal ceremonies are covered, and a particularly evocative case contains the elegant blue dress worn by Crown Princess Victoria in 1995, beside the silver clothes of Gustav III (1746–1792). Like most Swedish museums, it's particularly child-friendly with a dressing-up room for the girls and helmets and swords for the boys to try. Underneath, vaulted cellars house a formidable collection of royal vehicles and the stuffed bodies of the monarch's horses, including Streiff, Gustav II Adolf's mount when he rode fatally into battle in 1632. It's a ghostly place, with the sound of clopping hooves on cobbles accompanying you as you walk past the gilded carriages and winter sledges. ⏲ *1 hr.*

7 ★★★ kids Skattkammaren. The vaulted, underground Treasury is another treat, a jewel box of regalia where some of the exquisite state symbols of power are on display. Don't miss Karl Gustav X's (1622–1660) pale blue and gold crown with its distinctly Russian look, Erik XIV's (1533–1577) crown made in Stockholm in 1561 with its huge ruby and pearls, and Gustav

Practical Matters—Kungliga Slottet

Kungliga Slottet Gamla Stan. ☎ 402 61 30. Royal Apartments, Bernadotte Apartments, Treasury and Tre Kronor Museum: Jan 2–7 noon–3pm. Feb 14–May 14 Tues–Sun noon–3pm; May 15–31 10am-4pm. June–August 10am–5pm. Sep 1–14 10am–4pm; Sep 15–Dec 30 Tues–Sun noon–3pm. Mid-May–Aug 10am–4pm; Sept–mid-May Tues–Sun noon–3pm. Gustav III's Museum of Antiquities: May 15–Sep 14 same hours as above. Closed during official functions. Single attraction: Adults 100 SEK, children 7–18 years old 50 SEK, under-7s free. Combination ticket for the Royal Apartments, Bernadotte Apartments, Treasury, Tre Kronor & Gustav III's Museum: Adults 140 SEK, children 70 SEK. Guided tour included in ticket price.

The Royal Chapel Jun–Aug Wed, Fri, noon–3pm, Mass Sun 11am. www.royalcourt.se. T-bana Gamla Stal, Kungsträdgården. Bus 2, 43, 55, 76.

Vasa's (1496–1560) great sword of state. ⏱ *45 mins.*

8 ★★ **Royal Chapel.** If you're here on a Sunday, you can attend mass at the Royal Chapel. Otherwise, opening hours are restricted. The gorgeous chapel, designed by Tessin the Younger, was completed by Carl Harleman in the mid-1700s. It has a painted ceiling, 17th-century bronze crowns, and items rescued from the original fortress such as the late 17th-century benches made by Georg Haupt. ⏱ *20 mins.*

9 ★ **Kungliga Myntkabinettet.** The Royal Coin Cabinet is housed in a three-storey building outside the palace and tells the story of money from the 19th century to today. Here you'll see the first Swedish coin of the late 10th century from King Olof of Sigtuna and the world's largest 'coin', the 'rai-stone' from Micronesia. ⏱ *30 mins. Slottsbacken.* ☎ *519 553 04. Admission 50 SEK adults, under-17s free. Free on Mondays, free with Stockholm Card. Summer 9am–5pm, winter 10am–5pm.*

10 **Palace Café.** After all that you'll need refreshment, so sip a coffee in the café that looks out onto the courtyard and you might well get a glimpse of the Royals as they drive themselves in and out of the palace. *$.*

The Royal Coin Cabinet.

Art & Design

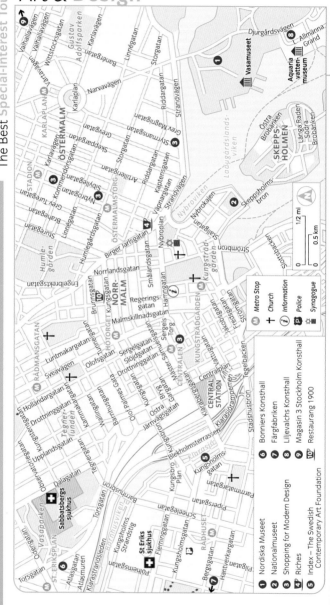

Map labels:
Valhallavägen · Valhallavägen · Wittstocksgatan · Gustav Adolfsparken · Karlavägen · Banérgatan · Linnégatan · Storgatan · Djurgårdsvägen · Allmänna Grand

Vasamuseet

Aquaria vatten-museum

Narvavägen · Karlaplan · Riddargatan · Strandvägen

ÖSTERMALM · KARLAPLAN · Grevgatan · Styrmansgatan · Grev Magnigatan

Karlavägen · Kommendörsgatan · Sibyllegatan · Nybrogatan · Skeppargatan · Storgatan · Artillerigatan · Riddargatan · Kaptensgatan · Strandvägen

Östra Brobänken · Långa Raden · Södra Brobänken · SKEPPS-HOLMEN · Ladugårdslands-viken

STADION · Grev Turegatan · Karlavägen · Linnégatan · Sturegatan · Brahegatan · ÖSTERMALMSTORG · Humlegårdsgatan

Nybroplan · Vasgatan · Nybrokajen · Skeppsholms-bron

Engelbrektsgatan · Birger Jarlsgatan · Smålandsgatan · Kungsträd-gården · Strömbron

Norrlandsgatan · Brunnsgatan · NORR-MALM · Regerings-gatan · Malmskillnadsgatan · Hamngatan · KUNGSTRÄDGÅRDEN · Jakobsgatan · Fredsgatan · Strömgatan

Slottsbacken

Rådmansgatan · Luntmakargatan · Sveavägen · Olofsgatan · Sergelgatan · Sergelgatan · Slöjdgatan · Drottninggatan · Mäster Samuelsgatan · Sergels Torg · CENTRALEN · Arsenalsgatan

Tegnérgatan · Kammakargatan · Olof Palmes Gate · Barnhusgatan · Kungsgatan · Östra Järnvägsgatan · Gamla Brogatan · Klara Norra · Vattugatan · Centralplan · Tegelbacken

CENTRAL STATION · Klarabergsgatan · Klarabergsviadukten · Stadshusbron

Holländargatan · Drottninggatan · Upplandsgatan · Wallingatan · Tegnérlunden · Blekholmsterrassen · Klarastrand

Kungsbro Plan · Kungsholms-gatan · Piperšgatan

Observatorielunden · Dalagatan · Torsgatan

Sabbatsbergs sjukhus

ST. ERIKSPLAN · Vasaparken · Atlasgatan · Atlasmuren · Klarastrandsleden

Kungsbro Strandstig · Fleminggatan · Kungsholms-gatan · Scheelegatan · Parmmätargatan

St Eriks sjukhus

RÅDHUSET · Bergsgatan · Pilgatan · Hantverkargatan · Kungsholmsgatan · Polhemsgatan · Kungsholmstorg

Legend:

- **M** Metro Stop
- **+** Church
- **(i)** Information
- **P** Police
- **✡** Synagogue

0 — 1/2 mi
0 — 0.5 km

Listings:

1. Nordiska Museet
2. Nationalmuseet
3. Shopping for Modern Design
4. Riches
5. Index – The Swedish Contemporary Art Foundation
6. Bonniers Konsthall
7. Färgfabriken
8. Liljevalchs Konsthall
9. Magasin 3 Stockholm Konsthall
10. Restaurang 1900

Sweden has a well-deserved reputation as a leader in art and design. At the 1925 World Exhibition in Paris, the clean lines, bold colors, and simple shapes using natural materials came as a revelation to a world still drowning in overblown country-house style. Then we were liberated with light wood furniture replacing heavy mahogany. START: **T-bana to Kungsträdgården.**

1 ★★ kids Nordiska Museet.
This museum places modern design in historical context, showing you the interiors of ordinary houses and how styles have changed over the decades. The small room settings are particularly evocative, charting what the younger generation saw as progress and the older lot saw as garish bad taste in design (p 13, bullet **1**).

2 ★★★ Nationalmuseet. Walk around Design 19002000 to see the development of Swedish (and international) design over the past 100 years. It's divided into the Stockholm Exhibition of 1930, the Scandinavian Design movement of the 1950s, and Swedish New Simplicity from the 1990s when Sweden once again took the lead in modern design. It includes both the familiar

and the unfamiliar and is a powerful collection (p 14, bullet **3**).

3 ★★★ Shopping for modern design. For 20th-century Scandinavian furniture, lighting ceramics, and glass from a whole swathe of masters, try Andrew Duncanson's **Modernity**. The clean lines of furniture by Bruno Mathsson (1907–1988) such as his laminated wood and plaited webbing chairs can be seen at **Studio B3**; while **Carl Malmsten** (1888–1972) went against the trend and down the path of renewing traditional Swedish craftsmanship for his light wooden furniture. For an idea of what your home could look like on a large budget, go to **Svensk Tenn;** for colorful accessories, try **10 Swedish Designers**. If you have the time and energy,

1976 Room Setting at the Nordiska museet.

travel outside the center to the biggest **Ikea** store in the world (www.ikea.se). For details of shops, see p 98.

see p 98.

4 ★★ **Riches.** Über-fashionable, this is where design-conscious Sweden comes to graze. It's an old restaurant, originally conceived as a typical brasserie, but has recently been jazzed up with leather banquettes and startling lights. Dress up, you're here to be seen. *Birger Jarlsgatan 4, Östermalm.* ☎ *679 68 42. $$.*

5 ★★ **Index – The Swedish Contemporary Art Foundation.** Originally, a photographic gallery, the foundation puts on 6–8 exhibitions a year, emphasizing the experimental by both international artists and Swedish unknowns. ⏱ *1½ hrs. Kungsbrostrand 19.* ☎ *640 60 60. www.indexfoundation.se. Tues–Fri*

noon–4pm, Sat, Sun noon–5pm. T-bana T-Centralen.

6 ★★ **Bonniers Konsthall.** This family-run, non-profit making art gallery was set up in honor of the founder's daughter, Jeanette Bonnier, after she died in a car accident. The impressive building, designed by Swedish architect, John Celsing, is a glass structure shaped like an iron, with light flooding into spaces where young artists exhibit. Enjoy the excellent café or join in a talk or seminar. ⏱ *1 hr. Torsgatan 19.* ☎ *736 42 48. www.bonnierskonsthall.se. Admission 50 SEK adults, under-18s free. Wed 11am–8pm, Thurs–Sun 11am–5pm. T-bana St Eriksplan.*

7 ★★ **Färgfabriken.** The Center for Contemporary Art and Architecture or 'laboratory of the contemporary' has an experimental, cutting-edge approach. Founded in 1995 in an old 1889 factory, its wide program of art, video, and installation

Liljevalchs Konsthall was designed by Carl Bergsten in 1913-1916.

The Stockholm Art Scene

Stockholm is becoming known for its vibrant art scene with both non-profit making and commercial galleries a vital part. For young Swedish artists, visit **Natalia Goldin** in Vasastaden (www.nataliagoldin.com). Galleri Charlotte Lund in Östermalm (www.gallericharlottelund.com) is a high profile gallery for international and young artists. In Södermalm, try the art collective **Candyland** (www.candyland.se) and **ID:I**, a non-commercial co-operative of artists who each take over the gallery for three weeks at a time (www.idigalleri.org). For more information, pick up a copy of the free guide *Konstguiden*, available from most galleries. Many galleries close from mid-June to mid-August.

events include architecture and design in several exhibition spaces.
1½ hrs. Lövholmsbrinken 1, Liljeholmenorsgatan 19. ☎ 645 07 07. www.fargfabriken.se. Admission 40 SEK adults, under-18s free. Thurs–Sun noon–6pm during exhibitions. T-bana Liljeholmen

⑧ ★★ kids Liljevalchs Konsthall. The Liljevalchs is renowned for its major exhibitions and collections of international, Swedish, and Nordic art from the 20th century. The highlight is the *Spring Salon* (end of January to mid-March) that showcases works by unknown artists. Built thanks to the wealth of industrialist Carl Fredrik Liljevalch (1837–1909), the gallery was designed by Carl G. Bergsten (1879–1935) and built in neo-classical style in 1913–1916.
1 hr. Djurgardsvägen 60.
☎ 50 83 13 30. www.liljevalchs.stockholm.com. Tues–Sun 11am–5pm (Tues–Thurs to 8pm). Bus 47. Tram 7. Ferry to Djurgården (summer).

⑨ ★★★ Magasin 3 Stockholm Konsthall. This privately-funded gallery opened in 1987 and has 6–8 exhibitions a year concentrating on 3-dimensional work. The gallery also commissions site-specific installations. Previous exhibitions in this former 1930s warehouse include photographs by Julia Margaret Cameron (1815–1897) alongside those of Miroslav Tichy (b. 1926); Gilbert & George, Pipilotti Rist, and Mona Hatoum. There are also talks, lectures, and film screenings.
1 hr. Frihamnen. ☎ 545 680 40. www.magasin3.com. Admission 40 SEK adults; under-20s free. Entrance fee gives you a season ticket to that season's exhibitions. Thurs noon–7pm, Fri–Sun noon–5pm. Guided tours Sat 2pm. Bus 1, 76.

⑩ ★★ Restaurang 1900. You have two options here; eat in the restaurant with its design echoes of 1900s classics, or drink at the circular, contemporary, and very cool bar, which is highly rated for its cocktails (p 119). *Regeringsgatan 66.* ☎ 20 60 10. www.r1900.se. $$$.

Gourmet Stockholm

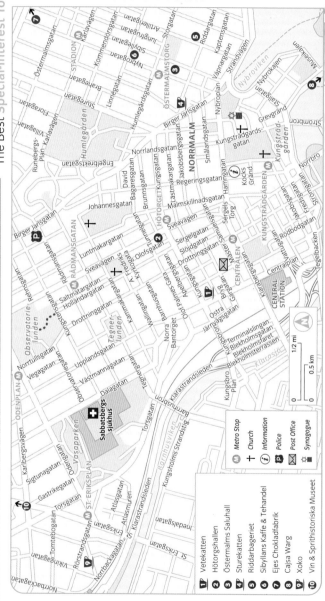

Metro Stop
+ **Church**
(i) **Information**
P **Police**
⊠ **Post Office**
✡ **Synagogue**

0 — 1/2 mil

0 — 0.5 km

1 Vetekatten
2 Hötorgshallen
3 Östermalms Saluhall
4 Sturekatten
5 Riddarbageriet
6 Sibyllans Kaffe & Tehandel
7 Ejes Chokladfabrik
8 Cajsa Warg
9 Xoko
10 Vin & Sprithistoriska Museet

E at, drink, and be poor, but have fun on the way. Until I came to Stockholm for the first time, I had no idea that the city must rate as one of Europe's gourmet capitals. Apart from top dining, café life offers good cooking and different venues from the cozily old-fashioned to the strikingly modern. The other great surprise is the food markets where you can stock up on all kinds of exciting produce. START: **T-bana to Kungsträdgården.**

1 ★★ kids **Vetekatten.** Start as you mean to go on at this delightful old-fashioned café and pastry shop. It's all rather prim and proper, just as your great aunt would like. Classic Swedish pastries, teas, and coffees are taken in a series of small rooms with old furniture and pretty textiles—you feel as if you're in an old Swedish home. The shop also sells all its cakes and bread so you can stock up for your picnic. *Kungsgatan 55.* ☎ *21 84 54. $.*

2 ★★ **Hötorgshallen.** Descend into the basement under the Filmstaden Sergel multiplex and you step away from Stockholm into an international world. The food market was built in the 1950s and renovated in the 1990s. What it lacks in soul it makes up for in choice. Whereas Östermalm is essentially Swedish, Hötorgshallen offers a varied stock—Indian spices, Turkish stuffed vine leaves, sweet Greek delicacies. If you want to eat here, make for **Kajsas Fish** restaurant for its fabulous fish soup and grilled fresh fish (☎ 20 72 62). ⏱ *1 hr. Hötorget. www.hötorgshallen.se. Indoor market: May–Aug Mon–Fri 10am–6pm; Sept–Apr Mon–Thurs 10am–6pm, Fri 10am–4pm. Outdoor market: Mon–Fri 10am–7pm, Sat 10am–5pm, Sun noon–5pm. T-bana Hötorget.*

3 ★★★ **Östermalms Saluhall.** At this food hall you can find fish

Cheeses on sale at Östermalms famous food hall.

that were happily swimming around a few hours before from Melanders Fisk, fresh truffles and seasonal game from B. Andersson, and rich, dark brown bread from the bakery of Amandus Brödbrod—what more could any self-respecting foodie desire? This is one of Europe's great food halls, where you walk past stalls with moose heads staring down at you and chocolate stands that groan under the sweet weight. And it's full of excellent cafés and restaurants to tempt you. ⏱ *1 hr. Östermalstorg, www.ostermalms hallen.se. Mon–Thurs 9.30am–6.30pm, Fri 9.30am–4pm; Jun–Aug Sat 9.30am–2pm. T-bana Östermalmstorg. (See p 16, bullet* **6** *).*

Take an old-fashioned break at Sturekatten.

5 ★★ **Riddarbageriet.** Don't miss this famous bakery, which produces some of the best bread and cakes in Stockholm, with the highest praise going to Johan Sorberg's sourdough loaves. You can have tea or coffee (and some of those cakes) at the few small tables inside. *Riddargatan 15.* ☎ *660 33 75. Mon–Fri 8am–6pm, Sat to 3pm. T-bana Östermalmstorg.*

6 ★★ **Sibyllans Kaffe & Tehandel.** A real treat awaits you at this posh tea and coffee shop with its old-fashioned jars full of specialist blends. The shop has been here since World War I, as have, so it seems, some of its clients. *Sibylle-gatan 35.* ☎ *662 06 63. www. sibyllanskaffetehandel.com. T-bana Östermalmstorg.*

4 ★★ **kids Sturekatten.** Enter through an archway and go upstairs to this little café. Here, in a series of different rooms all decorated with comfortable chairs and old paintings, you can settle down to traditional Swedish *prinsesstarta* (cream and marzipan mix) or the fabulous *äppelpaj* (apple pie). Service is as friendly as the surroundings. *Riddargatan 4.* ☎ *611 16 12. $.*

7 **Ejes Chokladfabrik.** Established in 1923 and supplying chocolates to the Royal Family, this is the place for upmarket chocolate. Everything is handmade from the best Belgian ingredients here on the premises, leaving nothing to chance. *Erik Dahlgsgatan 25.* ☎ *664 27 09. www.ejeschoklad.se. T-bana Karlaplan.*

Top dessert chef makes the cakes at Xoko.

The Wine and Spirit Museum.

8 ★★ Cajsa Warg. Named after Sweden's most famous cookery book writer who lived from 1703 to 1769, this wood-paneled shop in Södermalm is a good choice for carefully sourced, organic foods (local, Swedish, and international). Staff test everything they stock, and provide a selection of cooked foods as well. This is the place for a picnic: either make your own choice or buy one of their tasty recommendations. *Renstiernas Gata 20.* ☎ *642 23 50. www.cajsawarg.se. Mon–Fri 8am–9pm, Sat, Sun 10am–9pm. Bus 2, 3, 59, 76.*

9 Xoko. Mecca for the sweet-toothed, Xoko is the inspiration of chocolatier and dessert chef, Magnus Johansson. He created the desserts for King Carl-Gustav's 60th birthday banquet and does the honors with the desserts at the Nobel Laureate banquet, so you know you can expect the best. The sublime desserts come at a price, but one well worth paying. *Rörstrandgatan 15.* ☎ *31 84 87. www.xoko.se. $$$*

10 ★ Vin & Sprithistoriska Museet. In 1923, the building that now houses the Wine and Spirits Historical Museum was a warehouse; in 1989 it was converted into this quirky, interesting, and extensive museum. The story is of Sweden's history of alcohol production—and consumption—from the Middle Ages when strong liquor (*brännvin*) was used for medicinal purposes and, more unusually, to make gunpowder. The route takes you past brewing equipment, a wine merchant's shop from around 1900 (patronized by playwright August Strindberg), and a home distillery of 1830 when potatoes were used to make schnapps. The audio tour in English brings it all alive. But the most enjoyable bit comes at the end, when you can test your sense of smell with 55 spices and herbs used in vodka and liquors, and then move on to listen to 200 jolly drinking songs. The museum website gets lots of requests for the songs and words (they have over 2,000 songs in their archives) for the Midsummer celebrations. *Dalagatan 100.* ☎ *744 70 70. www.vinosprit historiska.se. Admission 40 SEK adults, under-17s free. Free with Stockholm Card. Free audio guide in English. Tues 10am–7pm, Wed–Fri 10am–4pm, Sat, Sun noon–4pm. Bus 2, 4, 65.*

Drottningholm

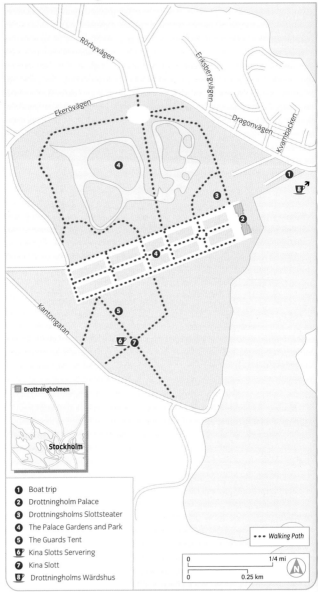

Rörbyvägen

Eriksbergsvägen

Ekerövägen

Dragonvägen

Kvarnbacken

❹

❸

❷

❹

Kantongatan

❺

🄶 ❼

Drottningholmen

Stockholm

❶ Boat trip
❷ Drottningholm Palace
❸ Drottningsholms Slottsteater
❹ The Palace Gardens and Park
❺ The Guards Tent
🄶 Kina Slotts Servering
❼ Kina Slott
🄱 Drottningholms Wärdshus

••• Walking Path

0		1/4 mi
0	0.25 km	

Drottningholm Palace has been the Royal Family's home since 1981. There's plenty to see at this UNESCO World Heritage Site and it's a great place for a picnic. 10km west of Stockholm on the island of Lovön, it makes a perfect excursion by boat, but if you're pushed for time, go by boat and return by bus and T-bana.

START: **Boat to Drottningholm from Stadshusbron on Kungsholmen.**

❶ ★★★ kids Boat trip. The skyline of Riddarholmen and the imposing Stadshuset recede into the distance as you slip away from central Stockholm. Smart residential areas give way to hidden creeks, marshland, and bays with moored boats during the one-hour journey. The trip itself is a pleasure, particularly if you take an old 1900s steamboat. *1 hr. Stadshusbron. www.strommakanabolaget.se. By boat: buy tickets at the booth or online. May 1–Sep 13, daily and hourly 10am–3pm. Return daily and hourly 11am–4pm. Return ticket 150 SEK, one way 110 SEK. By T-bana: Brommaplan, then bus 177, 178, 301, 323.*

❷ ★★★ kids Drottningholm Palace. The Palace is a Royal family home and so you can see only one impressive part of it. Designed by the royal architect Nicodemus Tessin the Elder (1615–1681), it was inspired by Versailles (see box p 43). Its State Rooms are decorated with polished marquetry floors, painted ceilings, lavish furnishings, and portraits of past kings. The central part is built around a huge stairwell with *trompe l'oeil* paintings giving an infinite perspective. Levées or morning receptions were held in Queen Hedvig Eleanora's **State Bedroom**; Queen Lovisa Ulrika's **Library** was decorated by Jean Eric Rehn (1717–1793) in lavish style; and antique wood-burning porcelain stoves in some rooms add a domestic feel. *1 hr. ☎ 402 62 80. www.royalcourt.se. Adult 80 SEK, child 7-18 years 40SEK, under 7s free. May–Aug daily 10am–4.30pm Sep daily noon–3.30pm, Oct–Apr*

Take the old-fashioned 1900s steam boat to Drottningholm.

A battling Hercules faces the back of the palace.

Sat, Sun noon–3.30pm. Guided tours in English May Sat, Sun 10am, noon, 2pm, 4pm, Jun–Aug daily (same times), Oct–Apr Sat, Sun noon, 1pm, 2pm.

❸ ★★ **kids** **Drottningholms Slottsteater.** The 1776 Court Theater looks modest, but inside the world's oldest theater is a wonderful piece of design, the scenery all moved by wooden hand-driven machinery and still in working order. Designed by architect Carl Fredrik Adelcrantz (1716–1796), the theater retains its original 18th-century stage and hand-painted decorations. Sound effects may be simple but they work: a wooden box filled with stones makes thunder; other apparatus make waves and wind. Watch all this in action at the summer opera festival (p 139). ⏲ *1 hr. Admission 60 SEK adults, under-16s free. Free with Stockholm Card (see p 11). Guided tours in English daily May noon–4pm; Jun–Aug 11am–4pm, Sat 1–3pm.*

❹ ★★★ **kids** **The Palace Gardens and Park.** Three Baroque gardens stretch out from the back

of the palace. The Embroidery Parterre, laid out in 1640, takes you past a dramatic statue of Hercules to the Water Parterre with its topiary and fountains. Beyond lies the enclosed Theatre Bosquet. The whole vista is flanked by rows of symmetrically-cut chestnut trees. To the north, the English Park is dotted with lakes, small islands, and buildings such as the late 18th-century Governor's Residence, a small gatehouse, and a Gothic Tower of 1792. With these wonderful follies and a perfect *rus in urbe* setting, I expect Marie Antoinette to pop out from behind a tree. ⏲ *1 hr.*

❺ ★ **The Guards Tent.** From afar it looks like an elaborate marquee, but this was built in 1781 as the quarters for Gustav III's dragoons. It was designed by Adelcrantz as a 'tent in a Turkish army camp' and is now the museum of Drottningholm's Royal Guard. *30 mins. Mid-Jun–mid-Aug 11am–4.30pm.*

❻ **kids** **Kina Slotts Servering.** Buy coffee and cakes in the dimly lit vaults of what was the kitchen of

Royal Architects

The Tessin family had a huge influence on Swedish architecture, town planning, and landscaping. **Nicodemus Tessin the Elder's** (1615–1681) European travels gave him a passion for the new, flamboyant Baroque style. His greatest work was Drottningholm Palace, which his son, **Count Nicodemus Tessin the Younger** (1654–1728) completed after his father's death. The younger Tessin also traveled around Europe, but under Swedish royal patronage, giving him such status that King Louis XVI turned on the fountains at Versailles especially for him. When the Royal Palace in Stockholm was destroyed by fire, Tessin created its replacement, although it had not been completed when he died in 1728. He also drew up master plans for the development of Stockholm, designed various churches, and built his own magnificent home, Tessinska Palatset in Slottsbacken, which has been the residence of the Governor of Stockholm County since 1968.

the Chinese Pavilion and then sit outside in the sunshine. *$*.

7 ★★ **Kina Slott.** The original Chinese Pavilion, pre-fabricated in Stockholm, was put up in secrecy for Queen Lovisa Ulrika's 33rd birthday in 1753 as a gift from her husband, King Adolf Frederik. It didn't

The secret 'Confidence'.

last long and was replaced 10 years later by this pretty, low, curved building, restored to its original bright colors in the 1990s and furnished with Chinese and Japanese artifacts. Beside it stands 'The Confidence', a separate building designed as a private dining room. No servants entered the room; instead a ready-laid table came up through the floor from the underground kitchens. On the other side is a 1760s billiard room and King Adolf Frederik's lathe workshop—it was all the rage for 18th-century royals to practice woodturning. *As Palace, but closed Oct-Apr. Adult 70 SEK, child 7-18 years 35 SEK, under 7s free. Free with Stockholm Card (see p 11).*

8 ★★ **Drottningholms Wärdshus.** Walk out of the Palace grounds to this restaurant housed in a building from the 1850s. The cooking is European and as elegant as the setting. It's top dining at top prices, but then it should be—it's the Swedish Royal family's local after all. *Malmbacken.* ☎ *759 03 08. www.drottningholms wardshus.se. $$$.*

Winter in Stockholm

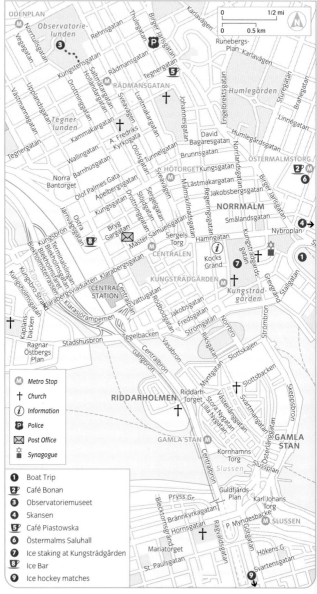

0	1/2 mi
0	0.5 km

Metro Stop ⓜ
Church ✝
Information ⓘ
Police 🅿
Post Office ✉
Synagogue ☰

1 Boat Trip
2 Café Bonan
3 Observatoriemuseet
4 Skansen
5 Café Piastowska
6 Östermalms Saluhall
7 Ice staking at Kungsträdgården
8 Ice Bar
9 Ice hockey matches

Winter in Stockholm is a magical time. The sea freezes over and skaters take to the open-air ice rinks, the seasonal markets open, and the shops are decorated with some of the most beautiful winter windows. The days might be short but the city makes up for it with its sparkling lights and street lanterns. START: **T-bana to Kungsträdgården.**

① ★★★ kids **Boat trip.** The ice crackles, the boat slowly moves forward; this is a boat trip with a difference because it's on a ship that can become an icebreaker if necessary. Slipping through the frozen sea as you edge out of Stromkajen towards the Fjärderholmarna islands, you get a totally different view of Stockholm from the wintery sea. It's a wonderful experience. 1 hr 15 mins. *Strömkajen. City Discovery. www. city-discovery.com. Fri, Sun. Contact them via the website for times and prices. T-bana Kungsträdgård.*

② ★ **Café Bonan.** You'll need plenty of refueling stops to help keep you warm, and this dimly lit place is invariably full of customers drinking rich dark hot chocolate and eating sweet pastries. *Humlegardsgatan 9.* 662 49 04. $.

③ ★ kids **Observatoriemuseet.** The small, old Observatory Museum is only open in winter when the sky is dark enough to see the stars. The museum is housed in a hilltop observatory built for the Royal Swedish Academy of Sciences in the late 1740s, and opened in 1753. Guided tours take you through the observation rooms furnished with 18th-century instruments belonging to astronomer Pehr Wargentin (1717–1763) who lived and worked here. Climb the narrow staircase to the dome for a fabulous view of the city spread below you. On Tuesdays and Thursdays you can gaze at the heavens through a telescope, weather permitting. In 1931, the observatory moved its scientific research to Saltsjobaden in the Stockholm archipelago. 1 hr. *Drottninggatan 120.* 54 54 83 90.

Keeping warm in Skansen.

Café Piastowska's warm, cosy interior.

www.observatoriet.kva.se. Admission 50 SEK adults, 25 SEK children 7–18 years. Jan: Sun noon–3pm, guided tour in English at 1pm. Oct–Mar Tues, Thurs 6–9pm with guided tours in English hourly. Cupola open 6–7pm. T-bana Radmansgatan.

④ ★★★ kids Skansen. An openair museum might not seem the place for a winter visit, but Skansen pulls the stops out in winter with its Christmas markets, the annual Santa Lucia celebrations on December 13 with its huge firework display lighting up the sky, and finally its New Year's celebrations. Walking through the buildings as the snow gently falls really takes you away from it all and you feel as if you have truly stepped back in time. It also makes you very happy to be living in the 21st-century with all its creature comforts. *See p 49.* ⏱ 2 hrs. Bus 47.

⑤ Café Piastowska. A warming bowl of *borscht* or a plate of Swedish meatballs is just what you should order at this tiny, cozy, friendly venue. There are tables outside in summer,

but the point of the place is the cluttered interior, hearty food, and good beer. The last time I was there, a suitably laidback and somewhat old-fashioned couple performed, he on the guitar, she singing the equivalent of *Blowing in the Wind.* Perfect for a melancholy winter evening. *Tegnergatan 5.* ☎ 21 25 08. $$.

⑥ ★★★ Östermalms Saluhall. In winter this food hall is full of game and seasonal delights. It's particularly attractive in the run up to Christmas, with festive food on sale throughout the covered market. And it's great for unusual presents of food to take home. ⏱ 1 hr. Östermalmstorg, www.ostermalms hallen.se. Mon–Thurs 9.30am– 6.30pm, Fri 9.30am–4pm; June–Aug Sat 9.30am–2pm. T-bana Östermalmstorg. (See p 16, bullet ⑥.)

⑦ ★★ Ice skating at Kungsträdgården. There's a small open-air ice rink here in winter, which is best at night when you can skate under the floodlights. It's popular and well-established (it's been running here since 1962) and it's free to use so all you have to pay for is skate rental. ⏱ 1 hr. Mon– Thurs 9am–6pm, Tues, Thurs 9am–9pm, Sat, Sun 10am–6pm. Skate rentals ☎ 20 01 77. 40 SEK per hour adults, 20 SEK per hour for those up to 18 years old. T-bana Kungsträdgården.

⑧ Ice Bar. On the basis that you're so cold already nothing will affect you, try the Ice Bar. At –5°C (23°F) you'll be grateful for the furlined coats and warm boots that come with the ice-cold vodka. *Nordic Sea Hotel.* ☎ 505 630 00. $$. *See p 150.*

Christmas Markets

Stockholm's Christmas markets are as colorful as anywhere in Europe. Particularly worth looking out for are Swedish Christmas sweets, reindeer meat, and smoked sausages. Keep warm with copious mugs of *glogg* (mulled wine). The market at **Skansen** (p 49) is held at weekends in December until Christmas Eve. It's a good source for craft products, from handmade candles and Christmas food to traditional Christmas ornaments and the famous Dala horses, originally carved by lumberjacks when they weren't cutting down the forests in the Dala region. **Stortorget** in Gamla Stan is another place to make for with the historic surroundings adding to the atmosphere. The market runs from 24 November to 24 December (p 59, bullet ③). **Sigtuna** has a fair on the four Sundays before Christmas (see Sigtuna, p 156). For that royal touch, go to **Drottningholm** Slott on the first weekend in December (p 41).

⑨ ★★ kids Ice hockey matches. It's fast and furious as native teams such as Djurgården IF and international names like the NHL Pittsburg Penguins and the Ottawa Senators battle it out in front of capacity crowds. Matches take place at Hovet, the old ice hockey stadium within the Globen complex and in Globen itself, the huge spherical construction that stands out for miles. Djurgården IF is the major Stockholm team and plays in the Elitserien, the Swedish Elite League, one of the top European leagues. *Arenavägen, Johanneshov. Tickets* ☎ *077 131 00 00. www.globen arenas.se/en. T-bana Globen.*

Ice skating at Kungsträdgarden.

Skansen

1 The Town Quarter
2 Northern Skansen's Farm Dwellings
3 Wild animals
4 Eastern Skansen
5 Southern Skansen
6 Central Skansen
7 Solliden Stage
8 Solliden Restaurant

In 1891, Artur Hazelius founded Skansen, the world's first open-air museum. It's a huge park, with over 150 buildings and a zoo. It was opened at a time when industrialization was threatening the rural way of life and the idea was to preserve some of the buildings and culture of old Sweden. I'm always amazed by the small size of the buildings and how close people lived to each other. **START: Bus 47, Tram 7 or summer ferry to Djurgården from Nybroplan.**

1 The Town Quarter. Ten old houses, bought up by the municipality of Stockholm to clear the way for modern properties in Södermalm, were brought to Skansen in 1926–1933 to start the Town Quarter. Here you find the **Glassworks**, established in 1936, where you can watch glass being blown, and then buy the delicate results in the shop. The **Furniture Factory, Engineering Works, Pottery,** and **Shoemaker's House** stand cheek-by-jowl with the **Bookbindery** and a **worker's home**. Skansen also has a serious purpose—endangered species, especially the common plants once found in the gutters and alleyways of old Stockholm, are planted outside the **Shoemaker's House**. Step into **Charles Tottie's Residence** built by Sweden's

The Old Shop in the Town Quarter.

richest merchant in the 18th century to see how the other half lived. The dining-room has sweet-smelling cedar paneling while the drawing room is in Cuban mahogany. Skansen naturally has the **Hazelius Mansion**, the birthplace of the founder. The house was built around 1720 as a silk factory, and only converted into a house in 1803. Next door, the **Pharmacy** is full of old equipment for weighing chemicals and distilling liquids to make medicines. If you're flagging, go into **Petissan**, a little café that once served coffee to engineering students in Södermalm in the late 19th century. Just below the Town Quarter you find the 19th-century **Tobacco and Match Museum**, appropriately enough as it was a Swede who invented the safety match in 1844.

2 Northern Skansen's Farm Dwellings. The early 19th-century **Älvros Farmstead** comes from north Sweden where farmers lived by rearing animals and tending the land or from forestry, hunting, and fishing. It was a hard life with everyone sleeping in one room beside an open fire, though not as primitive as the **Sami Camp**. The Sami (Laplanders) built turf and wood huts as they followed the herds of reindeer. In contrast, the **Delsbo Farmstead** shows a well-to-do farm of 1850, with a splendidly decorated doorway, all frills and furbelows. Don't miss the beautifully carved wooden 14th-century **Vastveit Storehouse**,

The Sami camp with the Nordiska museet in the background.

one of the oldest buildings at Skansen.

❸ Wild animals. You can see elk, horses, lynxes, foxes, polecats, wild boars, and European bison in one section, though by far the most popular animals here are the brown bears. They may be Sweden's largest predator, but they look remarkably cute. There are also rare breeds such as fluffy goats, southern Swedish country cows that were believed to have died out in 1993, and the Gotland pony. The **Children's Zoo**, open May to September, has small animals; children can ride on horses and ponies at the Stables.

❹ Eastern Skansen. The **Finn Settlement** buildings came from Varmland where Finnish farmers settled in the 16th century to escape oppression and raids from Russia. The Finns were given land where they built farms and lived off the slash-and-burn style of cultivation. The settlement has a wooden building for drying and threshing corn, a smoke cabin, storehouse, and barn. In the early 19th century excessive alcohol consumption encouraged the temperance movement, led by people such as Peter Sieselgren, a Swedish priest who persuaded Parliament to prohibit distilling spirits at home in 1855. The small **Temperance Hall** was just one of hundreds of such places, which both educated and entertained the locals.

❺ Southern Skansen. A lot of the fun of this outdoor museum is in the details. In the small house in the **Oktorp Farmstead**, you can imagine the farmer sitting in his 'high seat' warming his feet at the open fire, while beggars lurked in the kitchen behind a special beam to keep them, literally, in their place.

❻ Central Skansen. Seglora Church dates from 1730. It was shut up, abandoned in 1903, and transported here in 1916. The simple wooden church with its wooden floors and old-fashioned box pews is now one of Sweden's most popular wedding venues. Market Street leads you past the country market stalls to **Bolinastorget**, popular for both Midsummer celebrations and the Christmas market that is one of Stockholm's winter highlights (see p 47). Finally, **Skogaholm Manor** makes me want to decorate my own house in Scandinavian fashion. It's gracious without being too grand, furnished in Swedish rococo style, and has a wonderful collection of blue and white china in the pantry. There's a Chinese drawing room, a

Practical Matters—Skansen

Skansen, Djurgårdsslätten 49–51. ☎ 442 80 00. www.skansen.se. Tickets range from 90–12 SEK for adults and 30–50 SEK for children 6-15 years old, depending on the time of year. Free with Stockholm Card (see p 11). Open May 1–Jun 19 and Sep, 10am–8pm, Jun 20–Aug 31 10am–10pm. For other times, telephone or check on the website. Bus 47, tram 7, ferry to Djurgården (summer).

nursery, bedchamber, and parlor. Well, I can always dream.

7 Solliden Stage. When the stage was built in 1938, its broadcasting equipment made it the most modern in the country and every major name came to perform here, such as the Swedish tenor Jussi Björling who gave an annual concert until his death in 1960. Today there are events throughout the year, from concerts to folk-dance displays.

8 Solliden Restaurant. You get a good view of Stockholm from the main restaurant. It's a lovely building with decorations by well-known artists and serves a tempting smörgåsbord. The **Tre Byttor** occupies three small rooms and is a replica of an 18th-century tavern. It serves dishes such as carpaccio of venison and a Swedish platter of three different kinds of herring. ☎ 566 370 00. www.profilrestauranger.se. $$.

Wild brown bear and her cub in the grounds of Skansen.

Stockholm with Kids

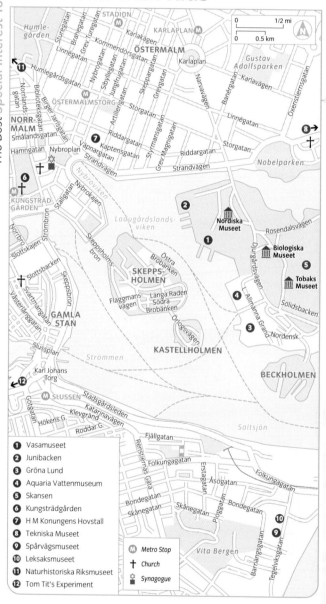

1 Vasamuseet
2 Junibacken
3 Gröna Lund
4 Aquaria Vattenmuseum
5 Skansen
6 Kungsträdgården
7 H M Konungens Hovstall
8 Tekniska Museet
9 Spårvägsmuseet
10 Leksaksmuseet
11 Naturhistoriska Riksmuseet
12 Tom Tit's Experiment

Ⓜ Metro Stop
✝ Church
⌂ Synagogue

Stockholm is one of the most child-friendly cities in Europe. Even museums become fun with their properly thought-out entertainment and special rooms for drawing, painting, and dressing up (see Livrustkammeren, p 30). If all else fails, the great outdoors beckons at Gröna Lund, Sweden's oldest amusement park. This is a long day; I recommend splitting it into two and pick and choose according to your family's tastes. START: **Bus 47, Tram 7, ferry to Djurgården (summer).**

1 ★★★ kids **Vasamuseet.** If you take them to only one 'grown-up' museum, make sure it's the Vasa where the old ship looms, huge and apparently invincible, above us mere humans. See p 8. ⏱ 1½ hrs.

2 ★★★ kids **Junibacken.** Even if your child hasn't heard of Astrid Lundgren, Sweden's most famous children's author, they'll love it here where her famous characters, Pippi Longstocking, Emil and the Lion-heart Brothers, and others, live in their own wonderland. In Pippi's Villa Villekulla, children can ride her horse and play in her kitchen. The main action is a mini-train journey through the stories; with an English commentary through enchanting scenes. Take some distractions of your own because the lines in summer can be long. There's a good café and a well-stocked shop. ⏱ 1 hr. Galärvarvsvägen, Djurgården ☎ 587 230 00. www.junibacken.se. Admission 110 SEK adults, 95 SEK children 3–15 years, under-3s free. Free with Stockholm Card (see p 11). Jan–May, Sep–Dec, Tues–Sun 10am–5pm, June; Aug 10am–5pm; Jul 9am–6pm. Bus 47. Tram 7. Ferry to Djurgården (summer).

3 ★★★ kids **Gröna Lund.** This is a real favorite with children, so keep this one for the afternoon if you want to visit other attractions. Though many rides are not as terrifying as some modern parks (built in 1883 this family-owned amusement park is Sweden's oldest), the free-fall 'Power Tower', at 80m (262 feet) high Europe's highest, challenges

Models at the Vasa Museum.

Thrills at Gröna Lund.

even the very brave. The roller-coaster, Kvasten (Broomstick), twists and turns and carries you beneath the tracks. Older rides are gentler. Evening concerts are held once a week. ⏱ *2 hrs. Allmänna Gränd 9.* ☎ *587 502 00. www.gronalundcom. Admission 70 SEK ages 7–64 years (more for evening concert); over-65s and under-6s free. Individual ride 20 SEK, multi-ride, all day passes from 280 SEK, under-3s free rides. Free with Stockholm Card (see p 11). Summer times (May–Sep) vary between 11am–10pm and 11am–11pm; call for details. Closed end Sep–end Apr. Bus 47. Tram 7. Ferry to Djurgården (summer).*

❹ ★ kids Aquaria Vattenmuseum. This small imaginative aquarium takes you through

Kids jumping in Kungsträdgården.

different habitats. Step into a rain-forest complete with thunderstorms and then walk over a rope bridge looking down at piranhas and catfish. There's a Nordic waters' display, and a glass tunnel where you're inches away from the sharks swimming. The intrepid can climb down into a sewer for a fish eye's view of what goes on underground— but you might prefer not to know. ⏱ *1 hr. Falkenbergsgatan 2.* ☎ *660 90 89. www.aquaria.se. Admission 80 SEK adults, 40 SEK children 6–15 years. Free with Stockholm Card (see p 11). Mid-June–end Aug 10am–6pm; Sep–mid-June Tues–Sun 10am–4.30pm. Bus 47. Tram 7. Ferry to Djurgården (summer).*

❺ ★★★ kids Skansen. This will be the other attraction vying for your older children's attention, and the young ones will be enchanted by the zoo and particularly the bears. (See p 49.) ⏱ *2 hrs.*

❻ ★★ Kungsträdgården. The long esplanade that goes down to the water was once the royal kitchen garden. Today it's a delight-ful park with summer concerts, mime artists, and children's activi-ties, such as a summer trampoline (50 SEK for 5 minutes). ⏱ *1 hr.*

❼ ★★ H M Konungens Hovstall. Meet just before 2pm for a guided tour of the Royal Mews, a working royal department. The King's coachmen show you around the beautiful working harnesses, the 19th- and 20th-century carriages, and the 14 large Swedish half-blood horses that you see exercising in the riding arena (they may be on holiday in the summer). Plus, there's the garage with 11 royal cars. ⏱ *1 hr. Väpnargatan 1.* ☎ *402 61 06. www.kungahuset.se. Admission 50 SEK adults, 20 SEK under-18s. Jun 23–Aug 15 Mon–Fri 2pm; Aug 23–Nov 30, Jan 12–Jun 1 Sat, Sun 2pm. T-bana Östermalmstorg/ Kungsträdgården. Bus 47, 62, 69.*

⑧ ★★ kids Tekniska Museet. The Museum of Science and Technology is full of interactive exhibits geared to children, particularly in the Space section. When they're tired, take them to Cino 4, for a 4-D movie, the 4th dimension being extra technical effects (see p 68, bullet ❹). ⏱ *1½ hrs. Museivägen 7, Norra Djurgården.* ☎ *450 56 00. www.tekniskamuseet.se. Admission 60 SEK adults, 30 SEK children 6–19 years, under-6s free. Free Wed 5–8pm. Free with Stockholm Card (p 11). Mon–Fri 10am–5pm (to 8pm Wed), Sat, Sun 11am–5pm. Guided tours daily. Bus 69.*

⑨ ★★ kids Spårvägsmuseet. The 60 vehicles—from an 1877 horse-drawn tram to the transport of the future—really do keep children entertained. You can pretend to drive a 1960s tram, ride a miniature underground, and buy Brio trains in the shop. ⏱ *1 hr. Tegelviskgatan 22.* ☎ *462 55 31. www.spårvagsmuseet.sl.se. Admission 30 SEK adults, 15 SEK children 7–18 years, under-7s free. Free with Stockholm Card (see p 11). Mon–Fri 10am–5pm, Sat, Sun 11am–4pm. T-bana Slussen then bus 2, 53.*

⑩ ★★ kids Leksaksmuseet. Stockholm's Toy Museum is the place where I finally realized I've never grown up. Exhibits change all the time with new toys appearing like magic. Musical instruments, mechanical toys, models, dolls' houses, there's something from everybody's childhood there. It shares an entrance with the Transport Museum. ⏱ *1½ hrs. Tegelviksgatan 22.* ☎ *641 61 00. Admission 30 SEK adults, 15 SEK children 7–18 years, under-7s free. Free with Stockholm Card (see p 11). Mon–Fri 10am–5pm, Sat, Sun 11am–4pm. T-bana Slussen then bus 3, 55.*

⑪ ★★ kids Naturhistoriska Riksmuseet. You can't miss the enormous Natural History Museum. This huge building designed by Axel Anderberg (1860–1937), who also designed the Royal Opera House (see p 83) is certainly dramatic.

Hours of curiousity satisfied in the space section of the Tekniska Museet.

Huge creatures at the Natural History Museaum.

Completed in 1916, it's one of the 10 largest museums of its kind with more than 9 million objects, consisting of fungi, animals, minerals, and plants from all over the world. It's divided into different exhibitions: *Life in Water* brings you up close to giant squid; in *Marvels of the Human Body* interactive exhibits let you measure the electricity in your heart; meteorites from outer space are revealed in *Treasures from the Earth's Interior*; while *4.5 Billion Years* is quite simply The History of Life on Earth with dinosaurs to keep the children amused. The other great attraction is **Cosmonova**, Sweden's only IMAX 3-D cinema (see p 138). *Frescativagen 40.* ☎ *519 540 00. www. nrm.se. Main museum free. Admission to exhibitions 70 SEK adults, under-17s free. Free with Stockholm Card (see p 11). Cosmonova 85 SEK adults, 50 SEK children 5–18 years. Exhibitions + one Cosmonova show 120 SEK adults, 50 SEK children 5–18 years. Tues, Wed, Fri 10am–7pm, Thurs 10am–8pm, Sat, Sun 11am–7pm. Last show at Cosmonova starts one hour before the Museum closes. T-bana Universitetet; bus 40, 540.*

⑫ ★★ **kids** **Tom Tit's Experiment.** Even children with no apparent interest in science will find this award-winning attraction (I use the word advisedly) absorbing. Opened in 2006 in the former Alfa-Laval factory, Sweden's largest Science Center covers four floors of interactive, participatory fun, while also teaching valuable scientific lessons. Try the section devoted to the body where you can remove the internal organs of a life-size human; or the water section (aprons are provided) with its vortex of swirling water; or get thrown around by Sweden's biggest robot (you are strapped in) There are different events daily—rat racing anyone? It's worth the trek out south of Stockholm. After all, this might be the place where your child decides to become the next Einstein. ⏱ *2 hrs. Storgatan 33, Södertälje.* ☎ *522 525 00. www. tomtit.se. Tickets 165 SEK adults, 145 SEK children 3–17 years (some height and age restrictions). Free with Stockholm Card (see p 11). Weekdays 10am–4pm, weekends 11am–5pm. Pendeltag to Södertälje Centrum, then bus 754 and 755 to Centrifugen.* ●

Gamla Stan & Riddarholmen

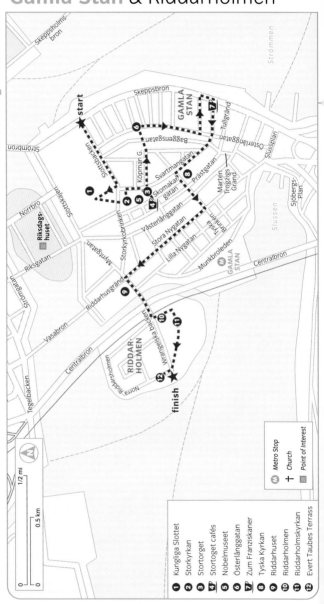

START ★

Skeppsholms-
bron

Strömmen

Skeppsbron

GAMLA
STAN

❼

Tullgränd

Österlånggatan

Baggensgatan

❻

Storkyrkobrinken

Storsbron

Strömbron

Norrbro

Köpman G.

Svartmangatan

❸

Skomakare-
gatan

❽

Prästgatan

Mårten
Trogzigs
Gränd

Slussplan

Sjöbergs-
Plan

Slussen

**Riksdags-
huset** 🔲

Riksgatan

❶

Myntgatan

❷ ❺
❹

Västerlånggatan

Stora Nygatan

Lilla Nygatan

Munkbroleden

GAMLA
STAN Ⓜ

Centralbron

Strömgatan

Vasabron

Riddarhusgränd

❾

Riddarholmsbron

RIDDAR-
HOLMEN

Norra Riddarholmen

Centralbron

Wrangelska backen

❿

⓫

Tegelbacken

⓬

FINISH ★

🅰

| 0 | 1/2 mi |
| 0 | 0.5 km |

Ⓜ *Metro Stop*

✝ *Church*

🔲 *Point of Interest*

❶ Kungliga Slottet
❷ Storkyrkan
❸ Stortorget
❹ Stortorget cafés
❺ Nobelmuseet
❻ Österlånggatan
❼ Zum Franziskaner
❽ Tyska Kyrkan
❾ Riddarhuset
❿ Riddarholmen
⓫ Riddarholmskyrkan
⓬ Evert Taubes Terrass

In the 13th century the whole city, protected by a defensive castle, was crowded onto the tiny island of Gamla Stan (Old Town), the inhabitants earning their living from the trade between Lake Mälaren and the Baltic Sea. By the 18th century, 10,000 people lived here. What you see today is a wonderful area of restored medieval and 18th-century houses, dominated by the huge Kungliga Slottet (Royal Palace). START: **T-bana to Gamla Stan. Bus 2, 43, 176 to Kungliga Slottet. T-bana to Kungsträdgården and walk.**

① ★★★ kids Kungliga Slottet. Walk up to the Royal Palace from Skeppsbron where a statue of Gustav III, sculpted in 1799 in memory of the 'charming king' who was murdered in 1792, faces the palace. To your right, enter the curved outer courtyard where the Changing of the Guard takes place daily. The palace is magnificent and should be on everyone's must-do list (see p 29). 2 hrs.

② ★★ Storkyrkan. Stockholm's 700-year-old cathedral is a striking, lofty building. Inside it's a mix of styles: the medieval red tiles a background for the Baroque royal chairs designed by Nicodemus Tessin the Younger (1654–1728) in 1684. Other treasures include the 1489 St George and the Dragon by Berndt Notke of Lübeck carved from oak and real elk antlers, and The Parhelion painting showing an extraordinary light phenomenon over Stockholm in 1535 with six sparkling rings of light in the skies—a sure sign, to superstitious medieval minds, of the end of the world. Also look out for a 120cm (12 feet) high seven-branched candlestick. 30 mins. Trångsund 1. ☎ 723 30 16. Admission 25 SEK. Free for under 16s. Free with Stockholm Card (see p 11). May–Aug 9am–6pm, Sep–Apr 9am–4pm. Services Sat, Sun 11am. English tour of tower Jul–Aug 1pm. T-bana Gamla Stan. Bus 2, 43, 55, 76.

③ ★★ Stortorget This pretty medieval square was the scene of the notorious Stockholm Bloodbath in November 1520 when the Danish King Kristian II, who defeated the Swedish Regent, Sten Sture the Younger, betrayed his promise of an amnesty. A feast at Tre Kronor Fortress ended with the partygoers

The cathedral from the narrow streets.

Mårten Trotzigs Grand is the city's narrowest street.

arrested and more than 80 noblemen executed the next day. Today it's more peaceful with the Nobel Museum looking over the square's cafés and terraces. ⏱ *15 mins.*

4 ★ **Stortorget cafés.** Forget the infamous bloodbath over a fortifying cup of hot chocolate and a cake at **Chokladkoppen** (*Stortorget 18* ☎ *20 31 70. $*) or, if it's raining, dive into the next door **Café Kaffekoppen**. *Stortorget 20* ☎ *20 31 70. $.*

5 ★★ **kids Nobelmuseet.** You can stand for ages looking up at the ingenious display of Nobel prizewinners whose biographies, printed on large banners, slowly circle the ceiling like hangers in a dry cleaners. There's plenty to occupy you in this small museum: short films about the laureates, TV clips on sets located in the floor, and headphones for listening to various acceptance speeches—don't miss the highly entertaining speech by Isaac Bashevis Singer (1902–1991), who received the Nobel Prize for Literature in 1978. ⏱ *45 mins. Borshuset, Stortorget.* ☎ *534 818 00. www.*

nobelmuseet.se. *Admission 60 SEK adults, 20 SEK children 7–18 years, under-7s free. Free with Stockholm Card (see p 11). T-bana Gamla Stan. Bus 2, 43, 55, 76.*

6 ★★ **Österlånggatan.** While tourists stick to Västerlånggatan, locals prefer to shop in and around Österlånggatan, known for its small boutiques selling crisp table linen, scrubbed white painted furniture, and iron candleholders that will make your home look thoroughly Scandinavian. Don't miss the tiny alleyway that's a mere 90cm (less than 3 feet) wide, called Mårten Trotzigs Gränd after a German merchant who cannily married the mayor's daughter and so ensured his place in history. ⏱ *30 mins.*

7 ★ **Zum Franziskaner.** Claiming its place in history as Stockholm's oldest restaurant (1421), this rebuilt 1906 version looks pretty good with wooden floors, paneling, and 19th-century artifacts. Lunch, around 80 SEK, comes with a hot dish, bread, salad, and coffee. *Skeppsbron 44.* ☎ *411 83 30. $$.*

Riddarmolmen is a tiny island.

8 ★★ **Tyska Kyrkan.** The splendid German church is a reminder of the power of the German Hanseatic League, whose trading empire from the 13th to late 17th century included Gamla Stan. The church, built in 1638–1642 has a royal gallery, a 1660s pulpit, and a beautiful altar. ⏱ *20 mins. Svartmangatan 16A.* ☎ *411 11 88. www.stockholms domkyrkoforsamling.se. Jul, Aug 11am–5pm; Sep–June 11am–4pm. T-bana Gamla Stan. Bus 2, 43, 55, 76.*

9 ★★ **Riddarhuset.** The House of the Nobility, considered one of northern Europe's most beautiful buildings, was built in the Dutch Renaissance style (1641–1647) as a base for the nobility. The inside is as beautiful as the exterior, with several halls, a magnificent double staircase, and the Knights' Room with a ceiling painted by David Klöcker von Ehrenstrahl (1628–1698). 2,320 coats-of-arms of the noble cover the walls. It's also a wonderful concert venue (p 135). ⏱ *30 mins. Riddarhustorget 10.* ☎ *723 39 90. www.riddarhuset.se. Admission 50 SEK adults, 25 SEK students. Mon–Fri 11.30am–12.30pm.*

10 ★★ **Riddarholmen.** Walk over the Riddarholmsbron bridge onto this tiny island, a strange, deserted place at night when the offices housed in the magnificent 17th-century noble palaces have closed. A statue to the city's founder, the 13th-century Regent, Birger Jarl, dominates the spacious square. ⏱ *30 mins.*

11 ★★ **Riddarholmskyrkan.** The ghost town feel extends to the magnificent 14th-century Riddarholm church where many of Sweden's monarchs lie buried. The

Evart Taube entertains.

walls are decorated with coats-of-arms, but my attention was caught by the chapels and underground vaults. The Carolean chapel, built between 1671 and 1743, houses small ornate tombs to remind you of the frailty even of royal life. The tomb of the founder of the Bernadotte dynasty (the present Royal family) and of Gustav Adolphus Magnus are particularly bombastic. ⏱ *40 mins. Birger Jarls Torg.* ☎ *402 61 30. www.royalcourt.se. Admission 30 SEK adults, 10 SEK children 7–18 years, under-7s free. Free with Stockholm Card (see p 11). Mid-May–mid-Sep 10am–4pm. Tours in English Jun–Aug 2pm and 4pm. T-bana Gamla Stan.*

12 ★★ **Evert Taubes Terrass.** End the day in the early evening on the terrace steps, looking out onto the waters and over to the imposing Stadshuset (City Hall). This is where romantics hang out with a bottle of fizz, overlooked by the statue of Evert Taube (1890–1976), Sweden's much-loved singer and writer. ⏱ *40 mins. Norra Riddarholmshamnen. T-bana Gamla Stan.*

Djurgården

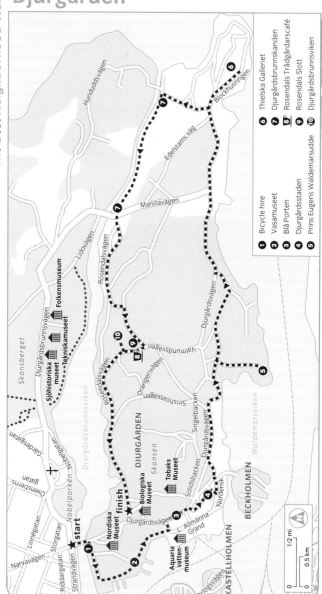

1 Bicycle hire
2 Vasamuseet
3 Blå Porten
4 Djurgårdsstaden
5 Prins Eugens Waldemarsudde

6 Thielska Galleriet
7 Djurgårdsbrunnskanden
8 Rosendals Trädgårdscafé
9 Rosendals Slott
10 Djurgårdsbrunnsviken

The former royal hunting ground on the delightful island of Djurgården (pronounced 'your-gore-den') is a green, forested area with very few houses. However, it does have some of Stockholm's best museums, the Vasa Museum, the Gröna Lund funfair, and the two museums founded by Artur Hazelius around 1900—the magnificent Nordiska Museum and the outdoor museum Skansen. You can either walk (although it's a long tour) or hire a bicycle as I did. START: **Bus 47, Tram 7, summer ferry to Vasamuseet.**

1 Bicycle hire. Djurgårdsbrons Sjocafé just over the ornate iron bridge connecting Östermalm and Djurgården is a good place to hire a bicycle. Bikes are 65 SEK an hour, or 250 SEK for the day, whichever is the cheaper, but they will need an ID so take your passport with you. Then cycle off down the relatively traffic-free roads and cycle paths around the island. *Galårvarvsvägen 2.* ☎ *660 57 57. Open Mar–Oct 9am–9pm. Bus 47. Tram 7. Ferry to Djurgården (summer).*

2 ★★★ kids Vasamuseet. No matter how many times I see this ship, walking into the Vasa museum always sends a shiver down my spine. It's one of the world's great sights and I always find something new to discover on the ship itself or in the surrounding displays that explain what is an incredibly romantic story. *2 hrs. See p 8, bullet* **3**.

3 ★★ kids Blå Porten. The 'Blue Door' is well worth seeking out, hidden beside the contemporary art gallery, Liljevalchs Konsthall (see p 35, bullet **8**). It's a delightful café with a wonderful secret garden, and is perfect for families. Get your food inside and your cakes from a groaning table and find a place outside. It's one of the best short stops if you're visiting any of the nearby museums. *Djurgårdsvägen 64.* ☎ *663 87 59. $$.*

Blå Porten is one of the city's most delightful outdoor cafés.

4 ★ Djurgårdsstaden. Get away from the crowds down the small streets on the south of the island. There aren't many old wooden houses left and most of them seem to be occupied by high-tech firms, but the area gives you a very real idea of old Stockholm. Cross over to Beckholmen—a small island with dry docks used first for commercial boats and subsequently by the Swedish navy—where a local pitch boilery gave the island its name. It's still a working area, and with its old equipment recalls its former days.

The garden at Prins Eugens Waldemarsudde.

5 ★★ **Prins Eugens Walde-marsudde.** Go past the impossibly handsome and huge Italian Embassy, located in a house called Oakhill down beside the water, to this other huge waterside mansion, designed by Ferdinand Boberg (1860–1946) who also designed the NK Department Store (p 94). It was owned by Prins Eugens (1865–1947), the son of Oscar II and the younger brother of King Gustav V. Eugens was a noted artist and his former mansion is full of the landscapes for which he rightly became famous. He was also a great patron and so this patrician house is full of early 20th-century Swedish art. Temporary exhibitions of important artists are held on the upper floors. Even if you don't go for the art, the house is a tour in itself, and there's an excellent shop.
⏱ 1 hr. Prins Eugens Vag 6. ☎ 545 837 00. Admission 85 SEK adults, under-18s free. Free with Stockholm Card (see p 11). Bus 47.

6 ★★ **Thielska Galleriet.** Seek out this wonderful example of a villa by architect Ferdinand Boberg (1860–1946) and its fascinating collection of Nordic art from the late 19th and early 20th century. Both belonged to the remarkably rich banker Ernest Thiel (1860–1947), who described himself as 'Something extremely surprising and dangerous for my time: a thinking banker.' However, all his intellect didn't save him from bankruptcy shortly after World War 1. The Swedish state then stepped in and bought both the house and the collection. All the major Swedish artists of Thiel's time are displayed here, plus works by Thiel's friend, Edvard Munch. It makes a fascinating gallery of works by—to foreign visitors at least—relatively unknown artists. ⏱ 1 hr. Sjötullsbacken 8. ☎ 662 58 84. www.thielska-galleriet.se. Admission 50 SEK adults, under-16s free. Free with Stockholm Card (see p 11). Mon–Sat noon–4pm, Sun 1pm–4pm. Bus 69.

7 ★★ **Djurgårdsbrunnskan-den.** Make your way north to where the Djurgårds canal empties into the sea. The route takes you beside the small canal, flanked by trees that turn it into an Impressionist painting. If you're tired and have no bicycle, the no. 69 bus from the

Thielska Gallery will take you to the canal bridge. From here it's a short stroll to the next stop.

8 ★★ Rosendals Trädgårdarscafé. This pretty organic market garden, shop, and superb café seem to be in the middle of the countryside. The café is housed in a greenhouse and you can take your home-cooked meal or coffee onto its garden terrace and relax in a thoroughly rural setting, disturbed only by birdsong and children's voices. *Rosendalsterrassen 12.* ☎ *54 58 12 70. www.rosendalstradgard. com. $$.*

Stop for a coffee and organic food at Rosendals Trädgårdarscafé.

painted ceilings, tiled stoves, and odd, interesting artifacts throughout. ⏱ *1 hr. Rosendalsvägen.* ☎ *402 61 30. www.royalcourt.se. Admission 70 SEK adults, 35 SEK children 7–18 years. Free with Stockholm Card (see p 11). Bus no. 47 or 69 then walk.*

9 ★★ kids Rosendals Slott. The small, two-storey high, royal summer retreat, built in the 1820s, was turned into a museum about the life of Karl XIV Johan (1818–1844) in 1913. The palace was prefabricated in Norrmalm and constructed here. It's well worth visiting (guided tours only) for its Swedish furniture and textiles. The fabric in the dining room is pleated to resemble a tent. You'll find wonderfully

10 ★ Djurgårdsbrunnsviken. From here walk or cycle along the quiet paths to the canal at the north of the island. Rosendalsvagen will take you back to the Djurgårds bridge and over to Strandvågen.

Rosendal's Slott.

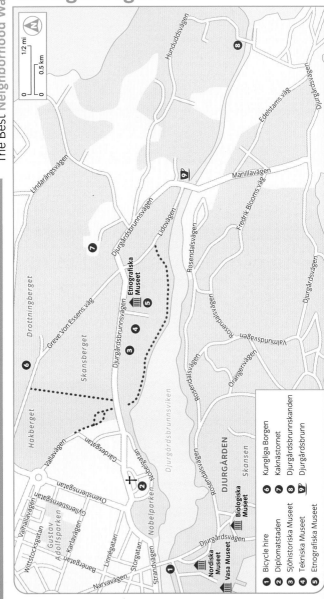

1/2 mi
0.5 km
0

Hunduddsvägen

Edelstams väg

Djurgårdsvägen

Manillavägen

Fredrik Blooms väg

Lindarängsvägen

Djurgårdsbrunnsvägen

Lidovägen

Djurgårdsvägen

Etnografiska Museet

Rosendalsvägen

Drottningberget

Greve Von Essens väg

Djurgårdsbrunnsvägen

Rosendalsvägen

Valmundsvägen

Skansberget

Rosendalsvägen

Orangerivägen

Hakberget

Gärdesgatan

Djurgårdsbrunnsviken

Rosendalsvägen

Vallavägen

Nobelgatan

DJURGÅRDEN

Skansen

Oxenstiernsgatan

Gyllenstiernsgatan

DJURGÅRDEN

Biologiska Museet

Wittstocksgatan

Gustav Adolfsparken

Banérgatan

Karlavägen

Linnégatan

Storgatan

Strandvägen

Djurgårdsvägen

Valhallavägen

Nordiska Museet

Vasa Museet

Narvavägen

Etnografiska Museet

1. Bicycle hire
2. Diplomatstaden
3. Sjöhistoriska Museet
4. Tekniska Museet
5. Etnografiska Museet
6. Kungliga Borgen
7. Kaknästornet
8. Djurgårdsbrunnskanden
9. Djurgårdsbrunn

Ladugårdsgärdet is the greenest part of Gärdet, an extensive residential neighborhood mainly built up in the 1920s and 1930s with Functionalist apartments for workers. Located on the island directly north of Djurgården, its royal associations began in the 15th century and continued under Karl XI (1655–1697) whose fort of Kungliga Borgen became a military training area from the 17th century on. Along the south shore there are a series of good museums. You can walk through this area or, as in Djurgården, take advantage of the quiet roads and green fields and hire a bicycle. START: **Bus no. 69 to Nobelparken for Diplomatstaden. Bus 47, Tram 7 of summer ferry to Djugården for bicycle hire.**

① ★★ kids Bicycle hire. See p 63 for details on the Djurgårdsbrons Sjocafé on Djurgården, just over the bridge from Östermalm, which is the nearest place for bicycle rental. *Galårvarvsvågen 2.* ☎ 660 57 57. Open Mar–Oct 9am–9pm. Bus 47. Tram 7. Ferry to Djurgården (summer).

② Diplomatstaden. As you can guess from the name, you'll find various foreign embassies in this area, a move that started when the British ambassador moved into Nobelgatan 7 in 1910. To the south lies the small

Nobelparken, named after Alfred Nobel (1833–1896); a little farther along Dag Hammarskjölds Vag you come to the brick **Engelska Kyrkan** (English Church) that was moved from the city center out to here in 1913, although it was only finished in the 1980s. 🕐 *30 mins.*

③ ★★ kids Sjöhistoriska Museet. This lovely building housing the National Maritime Museum stands beside a quiet stretch of water. The peaceful setting seems a far cry from the warlike maritime history that made Sweden the ruling

Sculpture in Nobelparken.

power in much of northern Europe and the Baltic Sea from 1611 to 1721. As well as Sweden's maritime history, the museum also tells the stories of shipbuilding in Sweden and of life on board. There's also a splendid maritime art collection as well as regularly changing exhibitions.

🕑 1½ hrs. Djurgårdsbrunnsvägen 24. ☎ 519 549 00. www.sjohistoriska.nu. Admission 50 SEK adults, under-18s free. Free with Stockholm Card (see p 11). Jun–Aug 10am–5pm, Sep–May Tues–Sun 10am–5pm. Guided tours daily 1pm (pre-book in English). Bus 69. See p 26, bullet ⑥.

④ ★★ kids **Tekniska Museet.** The National Museum of Science and Technology is designed very much with families in mind. It presents the history of Swedish technology and industry; inside the very large Machine Hall, pride of place goes to the country's oldest steam engine built in 1832. You'll also discover commercial aircraft, early Swedish cars from Saab, Scania, and Volvo, motorbikes, and a working model railway. But most families gravitate towards Teknorama where you can find out what it's like to be an astronaut at the *Adventure in Space* section following Sweden's only astronaut, Christer Fuglesang.

Strap your children into a machine that simulates weightlessness then let them find out what it's like to repair a space station. Then it's on to the Mine, which is suitably spooky and underground. Finally Sweden's only 4-D cinema, Cino 4, has daily shows in English. The 4th dimension involves extra technical effects. 🕑 2 hrs. Museivägen 7, Norra Djurgården. ☎ 450 56 00. www.tekniskamuseet.se. Admission 60 SEK adults, 30 SEK children 6–19 years, under-6s free. Free Wed 5–8pm. Free with Stockholm Card (see p 11). Mon–Fri 10am–5pm (to 8pm Wed), Sat, Sun 11am–5pm. Guided tours daily. Bus 69.

⑤ ★★ kids **Etnografiska Museet.** The first thing you see at the National Museum of Ethnography is a sculpture made out of old suitcases. In an increasingly technology-dominated world, it's a nice reminder of how so many of the valuable artifacts displayed in the museum were painstakingly brought back by travelers and scientists from the 18th century on—the explorer Sven Hedin (1865–1952) was one of the main contributors of Buddhas and Chinese artifacts. The museum is inventively laid out, placing its masks and ceramics, totem poles

The Japanese Tea house at the Etnografiska Museet.

The lofty Kaknåstornet tower dominates the skyline.

and statues, canoes and huts in delightful settings. In the gardens the secluded Japanese Teahouse, Zui-Ki-Tei (Pavilion of Auspicious Light), following the designs of a Japanese Professor, was built here in 1990. ⏱ *1½ hrs. Djurgårds-brunnsvägen 34.* ☎ *519 550 00. Admission 60 SEK adults, under-20s free. Free with Stockholm Card (see p 11). Tues, Thurs, Fri 10am–5pm, Wed 10am–8pm, Sat, Sun 11am–5pm. Bus 69.*

6 Kungliga Borgen. If you have the time and energy, strike north along Greve von Essens Vag to Kungliga Borgen, where you can see the remains of a fortress where generations of monarchs trained their troops. ⏱ *30 mins.*

7 Kaknästornet. On a clear day, this dominant tower, 155m (508 feet) high, gives a dramatic view across 60km of capital and countryside from its observation points 30 and 31 floors up. The huge tower was opened in 1967 as the major broadcast beacon for almost all radio and TV signals in the country and now provides satellite connections between European cities via five huge and daunting-looking dishes on the ground. To savor the view, you can linger over a coffee or a meal in the 28th-floor restaurant. ⏱ *30 mins. Mörka Kroken 28–30.* ☎ *667 21 05. www. kaknastornet.se. Bus 69.*

8 Djurgårdsbrunnskanden. From here you can do a circular walk, taking around 25 to 30 minutes, along Hunduddsvägen to where the Djurgård canal reaches the sea and return beside the still waters of the canal to a small bridge that connects this area with Djurgården.

9 ⭐⭐ **kids Djurgårdsbrunn.** It's tempting to flop down into a deckchair and sit for hours on the terrace here, looking onto the bridge over the canal. Good coffee, cakes, or a light lunch are recommended before you take the no. 69 bus back into town (p 114). *Djurgårdsbrunnsvägen 68.* ☎ *624 22 00. $$.*

Chill out at Djurgårdsbrunn.

West Södermalm & Långholmen

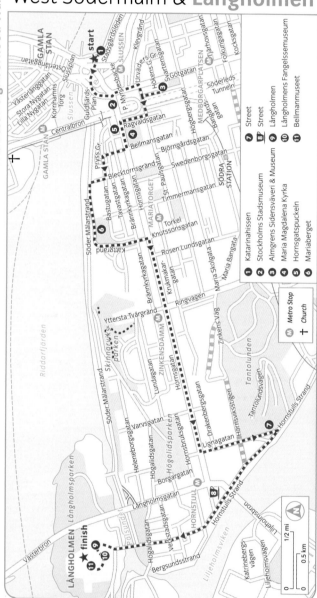

1 Katarinahissen
2 Stockholms Stadsmuseum
3 Almgrens Sidensväveri & Museum
4 Maria Magdalena Kyrka
5 Hornsgatspuckeln
6 Mariaberget
7 Street
8 Street
9 Långholmen
10 Långholmens Fängelsemuseum
11 Bellmanmuseet

Ⓜ Metro Stop
✝ Church

Södermalm, familiarly known as 'Söder', is a large island and was traditionally the working class area of Stockholm. As with working class areas everywhere, it is now being talked up as the new, cutting-edge part of the city. Certainly it is full of small boutiques, cafés, restaurants, and late-night clubs, although in parts you need to know where to look. Don't be shy; ask a resident for help; everyone here is fiercely proud of Söder. It's so large that I've divided it into two parts: the east and the smaller western part.
START: **T-bana to Slussen.**

Steep streets characterize Södermalm.

1 ★★ **Katarinahissen.** All visits to Söder must start or end at the top of the 37m (124 feet) high elevator that whisks you up in a few seconds to a glorious view over Stockholm laid out below you. *Stadsgården.* ☎ *642 47 86. Ride is 10 SEK. Free with Stockholm Card (see p 11). Jan–mid-May, Sep–Dec 10am–6pm, mid-May–Aug 8am–10pm. T-bana Slussen. See p 19, bullet* **2**.

2 ★ kids **Stockholms Stadsmuseum.** Appropriately for a city museum, the building, completed in 1685, has served as the city hall, then as law courts and prison, schools, and a tavern. It was designed by Nicodemus Tessin the Elder (1615–1681) and became a museum in the 1930s. This imaginative museum uses smells and sounds, as well as artifacts, pictures, and maps to demonstrate Stockholm through the centuries, from the Stockholm Bloodbath of 1520 to huge growth in the 20th century. ⏱ *45 mins. Ryssgården.* ☎ *508 316 00. Free admission. Tues–Sun 11am–5pm, Thurs 11am–8pm. T-bana Slussen.*

3 ★ kids **Almgrens Sidensväveri & Museum.** You normally don't associate Sweden with silk weaving, but in 1833, the enterprising Knut August Almgren opened a factory based on a secret technique of silk weaving that he ingeniously stole from the French while visiting Lyon. For decades he was the largest employer of female labor, offering his workforce healthcare, pensions, and a co-operative shop. Swedish high society adored the sensuous new material and the Almgren family carried on satisfying their fashionable clientele until 1974 when the factory closed. In 1991, a descendant of the original owner re-opened the factory as a working museum. Today you can discover the story and watch the 170-year-old looms in action. The shop sells silk scarves and fabric. ⏱ *45 mins. Repslagargatan 15.* ☎ *642 56 16. www.kasiden.se. Admission 65 SEK. Free with Stockholm Card (see* *p 11). Mon–Fri 9am–4pm, Sat, Sun 11am–3pm. Guided tours in Swedish Wed, Sat, Sun 1pm, Mon 1pm, 6pm. T-bana Slussen.*

④ Maria Magdalena Kyrka. Söder's oldest church was started in 1580, but not completed until the early 17th century. Its central plan is the model for all of Stockholm's later glorious Baroque churches. Today it is rather marooned on its commanding position. The short distance away from the main road gives its graveyard a particularly peaceful feel. Some of Sweden's poets are buried here, the best known outside Sweden being the troubadour, Evert Taube. ⏱ *15 mins. St Paulsgatan 10.* ☎ *462 29 40. www.mariamagdalena.se. Mon. Tues, Thurs–Sun 11am–5pm, Wed to 7.30pm. T-bana Slussen.*

⑤ Hornsgatspuckeln. Cross over the road to the small elevated, traffic-free section of Hornsgatan for a good selection of art and design galleries. Try **blås & knåda** (no. 26) for a wide variety of modern ceramics and jewelry; **Gallery Kontrast** (no. 8) for photography, and **The Glassery** (no. 38) for some startling and innovative glass items. The

Unusual glass at blås & knåda.

glamorous **Efva Attling** designs modern jewelry, and counts Madonna among her clients (no. 42). ⏱ *45 mins.*

⑥ Mariaberget. Walk down Guldfjardsterrassen to the sheltered path along Monteliusvägen, high above Söder Mälarstrand. You're rewarded with great views over the water and an idea of what old Södermalm was like. Small stone houses cluster in the narrow streets and alleyways and there's a little park full of mothers and children in the summer months. ⏱ *30 mins.*

⑦ ★★ kids Street. Take the T-bana from Mariatorget to Hornstull and walk south to the waterside area called Street. It was started by Englishman John Higson as a meeting place and modeled on London's Spitalfields market. Before 2000 there was nothing here; now it buzzes on summer weekends with entertainment, people partying, stalls of a variable kind, and a very good restaurant (see below). ⏱ *1½ hrs. Hornstull Strand. www.streetints stockholm.se.*

⑧ ★★ kids Street. On the water's edge and championing local and organic produce, the restaurant is a winner, literally—in 2007 it gained a Slow Food Award. Weekend brunch is particularly popular, but it's open all week and attracts the young, the arty, and the trendy. *Hornstull Strand 4.* ☎ *658 63 50. www. streetrestaurant.se. $$$.*

⑨ ★★ kids Långholmen. Walk directly north to the delightful island of Långholmen, separated from Södermalm by a small stretch of water crammed with moored boats. From 1724 to 1975 the island housed a large prison, which preserved Långholmen's peace from

A boat owner arrives for the weekend at Långholmen.

large-scale development. It's something of a green oasis, with a walking and cycling path and places to swim on the north shore, including the small sandy Klippbadet and Strandbadet coves. ⏱ **2 hrs.**

⑩ ★ kids Långholmens Fangelssemuseum. The prison museum is housed inside what is now a delightful hotel (see p 149). There were originally two prisons on the island, with around 700 cells, housing the usual murderers and thieves as well as journalists and politicians who had fallen foul of society. The last execution in Sweden took place here in 1910, using the guillotine that you can see along with 300 years of Swedish prison history.

⏱ **20 mins.** Långholmen Hotel, Långholmsmuren 20. ☎ 720 85 00. www.langholmen. com. Admission 25 SEK adults, 10 SEK children 7–14 years, under-7s free. Daily 11am–4pm. T-bana Hornstull then walk. Bus 4, 40 then walk.

⑪ Bellmanmuseet. Given the fame of the 18th-century troubadour Carl Michael Bellman (1740–1795), it's surprising there are so few places associated with him. So try to visit this late 17th-century house that contains a small museum devoted to him. He didn't live here, but frequently visited an opera singer friend who worked in the prison. The museum's café is a good place for a spot of light refreshment if you've decided to swim from the small nearby beach. ⏱ **45 mins.** Stora Henriksvik. ☎ 669 69 69/ www.bellman.nu. Admission 30 SEK adults, under-15s free. May, Sep, Oct Sat, Sun noon–4pm; mid-Jun–Aug daily noon–4pm. T-bana Slussen. Bus 4, 40.

A model on guard at the old prison on Långholmen.

Eastern **Södermalm**

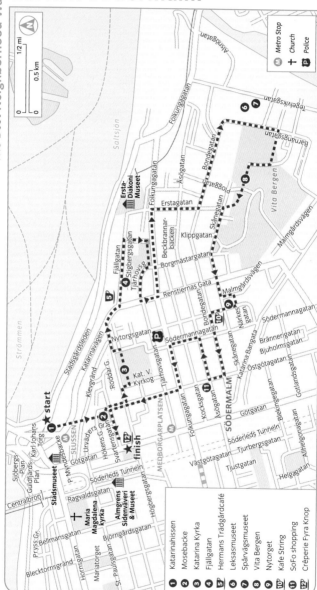

Metro Stop

✝ Church

P Police

❶ Katarinahissen
❷ Mosebacke
❸ Katarina Kyrka
❹ Fjällgatan
5️⃣ Hermans Trädgårdcafé
❻ Leksasmuseet
❼ Spårvägsmuseet
❽ Vita Bergen
❾ Nytorget
🔟 Kafe String
⓫ SoFo shopping
⓬ Crêperie Fyra Knop

Whereas western Södermalm is mainly residential, Eastern Södermalm enjoys a reputation for its trendy bars, cafés, and restaurants, many of them in SoFo (south of Folkungsgatan). Take a good pair of walking shoes because you'll find yourself criss-crossing SoFo frequently and the whole area is surprisingly hilly. START: **T-bana to Slussen.**

1 ★★ **Katarinahissen.** Whether you're going east or west, all routes on Södermalm start with this huge elevator from which you can see much of Stockholm. *See p 19, bullet* **2**.

2 ★ **Mosebacke.** This small area high up at the top of the Katarinahissen elevator became famous for entertainment in the 1850s with carousels, a summer theater, and open-air dance floors. A permanent theater was put up in 1859 along with the gateway leading onto Mosebacke Terrass. The theater's fortunes waxed and waned until it closed in 1958 for complete renovation. It re-opened in 1967 as **Södra Teatern** and has never looked back. Beside it stands **Mosebacke Etablissement**, one of Stockholm's best live music and performance venues. The café/bar provides a great summer spot on the outside terrace— I like to order a glass of wine or a coffee, mingle with the musicians who are invariably hanging out here,

and look out over the stunning view. ⏱ *15 mins.*

3 ★★ **Katarina Kyrka.** The modern altar is the only outward sign of the complete rebuild of this church in 1995, after a disastrous fire in 1990 destroyed its impressive Baroque interior. The reconstruction used 17th-century building techniques to reproduce the original church, designed by Jean de la Vallée (1620–1696), as faithfully as possible. It followed the central plan established in Maria Magdalena (see p 72, bullet **4**) where both altar and nave are located right in the middle of the building. Outside, the peaceful cemetery contains the simple grave of Anna Lindh, Sweden's foreign minister murdered in 2003. In summer, the church puts on a good program of concerts, or visit at lunchtime to listen to the organ and take in the beauty of your surroundings. ⏱ *20 mins. Högbergsgatan 13.* ☎ *743 68 00. Mon–Fri 11am–5pm, Sat, Sun 10am–5pm.*

Katarina Kyrka high on Södermalm.

Admission free. T-bana Medborgarplatsen.

4 ★★ **Fjällgatan.** Walk along Mäster Mikaels Gata (named after the city's first employed executioner), for a glimpse of the 18th-century houses built after the disastrous fire in 1723 that also badly damaged the nearby Katarina Kyrka (see bullet **3**). You'll emerge onto Fjällgatan, which you can follow right down to Fåfängan, gazing at Stockholm's waterside below you. ⏱ *30 mins.*

5 ★ **Hermans Trädgårdcafé.** 15 freshly made, inventive salads at lunchtime and a spectacular view makes Herman's a real attraction. As this vegetarian restaurant opens at 11am, you can also use it as a coffee and cake stop. *$$.*

6 ★ **kids Leksaksmuseet.** No matter where you come from—Sweden, the USA, planet Mars—children's toys are pretty universal and so the well-established Toy Museum

Old houses just of Hytorget.

will delight everyone. It's a large collection arranged in sections of steam engines and trains (always a favorite), cars, airplanes, peepshows, teddy bears, and dolls, including 16th-century dolls' houses. See p 55, bullet **10**. ⏱ *1½ hrs.*

7 ★★ **kids Spårvägsmuseet.** From the early days of public transport in Stockholm and the first horse-drawn tram of 1877 to the future of transport; it's all here. You'll also find information on the T-bana stations that have been decorated with pictures and different wall finishes, turning them into their own artworks. The museum itself is housed in an old bus station and, as at all transport museums, the sight of more than 60 trams, buses, and carriages from the late 1880s on curiously captivates a child's imagination. Special activities include a ride on a vintage bus on Saturdays and Sundays. See p 55, bullet **8**. ⏱ *1 hr.*

8 ★★ **Vita Bergen.** This hilly park (translated as 'White Mountains') is crowned by Sofia Kyrka, the church named after Sofia of Nassaua (1836–1913), Queen of Sweden from 1872–1907. The design won an architectural contest in 1899 and it opened in 1906. It's surrounded by just a few old wooden houses painted the traditional red and once owned by the working classes, today they are highly desirable, particularly as they are near that necessary accessory of the young professional, an allotment. ⏱ *45 mins.*

9 ★ **Nytorget.** Stop in this pretty garden square that has a street of old houses running off it. The little park is a local hit, full of children playing and people sitting on benches and organizing picnics. ⏱ *30 mins.*

⑩ ★ Kafe String. As laidback as you could ever want, the last time I was at this café I shared the place with four friends, locals playing an endless game of cards, a guy on his laptop perched on a chair on (yes, *on*) the windowsill, and a couple who were clearly in the throes of a burgeoning love affair. This attractive, quirky venue offers sandwiches, drinks, and coffee—and all the furniture to go home with should you need a table and chairs or even a motorbike to go with your latte. *Nytorgsgatan 38.* ☎ *714 85 14.* $.

The laid-back Kafe String where everything is for sale.

⑪ ★★ SoFo shopping. Okay, you've heard all about it, so now's the time to go shopping in the area. My advice is to wander at will in the streets that run between Renstiernans Gata and Götgatan. But for a little guidance, head to **Bondegatan**. For a good selection of secondhand and vintage clothing try the famous **Lisa Larsson Secondhand** (no. 43), and for 1960s furniture, visit **Södra Skattkammaren** (no. 44). Also worth seeking out is **cocktail** for some honest-to-goodness kitsch (34 Bondegatan), and for one of the best art and architecture bookshops in Stockholm, try the newly moved **konst-ig** at Asögatan 124. 🕒 *1½ hrs.*

⑫ ★ kids Crêperie Fyra Knop. Stockholm's only genuine crêperie is full of odd things such as fishing nets hanging around, giving it a certain nautical charm, while its sweet and savory crêpes are as good as you get in Brittany. It's open 5–11pm daily, and so is just the place for a quick bite before traipsing back to the center. *Svartensgatan 4.* ☎ *640 77 27.* $.

Great plastic kitsch at Cocktail.

Östermalm

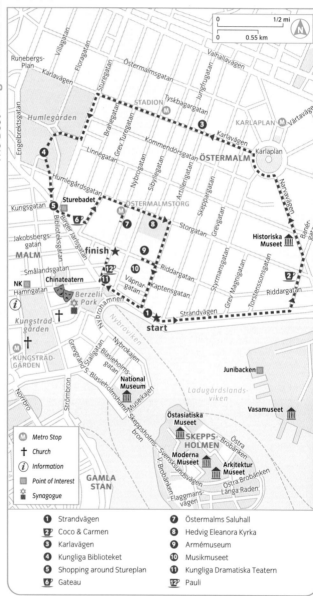

0   1/2 mi
0   0.55 km

Runebergs-Plan

Villagatan

Floragatan

Karlavägen

Stuvegatan

Östermalmsgatan

Valhallavägen

Jungfrugatan

Tyskbagargatan

STADION

❸

Värtavägen

KARLAPLAN

Engelbrektsgatan

Humlegården

Brahegatan

Grev Turegatan

Linnégatan

Kommendörsgatan

Karlavägen

Karlaplan

❹

Humlegårdsgatan

Nybrogatan

Sibyllegatan

Artillerigatan

ÖSTERMALM

Skeppargatan

Narvavägen

Kungsgatan

❺ Sturebadet

Birger Jarlsgatan

Bibliotekgatan

❻

ÖSTERMALMSTORG

❼

❽

Storgatan

Grevgatan

Historiska Museet

Banérgatan

Jakobsbergs-gatan

MALM

Smålandsgatan

finish ★

❾

Riddargatan

Styrmansgatan

Grev Magnigatan

Torstenssonsgatan

❷

Riddargatan

NK

Chinateatern

❶❷

❶❶

❶❷

Väpnar-gatan

Kaptensgatan

Hamngatan

Berzelii Park

Nybrohamnen

ⓘ

Kungsträd-gården

†

Strandvägen

❶
start ★

KUNGSTRÄD-GÅRDEN

†

Ⓜ

Grevgränd

S. Blasieholmsgatan

Nybrokajen

Blasieholms-gatan

Nybroviken

Junibacken

Ladugårdslands-viken

Vasamuseet

Norrbro

Strömbron

Stallgatan

Blasieholmshamn

Skeppsholms-bron

National Museum

Museikajen

Östasiatiska Museet

SKEPPS-HOLMEN

Östra Brobänken

GAMLA STAN

Moderna Museet

Arkitektur Museet

Svensksundsvägen

V. Brobänken

Flaggmans-vägen

Östra Brobänken

Långa Raden

Ⓜ Metro Stop

† Church

ⓘ Information

▣ Point of Interest

✡ Synagogue

❶ Strandvägen	❼ Östermalms Saluhall
❷ Coco & Carmen	❽ Hedvig Eleonora Kyrka
❸ Karlavägen	❾ Armémuseum
❹ Kungliga Biblioteket	❶⓪ Musikmuseet
❺ Shopping around Stureplan	❶❶ Kungliga Dramatiska Teatern
❻ Gateau	❶❷ Pauli

Östermalm developed in the 1870s when an expanding city pushed Stockholm north. Modeled on Paris, Östermalm was intended as the playground of the rich, with wide boulevards of elegant houses, gracious squares, and avenues. Today the sought-after area continues to have the best shopping, art galleries, exclusive designer boutiques, and a lively nightlife, while the green spaces of Gärdet and Djurgården stretch to the east. START: **T-bana to Östermalmstorg.**

❶ ★★ **Strandvägen.** One of the new boulevards built between 1880 and 1910, this is posh Stockholm at its best. Lime trees separate the sea from the grand Italian and French Renaissance style houses. You'll also find two of Stockholm's most famous interior design stores, **Carl Malmsten** (no 5b) and **Svenskt Tenn** (no 5), ideally placed here for their wealthy clients. 🕑 15 mins.

❷ ★ **Coco & Carmen.** Mingle with well-heeled locals over coffee and cakes, deli-style Caesar salad, or in summer, gazpacho soup at this delightful airy café sporting a smart blue-and-white awning. *Banérgatan 7.* ☎ *660 11 05. www.cococarmen.nu. $$.*

❸ **Karlavägen.** Walk up Narvägen to Karlavägen, two of the four great boulevards that, along with Strandvägen (❶) and Valkhallavägen, defined the new Östermalm in the late 19th century. Karlavägen is one of the many parts of the city with an outdoor sculpture gallery—the north side of Humlegården displays works such as *Living Iron* by Willy Gordon at Sturegatan, and *The City* by Lars Erik Husbert at Engelbrektsgatan. 🕑 15 mins.

❹ ★ **Kungliga Biblioteket.** The Royal Library is Sweden's copyright library, and has received a copy of every book printed in Sweden since 1661. With more than 3 million books and magazines, half a million posters, 300,000 maps, and

The Strandvägen waterfront.

hundreds of thousands of portraits and pictures, it's a formidable collection. The library, originally built in 1865–1878 but twice expanded, stands in Humlegården, the original hop garden for the royal household created by Gustav II Adolf in 1619. 🕐 30 mins. Humlegården. ☎ 463 40 00. www.kb.se. Jan 2–end May, mid-Aug–end Dec Mon–Thurs 9am–8pm, Fri 9am–7pm, Sat 10am–5pm; beginning June–mid-Aug Mon–Thurs 9am–6pm, Fri 9am–5pm, Sat 11am–3pm. T-bana Östermalmstorg.

⑤ ★★ Shopping around Stureplan. Smart Stockholm comes to shop around Stureplan. Walk down Birger Jarlsgaten and then turn into Bibliotekesgatan and Grev Turegatan for antiques, designer fashion, and jewelry. This area has a concentration of top names from **Georg Jensen** to local Swedish designers such as **Filippa K**, **J Lindeberg**, and the casual denim of **Acne**. And don't forget Sturegallerian—a world-class shopping mall built around the Jugendstil Sturebadet spa. See p 95. 🕐 1 hr. T-bana Östermalmstorg.

⑥ ★ Gateau. In Sturegallerian, make your way upstairs to the café where a snack adds at least a couple of inches to your waistline. Excellent cakes and pastries are the raison d'être at this famous bakery, which has branches all over Stockholm. *Sturegallerian, Stureplan.* ☎ 611 75 64. www.gateau.se. $$.

⑦ ★★★ Östermalms Saluhall. The chic food hall is one of Stockholm's great attractions. *See p 16, bullet ⑥.* 🕐 30 mins.

⑧ ★ Hedvig Eleanora Kyrka. The church opened in 1737 for the Swedish Navy and was made suitably impressive for the force that made Sweden a great nation. Inside, the light interior houses the altarpiece *Jesus on the Cross*, painted in 1738 by Georg Engelhard Schroder (1684–1750), and a splendid neo-classical pulpit. Although the organ is new, its façade was designed by Carl Fredrik Adelcrantz in 1762. Today, the church is well known for its regular classical music concerts (see p 139). 🕐 30 mins. Storgatan 2. ☎ 663 04 30. Daily 11am–6pm. T-bana Östermalmstorg.

⑨ ★★ kids Armémuseum. The Army Museum has been located in this former arsenal since 1879. The three-storey gracious white building houses a formidable history of 1,000 years of bloody warfare that, given Sweden's reputation for neutrality, comes as a slight shock, but empires are not won by wimps and peaceful means. The displays start on the top floor with the Viking Age and the Thirty Years War then descend to the 20th century. Much of it is shown in life-size settings that bring the reality home. 🕐 1 hr.

Hedvig Eleanora Kyrka.

Cavalry charge in the Army Museum.

Riddargatan 13. ☎ *788 95 60. www. armemuseum.org. Admission 60 SEK adults, under-18s free. Free with Stockholm Card (see p 11). Tues 11am–8pm, Wed–Sun 11am–5pm; July, Aug Tues 10am–8pm, Mon, Wed, Sun 10am–5pm. T-bana Östermalmstorg.*

⓾ ★★ kids **Musikmuseet.** If you're at all musical this small museum with around 6,000 instruments can give you hours of fun. There are some eccentric displays of instruments, placed as if they were being played, but with enough information to satisfy without over-whelming you. The real fun comes downstairs where I attempted to play a range of instruments from a harp to an electric guitar. ⊙ *1 hr. Sibyllegatan 2.* ☎ *51 95 54 90. www.stockholm.music. museum. Admission 40 SEK adults, under- 19s free. Free with Stockholm Card (see p 11). Tues–Sun noon–5pm. T-bana Kungsträdgården/Östermalmstorg.*

⓫ ★★ **Kungliga Dramatiska Teatern.** Built between 1902 and 1908 in Jugendstil style, the the-ater's white marble façade and bright gilded statues make it a work of art in its own right. Carl Milles (1875–1955) created the large sculptural group in the center section; Theodor Lundberg (1852–1926) produced the golden statues of Poetry and Drama, and Carl Larsson (1853–1919) painted the ceiling in the foyer of this gor-geous landmark, popularly known just as Dramaten. See p 140. ⊙ *1 hr. Nybrogatan 2.* ☎ *665 61 15. www. dramaten.se. Guided tours call for details. Free with Stockholm Card (see p 11). T-bana Kungsträdgården/Östermalmstorg.*

⓬ ★★ **Pauli.** Upstairs at Dramaten, you can visit this charming small restaurant without attending a per-formance. Good Swedish dishes are the order of the day. The walls are painted by the eponymous Georg Pauli (1855-1935), there's a portrait of Ingmar Bergman, and a summer terrace with views. *Nybrokajen.* ☎ *665 61 43. www.profil restauranger.se. $$$.*

The flamboyant Dramaten Theatre.

Norrmalm & **Vasastaden**

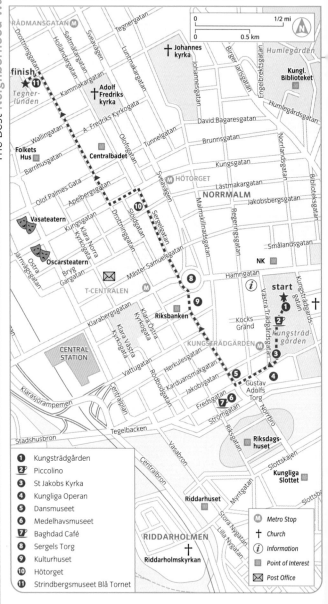

0   1/2 mi
0   0.5 km

1 Kungsträdgården
2 Piccolino
3 St Jakobs Kyrka
4 Kungliga Operan
5 Dansmuseet
6 Medelhavsmuseet
7 Baghdad Café
8 Sergels Torg
9 Kulturhuset
10 Hötorget
11 Strindbergsmuseet Blå Tornet

M Metro Stop
† Church
(i) Information
▢ Point of Interest
✉ Post Office

On this tour, we move away from the center and stroll north up to Vasastaden. Built at the end of the 1800s when Stockholm's population kept growing, the area is mainly residential and is bounded on the north side by large green open spaces.
START: **T-bana to Kungsträdgården.**

1 ★★ kids **Kungsträdgården.** All Stockholm finds its way here, either for the public events or just to watch the world go by. Originally the Royal Kitchen Garden—the King had to grow his cabbages and carrots somewhere—Stockholm's oldest park opened to the public in 1792. See p 54, bullet **6**. ⏱ *30 mins.*

2 ★ kids **Piccolino.** Join the locals in Stockholm's first espresso bar: **Piccolino** is a good place to sit outside and watch the world go by or take refuge during the winter months. ☎ *611 78 08. www. kunstradgarden.nu. $.*

3 ★ **St Jakobs Kyrka.** The red church, dedicated to the patron saint of pilgrims, is a mix of architectural styles. Started in 1588, it was completed in 1643. The 17th century is found in the baptismal font, church plate, and some of the porches. It

Piccolino was Stockholm's first espresso bar.

St Jakobs Kyrka is next to the Royal Opera.

then went through various renovations in the 19th century, including five stained glass panels by the altar. Now, the church is known for its music (see p 139). ⏱ *15 mins. Västra Trädgårdsgatan 2.* ☎ *723 30 38. T-bana Kungsträdgården.*

4 ★★ **Kungliga Operan.** The Royal Opera House is a magnificent, rather bombastic-looking building of 1898. The interior is superb, with ceiling paintings above the staircase inspired by the Paris Opera. The auditorium is all gold leaf and red velvet and has its fair share of ornately decorated boxes, including the Royal Box, which is placed stage left and so almost becomes part of the action. Ingmar Bergman produced some of the operas here, and it's also the home of the Swedish Royal Ballet. *See p 135. Guided tours summer only, daily at 1pm and 3pm. Tickets 75 SEK.* ☎ *791 44 00, www.operean.se.*

Sergels Torg.

⑤ ★★ **Dansmuseet.** This delightful museum will set your feet tapping and make every little girl who ever owned a pair of ballet shoes dream. The museum was founded in 1933 in Paris by Rolf de Maré (1888–1964), the Swedish aristocrat and art collector who managed the Swedish Ballet that took Paris by storm in the 1920s with its innovative style. The Swedish and non-European dance items were brought here when the museum in Paris closed in the 1940s. There's a good café with a terrace, and a well-stocked shop. ⏱ *40 mins. Gustav Adolfs Torg 22–24.* ☎ *441 76 50. www.dansmuseet.se. Admission free to collections; temporary exhibitions 40 SEK adults, under-18s free. May–Sep Mon–Fri 11am–4pm, Sat, Sun noon–4pm. Oct–Apr closed on Mondays.*

⑥ ★★ **Medelhavsmuseet.** The Museum of Mediterranean Antiquities has art and artifacts from Greece, Rome, Egypt, Cyprus and the near East housed in a splendid 17th-century classical building. Musical instruments, ancient sarcophagi, art, terracotta figures, and more show what the Ancient World respected and revered. ⏱ *45 mins. Fredsgatan 2.* ☎ *519 553 80. www.medelhavsmuseet.se. Admission 80 SEK adults, under-20s free. Free with Stockholm Card (see p 11). Tues, Wed 11am–8pm, Thurs–Sun noon–5pm. T-bana Kungsträdgården.*

⑦ ★ **kids Baghdad Café.** I love prolonging the Near East experience in the first-floor museum café, which specializes in dishes from the eastern Mediterranean. It's run by the owner of Halv Grek plus Turk

Kulturhuset in Sergels Torg.

The Kulturhuset looks onto Hötorget.

(see p 116) and offers the likes of chicken and couscous salad and a set lunch on weekdays at 95 SEK. Finish with ultra-sweet, tooth filling-defying baklava. *Fredsgatan 2.* ☎ *519 550 62. $$.*

8 ★★ Sergels Torg. Walk along Hamngatan and be lured into **NK**, Stockholm's poshest department store. Then make your way to Sergels Torg. Built on two levels during the 1960s and 1970s mania for the new, it's known for the glass sculpture surrounded by fountains in its center, erected in 1972 and designed by Edvin Öhrstrom (1906–1994) and, bizarrely, for political demonstrations. Dramatic lighting makes this rather brutal concrete center a better sight at night. ⏱ *10 mins.*

9 ★ kids Kulturhuset. A symbol of Swedish Modernism, the Cultural Center was designed by architect Peter Celsing (1920–1974) and opened in 1974. The large glass-sided building on the southern side of the square has three galleries with changing exhibitions, a library, two stages for music, dance, and drama, and a popular Children's Room with books (some in English), plus paints and paper for drawing and storytelling. Sterieteket is Sweden's only cartoon library and the building also houses Stockholm's Stadsteatern (see p 140). ⏱ *30*

mins. Sergels Torg. ☎ *508 315 08. www.kulturhuset.stockholm.se. T-bana T-Centralen.*

10 ★ Hötorget. The Hay Market started as a place to trade vegetables, milk, and meat and today stalls are still piled high with sweet strawberries, bright red tomatoes, and vivid colored flowers. The square is surrounded by the indoor international food market, Hötorgshallen (p 37), the PUB department store where Greta Garbo briefly sold hats, the Filmstaden Sergel multiplex (p 138), and Konserthuset (p 135). ⏱ *15 mins.*

11 ★ Strindbergsmuseet Blå Tornet. As you walk north up Drottninggatan, the chain stores give way to small boutiques and the Art Nouveau Centralbadet (p 17, bullet **9**). The street becomes more residential, just the place for August Strindberg (1849–1912) who moved into Blå Tornet (the Blue Tower) in 1908. An old-fashioned elevator takes you up slowly to the reconstructed bedroom, dining room, and study where a permanent exhibition shows his work as author, photographer, and artist, and vividly brings the old neighborhood to life. ⏱ *45 mins. Drottninggatan 85.* ☎ *411 53 54. www.strindbergsmuseet.se. Admission 40 SEK adults, under-18s free. Free with Stockholm Card (see p 11). Mar–Oct Tues noon–7pm, Wed–Sun noon–4pm; Oct–Feb Tues–Sun noon–4pm. T-bana Rådmansgatan.*

Skeppsholmen

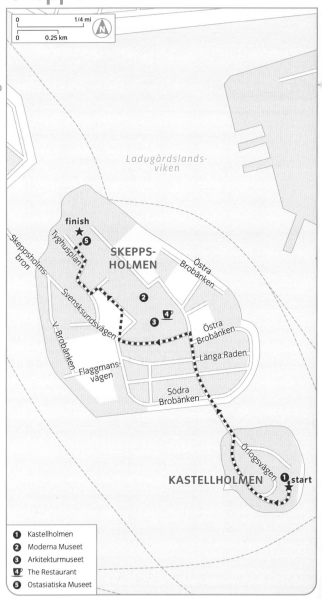

0 | 1/4 mi
0 | 0.25 km

Ladugårdslands-viken

finish

Skeppsholms-bron

SKEPPS-HOLMEN

Tyghusplan

Svensksundsvägen

V. Brobänken

Flaggmans-vägen

Östra Brobänken

Östra Brobänken

Länga Raden

Södra Brobänken

Örlogsvägen

KASTELLHOLMEN

start

❶ Kastellholmen
❷ Moderna Museet
❸ Arkitekturmuseet
❹ The Restaurant
❺ Ostasiatiska Museet

In the 17th century, Skeppsholmen provided the base for the all-conquering Swedish navy. It's a pretty island with a 1.6km walk around the seashore giving you views of all the major sights on the nearby islands. Beware on festivals and holidays when the 4-cannon battery blasts out. Tucked away at the bottom, the tiny island of Kastellholmen has a quaint seaside feel to it. START: **Bus 65 to the bottom of Skeppsholmen.**

1 ★★ Kastellholmen. Dominated by a rather new-looking Kastell (it was rebuilt in 1846–1848 after a gun cartridge factory unfortunately blew the old castle up), the tiny island of Kastellholmen is reached via a small bridge. The island is really a very large attractive granite rock where you can clamber up to find a natural seat and join the locals with a picnic. ⏱ *1 hr.*

2 ★★★ Moderna Museet. The Modern Art Museum comes as a surprise to first-time visitors who don't expect to find one of the world's great collections here in

The castle on the tiny island of Skeppsholmen.

Stockholm. Originally opened in 1958, it brought names such as Andy Warhol, Frank Stella, and Giacometti to a Swedish audience for the first time. The present building opened in 1998 when Stockholm was Cultural Capital of Europe, closed in 2002 due to damp problems, and then re-opened in 2004. Works are displayed in three sections: 1900–1945, 1946–1970 and 1971 to today. It's in reverse order, so walk to the back of the gallery first. It has a very well-stocked shop and shares a restaurant with the Architectural Museum. ⏱ *1½ hrs.*

3 ★★ Arkitekturmuseet. The Architectural Museum, housed in the old drill hall, shares an entrance and restaurant with the Moderna Museet and is a natural partner. More than 100 architectural models are laid out like a series of superior historical dolls' houses, taking you from a 2,000-year-old Viking longhouse to 20th-century bridges. After visiting real buildings such as the Stadshuset and the Royal Palace, you can gaze down at the miniature models to spot all the details you missed. There are numerous temporary exhibitions each year and the **Café Blom** is excellent for relaxing over a coffee, inside or out. ⏱ *45 mins. Exercisplan.* ☎ *587 270 00. www.arkitektur museet.se. Admission 50 SEK adults, under-19s free. Free Fri 4–6pm. Free with Stockholm Card (see p 11). Tues 10am–8pm, Wed–Sun 10am–6pm. Bus 65.*

4 ★ **The Restaurant.** I love booking for Saturday or Sunday brunch at the Modern Museum's restaurant. It's a popular place for a family get-together with a buffet of classic Swedish salmon, herrings, cold meats, potato dishes, vegetables, and a tempting dessert selection (265 SEK per person). During the week, there's a self-service lunch and, on Tuesdays, a bistro style selection from the grill. At other times, the coffee and cakes match the splendid view. *Skeppsholmen.* ☎ *519 552 82. www.moderna museet.se. $$$*

5 ★★ **Ostasiatiska Museet.** The East Asian museum's popularity has recently been boosted by the 2008 Beijing Olympics, because it has one of the world's greatest collections of Chinese art outside Asia. 1,200 objects from more than 5,000 years of history are on display.

Housed in a 17th-century building used to accommodate Karl XII's bodyguard, and designed by Nicodemus the Younger (1654–1728), the museum was founded by the Swedish archaeologist Johan Gunnar Andersson (1874–1960) who, in the early 1920s, came across an extraordinary collection of items from the Stone Age in China and was allowed to bring them back to Sweden. King Gustav VI Adolf (1882–1973) also left his collection of ancient Chinese arts and crafts—pottery, tools, and artifacts—to the museum. You'll discover Buddhist sculptures and works from Japan, India, and Korea, while the shop is an excellent source for Japanese tea sets and kimonos. ⏱ *1 hr. Tyghusplan.* ☎ *51 95 57 50. www.ostasiatiska.se. Admission 60 SEK, free up to 20 years old. Free with Stockholm Card (see p 11). Tues 11am–8pm, Wed–Sun 11am–5pm. Bus 65.* ●

Shopping Best Bets

Best **Art Books & Magazines**
★★ Konst-ig, *Åsögatan 124*

Best **1960s & Indie Music**
★★ Pet Sounds, *Skanegatan 53*

Best **for Commissioning your own Dinner Service**
★★ blås&knåda, *Hornsgatan 27*

Best **Old-fashioned Toys**
★ Bulleribock, *Sveagen 104*

Best **Pippi Longstocking Choice**
★ Kalikå, *Österlånggatan 18*; and ★ Junibacken Shop, *Galärvarvsvägen (p 94)*

Best **Posh Shopping Mall**
★★★ Sturegallerian, *Stureplan*

Best **Alvar Aalto Classic**
★★★ Jacksons, *Sibyllegatan 53*

Best **1930s Table Lamp**
★★★ Modernity, *Sibyllegatan 6*

Best **Traditional Swedish Craftsmanship**
★★★ Carl Malmsten, *Strandvägen 5B*

Shop at Stockholm's top design shop, Svensk Tenn.

Best **Design Drawing Room Look**
★★★ Svensk Tenn, *Strandvägen 5*

Best **Bright Bags**
★★ 10 Gruppen, *Götgatan 25*

Best **Ballet Music Cds**
★★ Dansmuseet Museum Shop, *Dansmuseet (p 83, bullet ⑤)*

Best **Clothing with a Conscience**
★★ Elkovaruhuset, *Österlånggatan 28*

Best **Classic Swedish Clothing**
★★ Filippa K, *Grev Turegatan 18*

Best **Chocolates Outside Belgium**
★★★ Ejes Chokladfabrik, *Erik Dahlsgatan 25 (p 38)*

Best **Kitsch for Friends Who Have Everything**
★★ Coctail de luxe, *Skanegatan 71*

Best **Trendy Jewelry**
★★★ Efva Attling, *Hornsgatan 45*

Best **Knicker Elastic**
★★ Björn Borg, *Sturegallerian*

Best **Luxury Writing Books**
★★ Ljunggrens, *Köpmangatan 3*

Best **Superior Swedish Souvenirs**
★★ Design Torget, *Kulturhuset;* and ★★ Skansen Shop, *Main Gate, Djurgårdsslätten (p 97)*

Best **Gourmet For Foodies**
★★★ Östermalms Saluhall, *Östermalmstorg*

Best **Creations from the Nobel Banquet Pâtisserie**
★★ Xoko, *Rorstrandgatan 15 (p 39)*

North Stockholm Shopping

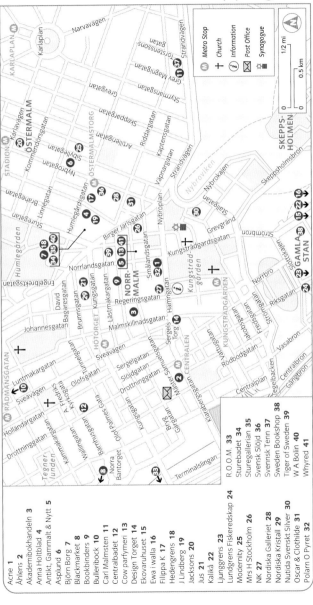

Map Legend
- Metro Stop
- + Church
- (i) Information
- ⊠ Post Office
- ✡ Synagogue

0 1/2 mi
0 0.5 km

Acne **1**
Åhlens **2**
Akademibokhandeln **3**
Anna Holtblad **4**
Antikt, Gammalt & Nytt **5**
Asplund **6**
Björn Borg **7**
Blackmarket **8**
Bookbinders **9**
Bulleribock **10**
Carl Malmsten **11**
Centralbadet **12**
Cow parfymeri **13**
Design Torget **14**
Ekovaruhuset **15**
Ewa i walla **16**
Filippa K **17**
Hedengrens **18**
J Lindberg **19**
Jacksons **20**
Jus **21**
Kalikå **22**
Ljunggrens **23**
Lundgrens Fiskeredskap **24**
Modernity **25**
Mrs H Stockholm **26**
NK **27**
Nordiska Galleriet **28**
Nordiska Kristall **29**
Nutida Svenskt Silver **30**
Oscar & Clothilde **31**
Polarn O Pyret **32**
R.O.O.M. **33**
Sturebadet **34**
Sturegallerian **35**
Svensk Slöjd **36**
Svensk Tenn **37**
Sweden Bookshop **38**
Tiger of Sweden **39**
W A Bolin **40**
Whyred **41**

South Stockholm Shopping

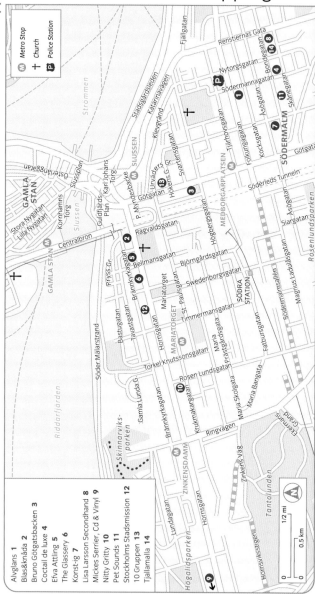

Alvglans **1**
Blas&knåda **2**
Bruno Götgatsbacken **3**
Coctail de luxe **4**
Efva Attling **5**
The Glassery **6**
Konst-ig **7**
Lisa Larsson Secondhand **8**
Mickes Serrier, Cd & Vinyl **9**
Nitty Gritty **10**
Pet Sounds **11**
Stockholms Stadsmission **12**
10 Gruppen **13**
Tjallamalla **14**

M Metro Stop
+ Church
P Police Station

SÖDERMALM
SÖDRA STATION
MARIATORGET
MEDBORGARPLATSEN
GAMLA STAN
ZINKENSDAMM
Rosenlundsparken
Skinnarviks-parken
Tantolunden
Högalidsparken
Riddarfjärden
Strömmen

Renstiernas Gata
Fjällgatan
Nytorgsgatan
Södermannagatan
Bondegatan
Åsögatan
Skånegatan
Tjärhovsgatan
Folkungagatan
Kocksgatan
Götgatan
Södermalmstorg
Stadsgårdsleden
Katarinavägen
Klevgränd
Urvädersgränd
Hökens G. Gr.
Svartensgatan
Götgatan
Söderleds Tunneln
Åsögatan
Siargatan
Rosenlundsparken
Björngårdsgatan
Swedenborgsgatan
Högbergsgatan
P. Myndesbacke
Ragvaldsgatan
Bellmansgatan
Brännkyrkagatan
St. Paulsgatan
Timmermansgatan
Fatbursgatan
Magnus Ladulåsgatan
Södermannalsallén
Maria Prästgårdsgata
Maria Skolgata
Maria Bangata
Pryss. Gr.
Bastugatan
Tavastgatan
Hornsgatan
Torkel Knutssonsgatan
Rosen Lundsgatan
Brännkyrkagatan
Krukmakargatan
Gamla Lunda G.
Lundagatan
Hornsgatan
Hornsviksstigen
Zinkens Väg
Eternans Grand
Ringvägen
Slussen
Stora Nygatan
Lilla Nygatan
Österlånggatan
Kornhamns Torg
Karl Johans Torg
Guldfjärds-Plan
Slussplan
Centralbron
Söder Mälarstrand

Stockholm Shopping A to Z

Bookshops

★ Akademibokhandeln

NORRMALM The Academy bookstore has a particularly good selection of books in English, maps, and travel books. *Mäster Samuelsgatan 32.* 🕿 *613 61 00. www.akademibokhandeln.se. AE, DC, MC, V. T-bana T-Centralen/ Hötorget. Map p 91.*

★ kids Alvglans SÖDERMALM

From the Belgian Spirou to Modesty Blaise, X-Men, and Spiderman, this specialist comic shop stocks all the greats and collectors' items. *Folkungagatan 84.* 🕿 *642 69 98. www.alvglans.se. AE, DC, MC, V. T-bana Slussen. Map p 92.*

★★ Hedengrens ÖSTERMALM

Since 1898 Hedengrens has been Stockholm's smartest bookstore stocking 80,000 titles in 9 languages from the arts to gardening; also holds exhibitions and regular book readings. *Sturegallerian, Stureplan 4.* 🕿 *611 51 28. www.hedengrens.se. AE, DC. MC, V. T-bana Östermalmstorg. Map p 91.*

★★ Konst-ig SÖDERMALM

This leading art bookshop stocks a formidably wide range of international titles and top international magazines. *Åsögatan 124.* 🕿 *20 45 20. www. konstig.se. T-bana Medborgarplatsen. Map p 92.*

★★ Sweden Bookshop GAMLA STAN

The Swedish Institute's popular bookshop is the best place to find books about Sweden, from literature to architecture, in 47 languages.

Slottsbacken 10. 🕿 *453 78 00. www.swedenbookshop.com. AE, DC, MC, V. T-bana Gamla Stan. Map p 91.*

CDs & Records

★ Mickes Serrier, cd & vinyl

SÖDERMALM Good vinyl and offerings from the likes of the Rolling Stones plus a good jazz section and everything from garage to soul on CD. *Långholmsgatan 20.* 🕿 *668 10 23. www.mickes-cdvinyl.se. MC, V. T-bana Hornstull. Map p 92.*

★★ Pet Sounds SÖDERMALM

The oldest and still known for the best indie music, although all the main names and music styles are here. *Skanegatan 53.* 🕿 *702 97 98. www.petsounds.se. AE, MC, V. T-bana Medborgarplatsen. Map p 92.*

Ceramics & Glass

★★ blås&knåda SÖDERMALM

Loosely and jokingly translated as 'blow and throw', this light and airy shop is run by a cooperative of around 50 glass and ceramic artists. Wide stock plus it sells members' works from functional to collectable. *Hornsgatan 26.* 🕿 *642 77 67. www.blasknada.com. AE, DC, MC, V. T-bana Slussen. Map p 92.*

★★ The Glassery

SÖDERMALM This relatively new gallery has up-and-coming names. If you're a collector or an aspiring one, come here for art glass by names such

Swedish Shape by Fredrik Nielsen—art glass at The Glassery.

as Simon Klenell and Frederik Nielsen. *Hornsgatan 38.* 📞 *25 11 95. www.theglassery.se. AE, DC, MC, V. T-bana Slussen. Map p 92.*

★★ **Nordiska Kristall** NORRMALM Swedish glass is rightly famous and here you'll find stunning examples of the art from names such as Kosta Boda (founded 1742) and Orrefors. *Kungsgatan 9.* 📞 *10 43 72. AE, DC, MC, V. T-bana T-Centralen. Map p 91.*

Children's Clothes & Toys
★★ **kids** **Bulleribock** VASASTADEN It started in the 1960s stocking only toys made of wood and natural materials, eschewing all things plastic. Now Bulleribock is wildly fashionable again. No computer games, just traditional playthings, mostly for children up to age 10. *Sveagen 104.* 📞 *673 61 21. www.bulleribock.nu. AE, MC, V. T-bana Radmansgatan. Map p 91.*

★★ **kids** **Kalikå** GAMLA STAN Great for a wide collection of striped tops, stuffed toys, and Pippi Long-stocking items, furniture, and bags in the shapes of houses and buses that grown-up girls will also covet.

Pippi Longstocking rag dolls at Kalikå.

Österlånggatan 18. 📞 *20 52 19. www.kalika.se. AE, DC, MC, V. T-bana Gamla Stan. Map p 91.*

★ **kids** **Polarn 0 Pyret** NORRMALM The 'Pal and the Tot' made its name in 1976 for comfortable, casual children's designs, and its signature stripes. The stripes are still around for children up to age 12. *Hamngatan 10.* 📞 *411 41 40. www.polarnopyret.se. AE, DC, MC, V. T-bana Östermalmstorg. Map p 91.*

Cosmetics
★★ **Cow parfymeri** ÖSTERMALM All the top cosmetics from Laura Mercier to L'Artisan Parfumerie with knowledgeable staff and professional make-up artists; expensive, but the best. *Mäster Samuelsgatan 9.* 📞 *611 15 04. www.cowparfymeri.se. AE, MC, V. T-bana Mariatorget. Map p 91.*

Department Stores/ Shopping Malls
★ **Åhléns** NORRMALM This huge chain started in 1899 with mail order, and opened the first Stockholm store in 1932. It's a mid-range store, good for fashion, beauty, home interiors, and electronics; also has a day spa. *Klarabergsgatan 50.* 📞 *676 60 00. www.ahlens.se. AE, DC, MC, V. T-bana T-Centralen. Map p 91.*

★ **Bruno Götgatsbacken** SÖDERMALM Known as Galleria Bruno, this small mall has a mix of international names (Miss Sixty) and Swedish (Whyred). The chic gather at the Ljunggrens bar/restaurant. *Götgatan 36.* 📞 *757 76 00. www. brunogallerian.se. CCs vary from shop to shop. T-bana Slussen/ Medborgarplatsen. Map p 92.*

★★★ **NK** NORRMALM The elegant Nordiska Kompaniet is the last name in Swedish high-class style. It's a favorite of Princess Victoria, is

NK is Stockholm's top department store.

★★ Ekovaruhuset GAMLA STAN
This boutique takes organic and eco to where it should be: chic and fashionable using Fair Trade practices. Hand-made designer prototypes from names such as Anja Hynynen and Modiga Barn. *Österlånggatan 28.* ☎ *22 98 45. www.ekovaruhuset.se. MC, V. T-bana Gamla Stan. Map p 91.*

★ Jus NORRMALM   One of the first of the new boutiques to encourage new talent in the late 1990s, both local and international, this chic venue stocks the likes of Ann-Sofi Back and the casual Burfitt. *Brunnsgatan 7.* ☎ *20 67 77. www.jus.se. AE, DC, MC, V. T-bana Hötorget. Map p 91.*

★★ Mrs H Stockholm ÖSTER-MALM   The outside looks traditional, but inside you'll find a wide stock of clothes, make-up, bags, and shoes from names such as Sonia Rykiel and Marc Jacobs, making this a target store for the fashionable. *Inside Passagen, mini mall, Birger Jarlsgatan 7.* ☎ *678 02 00. www.mrsh.se. AE, DC, MC, V. T-bana Östermalmstorg. Map p 91.*

★★ Nitty Gritty SÖDERMALM
One of the shops making Söder a shopping destination, Nitty Gritty has 7 adjoining shops for clothes, shoes, and accessories from names such as Dries Van Noten and Fred Perry; also has cds, books, a children's store, and a café. *Krukmakargatan 26.* ☎ *510 61 952. www.nittygritty.se. AE, DC, MC, V. T-bana Slussen. Map p 92.*

strong on clothes and beauty, and known for gourmet food and Swedish crafts. Café Entrée caters to weary shoppers. *Hamngatan 18–20.* ☎ *768 80 00. www.nk.se. AE, DC, MC, V. T-bana Kungsträdgården/Östermalmstorg. Map p 91.*

★★★ Sturegallerian ÖSTER-MALM   Chic Stockholm residents shop here when they've done with NK. It's a good mix of Swedish and international names for clothes and accessories plus revered bookshop Hedengrens (p 93). Plus restaurants and bars for people watching. *Stureplan. www.sturegallerian.se. CCs vary from shop to shop. T-bana Östermalmstorg. Map p 91.*

Fashion
★★ Blackmarket VASASTADEN
Go down the steps into this store for flamboyant labels from Henrik Vibskov, the new Minimarket, Jeremy Scott, and also Comme des Garçons and Peter Jensen; exhibition space plus seats for partners to wait. *St Eriksgatan 79.* ☎ *30 26 60. www.blackmarketstockholm.se. AE, MC, V. T-bana St Eriksplan. Map p 91.*

Fashion—Swedish Designers
★★ Acne ÖSTERMALM   Famous in Sweden and expanding (now in New York, Paris, and Oslo), Acne began as an advertising agency before turning to jeans in 1997. It's an all-round design store with casual chic as its inspiration. *Hamngatan*

10–14. ☎ 20 34 55. AE, DC, MC, V. T-bana Östermalmstorg. Map p 91.

★★ **Anna Holtblad** ÖSTERMALM The calm and cool interior of Anna Holtblad's store is a great setting for her strong shapes and colors, particularly in her signature knitwear, which has become the last name in Scandinavian chic. *Grev Turegatan 13.* ☎ 54 50 22 20. *www.anna holtblad.se. AE, DC, MC, V. T-bana Östermalmstorg. Map p 91.*

★ **Ewa i walla** GAMLA STAN For the romantic look, visit Ewa i Walla's small, crowded boutique. Her clothes float, are made of natural fabrics, and make you feel as if you're in a Bergman film; but definitely for the young. *Österlånggatan 23.* ☎ 245 887. *www.ewaiwalla.se. AE, MC, V. T-bana Gamla Stan. Map p 91.*

★★ **Filippa K** ÖSTERMALM This label is favored by Princess Victoria for its clean lines, simple shapes, and good quality. This is classic dressing for men and women. Founded in 1993 by Filippa Knutsson, it's now one of the leading Swedish brands, with stores in Stockholm and throughout northern Europe. *Grev Turegatan 18.* ☎ 45 888 88. *www.filippa-k. com. AE, DC, MC, V. T-bana Östermalmstorg. Map p 91.*

★★ **J Lindeberg** ÖSTERMALM Originally the progressive name in Swedish fashion, John Lindeberg is known for casual fashion and formal wear. He made his reputation with sporting styles favored by golfers. The label is now more mainstream and sold in 20 countries. *Grev Turegatan 9.* ☎ 678 61 65. *www. jlindeberg.com. AE, DC, MC, V. T-bana Östermalmstorg. Map p 91.*

★★ **Tiger of Sweden** NORRMALM Started by tailors Markus Schwamann and Hjalmar Nördstrom in 1903, Tiger has seen fashions come and go and emerged as one of the strongest Swedish labels with an emphasis on good cutting. Also has clothes for women, shoes, and accessories. *Jakobsbergsgatan 8.* ☎ 440 30 60. *www.tigerofsweden. com. AE, DC, MC, V. T-bana Östermalmstorg. Map p 91.*

★ **Tjallamalla** SÖDERMALM Small boutique with big ideas stocking new names for the young. *Bondegatan 46.* ☎ 640 78 47. *www. tjallamalla.com. AE, MC, V. T-bana Medborgarplatsen. Map p 92.*

★★ **Whyred** ÖSTERMALM Three former H&M employees set up Whyred in 1999, and it's now a name for cool style for men and women. Two stores in Stockholm, Whyred North and Whyred South (Gallerien Bruno in Södermalm). *Whyred North, Mäster Samuelsgatan 5.* ☎ 660 01 70. *www. whyred.com. AE, DC, MC, V. T-bana Kungsträdgården. Map p 91.*

Fashion—Vintage & Secondhand
★★ **Lisa Larsson Secondhand** SÖDERMALM Stockholm's best

Fab second-hand and vintage at Lisa Larsson.

Get those dancing shoes at Coctail de luxe.

known secondhand store stocks most styles and eras, from 1950s leather jackets to 80s party dresses. Designers such as Pucci stand next to names that sank without trace until turning up here; also stocks suits, shoes, and hats. *Bondegatan 48.* ☎ *643 61 53. www.lisalarsson secondhand.com. No CCs. Bus 2, 53, 59, 76. Map p 92.*

★★ **Stockholms Stadsmission** KUNGSHOLMEN   Five secondhand shops run by a homeless charity set up in the 1800s offer a wide range of just about everything. There are clothes and bric a brac in the Kungsholmen shop; the biggest range is outside the center, at Gröndal, south of Lilla Essingen. *Hormsgatan 58.* ☎ *642 93 35. AE, MC, V. T-bana Slussen. Map p 92.*

Fishing
★★★ **Lundgrens Fiskeredskap** GAMLA STAN   Founded in 1892, this old-fashioned specialist shop sells all the equipment that fishermen need. Expert staff help you make the right choices. *Storkyrkobriken 12.* ☎ *10 21 22. www.lundgrensfiske.com. AE, DC, MC, V. T-bana Gamla Stan. Map p 91.*

Gifts & Souvenirs
★★ kids **Coctail de luxe** SÖDERMALM   Plastic duck? Pink cuckoo clock? Improbable chandelier? Coctail de luxe and coctail supply all necessities of kitsch life and a few more you'd be hard put to imagine. They have furniture, too, in case you want to go all the way. *Skanegatan 71.* ☎ *642 07 40. www.coctail.nu. AE, DC, MC, V. Bus 2, 53, 59, 76. Map p 92.*

★★ kids **Design Torget** NORMALM   It began in 1993 in an empty shop in Kulturhuset where one of the founders of Design Torget worked as an architect. It expanded but kept the core philosophy of seeking out young designers and with design schools in Sweden. The stock is fresh, new, and varied. *Kulturhuset, Sergels Torg.* ☎ *50 83 15 20. www.designtorget.se. AE, MC, V. T-bana T-Centralen. Map p 91.*

★★ kids **Svensk Slöjd** ÖSTERMALM   If you're after souvenirs, come here for reindeer, textiles, wooden toys, and one of those famous Dala horses. *Nybrogatan 23.* ☎ *640 97 77. AE, MC, V. T-bana Östermalmstorg. Map p 91.*

Interior Design—Antiques & Secondhand

★★★ **Jacksons** ÖSTERMALM
For nearly 30 years, Jacksons has supplied top quality furniture, ceramics, glass, and textiles to the discerning. Specializing in the 20th century, they deal in the big Scandinavian and Nordic designers (Alvar Aalto to Carl Westman), and international names such as Mies van der Rohe. *Sibyllegatan 53.* ☎ *665 33 50. www.jacksons.se. AE, DC, MC, V. T-bana Östermalmstorg. Map p 91.*

★★★ **Modernity** ÖSTERMALM
Scotsman Andrew Duncanson stocks a wide range of 20th-century Scandinavian design, mainly post World War II, from the Egg Chair of Arne Jacobsen to jewelry by Swedish designers. Like Jacksons, Modernity is a familiar name at international arts, design, and antiques fairs. *Sibyllegatan 6.* ☎ *20 80 25. www.modernity.se. AE, DC, MC, V. T-bana Östermalmstorg. Map p 91.*

Interior Design—Contemporary Design & Furnishings

★ **Asplund** ÖSTERMALM   The Asplund brothers fill their store with new Swedish and international designs of candlesticks, furniture, and carpets and their own brand by Thomas Sandell. *Sibyllegatan 31.* ☎ *662 52 84. www.asplund.org. AE, MC, V. T-bana Östermalmstorg. Bus 56, 62. Map p 91.*

★★★ **Carl Malmsten** ÖSTERMALM   Carl Malmsten (1888–1972) was one of the Swedish modern masters of furniture design, championing traditional craftsmanship when it seemed under threat. His imaginative designs, light wood, and consummate craftsmanship worked and his designs and techniques—he founded two schools—still grace the homes of the design conscious. His grandson now runs the business.

Put a style together at Oscar & Clothilde.

Strandvägen 5B. ☎ *23 33 80. www. c.malmsten.se. MC, V. T-bana Östermalmstorg. Map p 91.*

★★★ **Nordiska Galleriet** ÖSTERMALM   This treasure trove mixes design classics of the past still being produced from names such as Arne Jacobsen with the eccentric creations of Philippe Starck and Swedish designer Johan Bohlin. *Nybrogatan 11.* ☎ *442 83 60. www. nordiskagalleriet.se. AE, DC, MC, V. T-bana Östermalmstorg. Map p 91.*

★ **Oscar & Clothilde** ÖSTERMALM   Most items here are reproduction, but cleverly chosen and put together to give the impression of an old Scandinavian home. *Nybrogatan 7.* ☎ *611 53 00. www. oscarclothilde.com. AE, DC, MC, V. T-bana Östermalmstorg. Map p 91.*

★ **R.O.O.M.** KUNGSHOLMEN
You'll find everything here, from furniture and furnishings to tableware, lamps, blankets, gift items, and even garden flares. *Alströmergatan 20.* ☎ *692 50 00. www. room.se. AE, DC, MC, V. T-bana Fridhemsplan. Map p 91.*

★★★ Svensk Tenn ÖSTERMALM
This classic store, founded by pewter designer Estrid Ericson in 1924, was expanded with functionalist furniture from Gunnar Asplund. Known for furniture and textiles by Josef Frank, whose designs still brighten the store—and numerous homes—today, the store also stocks contemporary designers and supplies the Royal family, so you're in good company. *Strandvägen 5.* ☎ *670 16 00 www.svenskttenn.se. AE, DC, MC, V. T-bana Östermalmstorg. Map p 91.*

★★ 10 Gruppen SÖDERMALM
Ten young textile designers set up this store back in 1970, producing geometric designs in bright primary colors. All 10 are no longer in charge, but their fabrics, bags, cushions, and oven gloves are still there. *Götgatan 25.* ☎ *643 25 04. www.tiogruppen.com. MC, V. T-bana Slussen. Map p 92.*

Jewelry
★★★ Antikt, Gammalt & Nytt
NORRMALM   A real gem of a shop for fashionistas and stylists after that outlandish piece of rhinestone or something designed in the 1940s

10 Gruppen in Södermalm.

and lying undiscovered. *Mäster Samuelsgatan 11.* ☎ *678 35 30. AE, DC, MC, V. T-bana Östermalmstorg. Map p 91.*

★★★ Efva Attling SÖDERMALM
The famous jeweler has had a varied career: from playing in the 1980s X Models band to designing clothes for Levi's and H&M. But she's best known for her jewelry in gold, silver, and precious stones. The wide range attracts clients such as Madonna; also in Birger Jarlsgatan. *Hornsgatan 44.* ☎ *642 99 49. www.efvaattlingstockholm.com. AE, DC, MC, V. T-bana Slussen. Map p 92.*

★★ Nutida Svenskt Silver
ÖSTERMALM   Sixty silver- and goldsmiths belong to the co-operative running this gallery. From silverware to the most delicate of silver enamel, the bold to the subtle. *Arsenalsgatan 3.* ☎ *611 67 18. www.nutida.nu. AE, MC, V. T-bana Kungsträdgården. Map p 91.*

★★★ W A Bolin ÖSTERMALM
Established in St. Petersburg in 1791, the Stockholm outlet opened in 1916. Guaranteed success from the start by the patronage of King Gustav V, Bolin continues to supply the Royal Family with vintage pieces from its own workshop as well as more modern jewels; exclusive, expensive, collectable. *Stureplan 6.* ☎ *54 50 77 70. www.bolin.se. AE, DC, MC, V. T-bana Östermalmstorg. Map p 91.*

Lingerie/Underwear
★★ Björn Borg ÖSTERMALM
When talking of Swedish lingerie and men's underwear, what other name could there be than former tennis star, Björn Borg? Great collection, suitable for all ages. *Sturegallerian, Stureplan.* ☎ *678 20 40. www.bjornborg.se. AE, DC, MC, V. T-bana Östermalmstorg. Map p 91.*

Prime Shopping Areas

High-end fashion shopping doesn't come much posher than in **Norrmalm**, around **Stureplan,** and in nearby streets such as **Birger Jarlsgatan**, **Grev Turegatan**, **Sibyllegatan,** and **Biblioteksgatan**. **Hamngatan** has NK, Stockholm's best department store and the Gallerian, good for everyday items. For antiques, good hunting grounds include **Vasastaden** and the streets of **Upplandsgatan** and **Odengatan**, and **Gamla Stan**. Serious antique hunters should look for shops that are members of Sveriges Konst och Antikhand-lareforening (SKAF). **Södermalm** has good vintage stores in and around **Bondegatan** and a host of small boutiques around **Götgatan** in SoFo.

Spas

★★★ Centralbadet NORRMALM

One of the most beautiful spas you'll ever visit. Take a treatment or just chill out in their pool and thermal pools, get fit in the gym, and sunbathe on the roof terrace in summer. *See p 17, bullet* ❾. *Drottninggatan 88.* ☎ *545 213 00. www.centralbadet.se. Entrance 120–170 SEK. AE, DC, MC, V. T-bana Hötorget. Map p 91.*

★★ Sturebadet ÖSTERMALM

This posh spa dates from 1885 and offers all major treatments, though it's pricier than Centralbadet. Admission gives you all the usual goodies such as pool, gym, and group exercise class. *See p 17, bullet* ❽. *Sturegallerian 36.* ☎ *545 015 00. www.sturebadet.se. Entrance 395–595 SEK. AE, DC, MC, V. T-bana Östermalmstorg. Map p 91.*

Stationery

★ Bookbinders NORRMALM

Get your life organized here with co-ordinated boxes, ranges of paper, photo albums, bound note-books, and more. Founded in 1927, the company still designs and pro-duces all its stock. *Norrlandsgatan 20.* ☎ *611 18 80. www.bookbinders design.com. AE, DC, MC, V. T-bana Östermalmstorg. Map p 91.*

★★ Ljunggrens GAMLA STAN

There's an international fan club for the shop's exquisite ranges of paper and paper products, boxes, and specially designed rubber stamps for creating your own artworks. Opened in 1913, the store was bought in 1989 by Barbara Bunke who trained as a graphic designer then bookbinder, and only stocks what she herself loves to use. *Köpmangatan 3.* ☎ *676 03 83. www.ljunggrenspapper.com. AE, DC, MC, V. T-bana Gamla Stan. Map p 91.* ●

Hagaparken

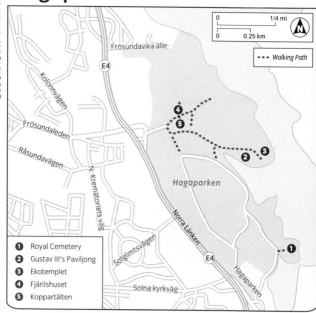

- **1** Royal Cemetery
- **2** Gustav III's Paviljong
- **3** Ekotemplet
- **4** Fjärilshuset
- **5** Koppartälten

Hagaparken was created by architect Fredrik Magnus Piper (1746–1824) as part of King Gustav III's grand design to build a new castle and the kind of romantic park that the English excelled in designing. Surprisingly few visitors come out here, but jump on the T-bana and bus and see why this part of the National Ekoparken (p 107) is such a favorite. START: **Bus 3 or 52 to the Karolinska Sjukhuset hospital, then short walk to the Park.**

1 ★ **Royal Cemetery.** Get off the no. 3 or 59 bus and walk northeast until you're in Hagaparken. The park was designed in the mid-18th century when Europe was having a full-blown love affair with all things Oriental. You'll see evidence of this passion in the form of a small Turkish Pavilion and a strange-looking Chinese Pagoda, a kind of folly open to the elements. Just beyond, you come to a tiny island and the Royal Cemetery. Recent monarchs buried

here, rather than in Riddarholm-skyrkan (see p 139), include Gustav VI Adolf (1882–1973), and his second wife, the former Lady Louise Mountbatten (1889–1965), who was the current Duke of Edinburgh's aunt. ⏱ *30 mins. May, Sun and public holidays 1pm–3pm Jun–Aug Thurs 9am–3pm.*

2 ★★ kids **Gustav III's Paviljong.** The path meanders beside the water up to this

Relax in Hagaparken.

neo-classical palace, plain outside, but glorious within—there's a magnificent hall of mirrors and classical Italian-style rooms. In March 1792, King Gustav III left here to go to the opera in Stockholm, and never returned. He was assassinated that night and his ambitious plans for the park died with him. ⏱ *45 mins* ☎ *402 61 30. www.royalcourt.se. Admission 70 SEK adults, 35 SEK children 7–18 years. Free with Stockholm Card (see p 11). Jun–end Aug Tues–Sun guided tours only noon, 1pm, 2pm, and 3pm.*

3 ★ **kids** **Ekotemplet.** The curious round structure behind the pavilion was designed in the 1790s as a summer dining room for the royal family. You can get married in this 'Temple of the Echo'—so-called because you can eavesdrop on private conversations, which may lead to divorce rather than marriage. Go west past Haga Slott, built in 1802–1804 for Gustav IV Adolf, and where the present King of Sweden, Carl XVI and his sisters were born and brought up. Today, it's an impressive conference center and is used by the government for receptions and accommodating official guests. ⏱ *25 mins.*

4 ★★ **kids** **Fjärilshuset.** If the children have now lost interest, head straight to the Butterfly House. The glass structure was the original greenhouse of the Palace but plants have now been replaced by exotic butterflies and birds that fly past you as you wander through the equivalent of a tropical rainforest. ⏱ *1 hr. Häga Trädgård.* ☎ *730 39 81. www.fjarilshuset.se. Admission 80 SEK adults, 40 SEK children 4–15 years. Free with Stockholm Card (see p 11). Apr–Sep Mon-Fri 10am-5pm, Sat, Sun, public hols 11am-6pm. Oct-Mar, closes one hour earlier.*

5 ★ **kids** **Koppartälten.** From the butterfly experience, walk to another folly, the Roman battle copper tents that were completed in 1790. Like the Drottningholmen tent (see p 42, bullet **5**), these delightful constructions were originally intended as stables. The horses have long gone, replaced by the Haga Park Museum and a café/restaurant. From here, walk back to the southern end of the park past the only evidence left of Gustav III's grandest design, the magnificent Versailles-inspired Palace. The king's death stopped the project in its tracks and all that is here are the foundations. ⏱ *1 hr.*

Green Stockholm

STOCKHOLM UNIVERSITY

Lilla Värtan

Norra Länken

Röslagsvägen

VASASTADEN

E20

Lidingövägn.

Erik Dahlbergsg.

Tegeluddsvägen

St. Eriksgatan

Odengatan

Sveavägen

Birger Jarlsgatan

Valhallavägen

Torsgatan

Klarastrandsleden

NORRMALM

ÖSTERMALM

Greve Von Essens väg

KUNGSHOLMEN

STOCKHOLM

Strandvägn

DJURGÅRDEN

Norr Mälarstrand

Västerbron

Riddarfjärden

LÅNGHOLMEN

Söder Mälarstrand

Saltsjön

Katarinavägen

Hornsgatan

SÖDERMALM

Söderleden

Folkungagatan

Årstaviken

Ringvägen

HAMMARBYHAMNEN

E4

222

Södra Länken

73

Södra Länken

ENSKEDEDALEN

Nynäsvägen

❶	Katarina Kyrka
❷	Långholmen
❸	Lasse i Parken
❹	Skogskyrkogården
❺	Tessinparken
❻	Bergianska Tradgården
❼	Ladugårdsgärdet
❽	Djurgården

ENSKEDE

Sockenvägen

73

| 0 | | 1 mi |
| 0 | | 2 km |

If you think your city is green, wait until you visit Stockholm. Local families treasure the small squares in the city center, as well as the green spaces of Djurgården (p 62) and Ladugårdsgärdet (p 66) where they go at weekends for picnics beside the water. To the north lies Hagaparken (see p 102) and the rolling landscape around the University. It's just what you expect in the eco-passionate city that created Ekoparken, the world's first National City Park (p 107). START: **T-bana to Medborgarplatsen.**

❶ ★ kids Katarina Kyrka.

Inside, this church has one of the most beautiful Baroque interiors I've seen, reproduced perfectly using old techniques after a disastrous fire in the 1990s destroyed everything of the original 1695 building except the outer walls. Outside, the church is surrounded by a peaceful graveyard. It's slightly off the usual Södermalm beaten track and therefore remains one of the island's most peaceful spots. *30 mins.* See p 75.

❷ ★★ kids Långholmen. The

island, which lies below the impressive Västerbron bridge, was kept free from major development because of the grim prison that

occupied Långholmen from 1724 to 1975. Only the prison—now a hotel— and a few houses, including the former home of the poet C M Bellman (p 73, bullet ⓫), disturb the landscape. It's great for picnics, and has one of my favorite swimming beaches. *1 hr. See p 72.*

❸ Lasse I Parken. On a road

leading down to the small bridge that crosses onto Långholmen, this charming restaurant is tucked away in its own garden. It's the perfect place for an al fresco coffee, snack, or full-blown evening meal, and looks and feels more like a private house than a restaurant. *Högalidsgatan 56.* ☎ *658 33 95. $$.*

The peaceful graveyard at Katarina Kyrka.

④ ★★★ Skogskyrkogården. Come here for the utter peace and tranquility of this world-famous cemetery 6km south of Stockholm and built on former gravel quarries that had become totally overgrown. A competition for its design, held in 1915, was won by two architects, Gunnar Asplund (1885–1940), Sweden's most influential and internationally renowned architect between the two world wars, and Sigurd Lewerentz (1885–1975). The cemetery itself, along with Asplund's Woodland Chapel, was opened in 1920. Later additions were Lewerentz's Resurrection Chapel (opened in 1925) and Asplund's Woodland Crematorium (opened in 1940), along with three chapels representing Faith, Hope, and the largest of the chapels, the Holy Cross—notable for the statue of *The Resurrection* by the artist John Lundqvist (1882–1972). In 1994, the cemetery became a UNESCO World Heritage Site. Both the unknown and the famous are buried here, including Greta Garbo (1905–1990), Asplund (1885–1940), and Black Metal hero, Per Yngve Ohlin (1969–1991). The Visitor's Center has an exhibition about the cemetery. ⏱ *2 hrs. Arenavägen 41.* ☎ *508 30 100. www.skogskyrkogarden.se. May–beginning Sep 11am–5pm. T-bana Skogskyrikogarden.*

⑤ Tessinparken. Tessin Park, named after the three generations of architects (see p 43) who had such an influence on Stockholm, is small with grass lawns, flowerbeds, a fountain, and the sculpture *The Egg*, by the Danish architect and sculptor, Egon Möller-Nielsen. The strange-looking concrete sphere is smooth and hollowed out, making it a magnet for children who love climbing in and out of its odd interior. The Park was opened in 1931, the first part of a town planning

The Victoria glass house at the Botanic Garden.

scheme just before the surrounding Funcionalist housing was built (1932–1937). The development was seen as a whole, with many architects involved in its planning. Compare it to 1930s architecture in other European countries, and you're struck by its freshness and modernity. ⏱ *45 mins. T-bana Karlaplan/Gärdet.*

⑥ ★★★ Bergianska Trädgården. The Botanic Garden stands beside the waters of Brunnsviken and attracts both botanic enthusiasts and those of us who just like to wander around beautifully planted gardens. The garden has been here since 1885 when the Royal Swedish Academy of Sciences moved from Vasastaden. In 1900, they built the circular domed Victoriahuset and, in 1995, it was joined by the modern Edvard Andersons Växthus, which houses Mediterranean and tropical plants. Entering the Botanic Garden, you first see the kitchen garden, and then flower borders of bright colors (particularly vibrant in Spring), a herb area, a pond full of giant water lilies,

Ekoparken

Ekoparken, the world's first National City Park, was established in 1995. It stretches from Ulriksdal in the north out into the archipelago with the inclusion of the Fjäderholmarna islands. The park—the equivalent in area of Stockholm's inner city—covers an astonishing 27 square km: 19 square km are land and 8 are water. This urban National Park includes some of Stockholm's great museums, making it a unique mix of both natural wonders and human cultural achievements. The biodiversity is impressive; certain plants and insects are only found here, and it has the densest concentration of oak trees in Europe.

and gently sloping meadows. There's also a market garden where people stagger away laden with all kinds of exotic plants and a good café with an outside terrace. ⏲ *1½ hrs. Frescati.* ☎ *545 917 00. www. bergianska.se. Edvard Andersons Växthus 50 SEK adults, Victoriahuset 20 SEK adults. Both free for under-15s. Free with Stockholm Card (see p 11). May–Sep Mon–Fri 11am–4pm, Sat, Sun 11am–5pm. T-bana Universitetet; bus 40 540. Train from Teknicks Högskolan to Frescati.*

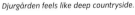

Djurgården feels like deep countryside.

7 ★★★ kids **Ladugårdsgärdet.** The 'field of barns', one of Stockholm's most natural and unspoiled areas, lies opposite Djurgården. Several museums lie along the water's edge; in the center, grassy meadows with grazing horses and children flying kites add to its particularly rural feel. *See p 66.*

8 ★ kids **Djurgården.** The island's long royal connection began when it was taken over by King Karl Knutsson in 1452. In 1580,

37

ROSENDAHLS WÄGEN.

Outdoor Sculpture in Stockholm

Stockholm has some magnificent outdoor sculpture. There are the expected tributes to past monarchs, such as **Gustav III** on Skeppsbron, commissioned from J T Sergel in 1799 in memory of this popular and cultivated King who was murdered in 1792. The city's founder, **Birger Jarl**, stands massively in the eponymous square on Riddarholm. Go to what is often called the city's most beautiful building, **Riddarhuset** (House of the Nobility) on Gamla Stan, for a series of sculptures on the roof that symbolize knightly virtues such as Nobility, Bravery, Prudence, and Strength (p 61). **Millesgården** on Lidingo is a museum devoted to the great sculptor Carl Milles and is an open-air garden of his sculptures (p 22). You can see Milles' superb **Gud på himmelsbågen** (God on the Rainbow) at Nacka Strand. Your first sight at the **Modern Art Museum** (p 87) is the outdoor sculptures from Alexander Calder, Yves Tingueley, Nicki de Saint-Phalle, and Picasso, whereas a walk along **Karlavägen** reveals a series of works by Swedish artists (p 79).

Djurgården was a royal park where Johan III (1537–1592) kept his deer; in the 17th century, Karl XI (1655–1697) enclosed the park for hunting; in the 19th century, the royal palace Rosendals Slott was built here as a summer retreat for the king. The Royal Family still administers and maintains the island although it became a public park in the late 19th century with the building of the Nordiska Museet and Skansen. It's easy to escape the crowds and wander through the meadows and along the paths that border the water, past simple old houses that cost a fortune. It's one of Stockholm's most popular islands and has two cafés that have to be included in anyone's outdoor favorites: **Blå Porten** (Blue Door) just near Liljevalchs Konsthall, (p 63, bullet ❸); and **Rosendals Trädgård**—a perfect oasis in the middle of the island (p 65, bullet ❽). ●

Dining Best Bets

Best **Old-School Swedish**
★★ Restaurangen Prinsen $$$$
Mäster Samuelsgatan (p 119)

Best **Old Favorite On the Way Up**
★★★ Carl Michael $$$$$ *Allmänna Gränd 6 (p 114)*

Best for **that Sublime Meal**
★★★ Mathias Dahlgren $$$$$
Grand Hotel (p 117)

Best **Up-and-coming Chef**
★★★ Leijontornet $$$$$ *Lilla Nygatan 5 (p 117)*

Best **Seaside Experience**
★★★ Pontus' Brasserie by the Sea
$$$$ *Tullhus 2 (p 119)*

Best **Desserts**
★★ Xoko $$$ *Rörstrandgatan 15 (p 39)*

Best for **Eating in the Garden**
★★ Blå Porten $$ *Djurgårdsvägen 64 (p 63)*; and ★★ Rosendals Trädgårdard $$ *Rosendalsterrassen 12 (p 65)*

Best **Vegetarian**
★ Hermans Trädgårdcafé $$
Fjällgatan 23 (p 76)

Restaurant Prinsen is a Stockholm institution.

Best for **Historic Surroundings**
★★ Den Gyldene Freden $$$$$
Österlånggatan 51 (p 114)

Best for **Top Cooking with Drama**
★★★ Operakallaren $$$$$ *Operahuset (p 118)*; and ★★★ Teater Grillen $$$$$ *Nybrogatan 3 (p 121)*

Best **Moules**
★★ Bistro Sud $$$ *Swedenborgsgatan 8 (p 113)*; and ★★ Brasserie Bobonne $$$ *Storgatan 12 (p 113)*

Best **Steak & Fries**
★★ Grill Ruby $$$ *Österlånggatan 14 (p 113)*

Best **Local Bistro**
★★ PA & Co $$$ *Riddargatan 8 (p 118)*

Best **Coffee & Cakes with Your Family**
★★ Sturekatten $ *Riddargatan 4 (p 38)*

Best for **Meatballs & Schnapps**
★★ Pelikan $$$ *Blekingegatan 40 (p 119)*

Best for **Surfing the World's Cuisines**
★★ Kungsholmen $$$$ *Norr Mälarstrand (p 117)*

Best for **Top Italian in Down-to-Earth Surroundings**
★★ Lo Scudetto $$$ *Åsögatan 163 (p 120)*

Best **Turbot**
★★★ Wedholms Fisk $$$$$
Nybrokajen 17 (p 122)

Best for **Foodies after Fish**
★★★ Lisa Elmqvist/Gerdas Fisk
$$$$ *Östermalms Saluhall (p 117)*

North Stockholm Dining

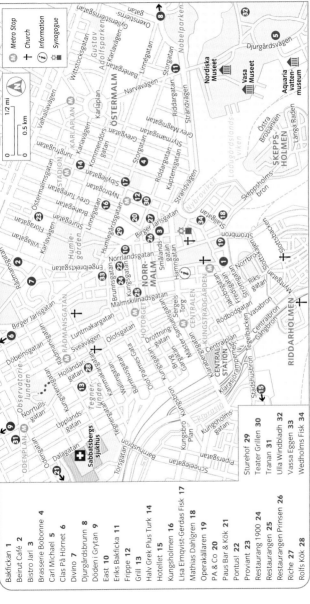

Legend:
- Ⓜ Metro Stop
- ✝ Church
- ⓘ Information
- ✡ Synagogue

Baklican 1
Beirut Café 2
Bistro Jarl 3
Brasserie Bobonne 4
Carl Michael 5
Clas På Hörnet 6
Divino 7
Djurgårdsbrunn 8
Döden i Grytan 9
East 10
Eriks Bakficka 11
Frippe 12
Grill 13
Halv Grek Plus Turk 14
Hotellet 15
Kungsholmen 16
Lisa Elmqvist-Gerdas Fisk 17
Mathias Dahlgren 18
Operakällaren 19
PA & Co 20
Paus Bar & Kök 21
Pontus! 22
Proviant 23
Restaurang 1900 24
Restaurangen 25
Restaurangen Prinsen 26
Riche 27
Rolfs Kök 28
Sturehof 29
Teater Grillen 30
Tranan 31
Ulla Windbladh 32
Vassa Eggen 33
Wedholms Fisk 34

Gamla Stan Dining

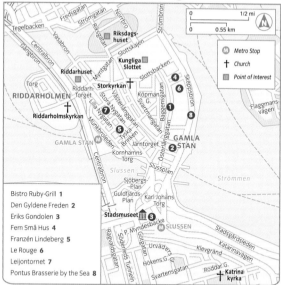

Bistro Ruby-Grill **1**
Den Gyldene Freden **2**
Eriks Gondolen **3**
Fem Små Hus **4**
Franzén Lindeberg **5**
Le Rouge **6**
Leijontornet **7**
Pontus Brasserie by the Sea **8**

Ⓜ Metro Stop
✝ Church
▨ Point of Interest

Sodermalm Dining

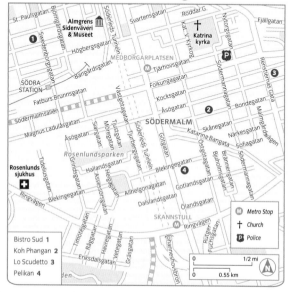

Bistro Sud **1**
Koh Phangan **2**
Lo Scudetto **3**
Pelikan **4**

Ⓜ Metro Stop
✝ Church
Ⓟ Police

Stockholm Dining A to Z

★★ Bakfickan NORRMALM
SWEDISH/BRASSERIE I like eating at the bar of the 'Hip Pocket' where it's more relaxed. It shares the same kitchen as Operabaren so expect superb tournedos Rossini, or go Swedish with smoked Baltic herring with potatoes, caviar, and chives. *Kungliga Operan, Karl XII's Torg.* ☎ 676 58 00. www.operakallaren.se. *Entrées 139–315 SEK. Prix fixe menus 365–440 SEK. AE, DC, MC, V. Mon–Fri 11.30am–11pm, Sat noon–10pm. T-bana Kungsträdgården. Map p 111.*

★★ Beirut Café NORRMALM
LEBANESE This Lebanese restaurant with a warm, low-lit interior takes you straight to the Middle East. Cooking is excellent; for variety I always order the meze selection at 280 SEK per person. *Engelbrektsgatan 37.* ☎ 21 20 25. www.beirut cafe,nu. *Entrées 195–240 SEK. AE, DC, MC, V. Dinner daily. T-bana Tekniska högskolan. Map p 111.*

★★ Bistro Jarl ÖSTERMALM
SWEDISH/FRENCH You're in the best shopping area in town, so this is not as bistro-like as it sounds. In fact, it's high-end Stockholm having fun on rich French-inspired cooking. The restaurant is elaborately decorated in gold and green with chandeliers; the bar buzzes. *Birger Jarlsgatan 7.* ☎ 611 76 30. www. bistrojarl.se. *Entrées 185–345 SEK. AE, DC, MC, V. Mon–Fri 11.30am–1am, Sat 1pm–2am. T-bana Östermalmstorg. Map p 111.*

★★ kids Bistro Ruby/Grill Ruby
GAMLA STAN *FRENCH/AMERICAN* This is Paris/Texas side by side. Bistro Ruby is traditional French given a Swedish twist; the Grill serves large well-cooked portions of steak and fries with a choice of accompaniments. The Bistro is more intimate; the Grill noisy and jumping. *Österlånggatan 14. Bistro:* ☎ 20 57 76. www.bistroruby.com. *Entrées 195–410 SEK. Dinner daily. Grill:* ☎ 20 60 15. www.grillruby.com. *Entrées 187–445 SEK. Dinner Mon–Sat, Lunch Sat. AE, DC, MC, V. T-bana Gamla Stan. Map p 112.*

★★ Bistro Sud SÖDERMALM
FRENCH This friendly venue for the sophisticated local media crowd offers typical bistro dishes such as moules as well as those with a more adventurous Swedish take. Good bar. *Swedenborgsgatan 8.* ☎ 640 41 11. www.bistrosud.se. *Entrées 125–285 SEK. AE, MC, V. Dinner daily. Closed July. T-bana Mariatorget. Map p 112.*

★ kids Brasserie Bobonne
ÖSTERMALM *BRASSERIE* I love this small friendly restaurant for its local feel and classic brasserie dishes from the blackboard, cooked in an open kitchen. If you're longing for a plate of moules marinières or a boeuf Bourguignon, book here. *Storgatan*

Ruby Grill.

12. ☎ 660 03 18. www.brasserie bobonne. com. Entrées 185–295 SEK. Prix fixe menu 498 SEK. AE. MC, V. Mon–Sat 10am–10pm. T-bana Östermalmstorg. Map p 111.

★★ **Carl Michael** DJURGARDEN *MODERN SWEDISH* This light gray and white restaurant opposite Gröna Lund is now under the auspices of Staffan Svederman and Mattias Rosenbaum, the sommeliers who also own Brasserie Godot. The cooking is a mix of the simple and the challenging, a veal sausage at lunch, cod with black pudding and fresh mushrooms for dinner. *Allmänna gränd 6.* ☎ 667 45 96. *www.carl michael.se. Entrées 182–298 SEK. AE, DC, MC, V. Lunch daily, dinner Tues–Sun. Bus 47. Map p 111.*

★ kids **Clas På Hörnet** VASAS-TADEN *SWEDISH* This is where I go for tradition—the inn dates back to 1731, the perfect setting for classic food such as crayfish in season, roast reindeer, and pike-perch, all in hearty portions. Candlelit and romantic. *Surbrunnsgatan 20.* ☎ 16 51 36. *www.claspahornet.com. Entrées 275–345 SEK. AE, DC, MC, V. Mon–Fri 11.30am–midnight, dinner Sat. T-bana Tekniska högskolan. Map p 111.*

★★ **Den Gyldene Freden** GAMLA STAN *SWEDISH* This is a real old-timer (since 1772) with three floors of snug corners and old-fashioned décor. But it has not dragged its feet and is producing new and adventurous dishes such as fish and shellfish fricassée with fennel, saffron, and cream. And just think, you might be sitting in the very same place as the famous singer-composer Evert Taube. *Österlånggatan 51.* ☎ 24 97 60. *www.gyldenefreden.se. Entrées 175–425 SEK. AE, DC, MC, V. Lunch Mon–Fri, dinner Mon–Sat. T-bana Gamla Stan. Map p 112.*

★★★ **Divino** NORRMALM *ITALIAN* This well-established Italian keeps its reputation as the best Italian in town with a loyal, wealthy clientele. Rich cooking, a superb Italian wine list, elegant décor, and knowledge-able (and enthusiastic) waiters help the luxury ingredients and high prices slip down very nicely. *Karlavägen 28.* ☎ 611 02 69. *www.divino.se. Entrées 295–340 SEK. AE, DC, MC, V. T-bana Råd-mansgatan. Map p 111.*

★★ kids **Djurgårdsbrunn** DJURGÅRDEN *SWEDISH* The canal-side setting is magical and the ter-race fills up fast in summer. The menu covers everything from moules frites to beef tartar and does it very well. *Djurgårds-brunnsvägen 68.* ☎ 624 44 00. *www.bockholmen.com. Entrées 195–295 SEK. AE, DC, MC, V. Bus 69. Map p 111.*

★★ kids **Döden i Grytan** VASAS-TADEN *ITALIAN* You only need to worry about the translation of the name 'Death in the pot' if you overeat, which is the temptation, given the size of the portions and the menu's wide range. Cooking is robust and plentiful; brick walls give

Beside the canal in Djurgårdsbrunn.

East's bar and restaurant are equally popular.

the place a trattoria feel. *Norrtulls-gatan 61.* ☎ *32 50 95. www.doden igrytan.se. Entrées 195–245 SEK. AE, DC, MC, V. Dinner daily. T-bana Odenplan. Map p 111.*

★ **East** ÖSTERMALM *ASIAN* With sushi and sashimi such a rage in health-conscious Sweden, East is rightly popular. It has a good location, stark minimalist décor, and an outdoor terrace to tempt, along with Oriental cooking from Thai to Japanese. The bar makes a great late-night meeting place. *Stureplan 13.* ☎ *611 49 59. www.east.se. Sushi from 96 SEK. Entrées 183–329 SEK. T-bana Östermalmstorg. Map p 111.*

★ **kids Eriks Bakficka** ÖSTERMALM *SWEDISH* I always take friends to Eriks Gondolen for a drink but for a casual meal, always eat at the little sister. This small local restaurant has home comfort dishes such as Eriks' cheeseburger and poached halibut with potato croquettes, beans, and smoked bacon. *Fredrikshovsgatan 4.* ☎ *660 15 99. www.eriks.se. Entrées 195–275 SEK. Prix fixe menus 460–530 SEK. AE,*

DC, MC, V. Lunch Mon–Fri, dinner Mon–Sat. T-bana Karlaplan. Map p 111.

★★ **Eriks Gondolen** SÖDER-MALM *TRADITIONAL SWEDISH* High above Södermalm at the end of the Katarina elevator, you come here for the views and the cooking rather than the standard décor. It's crowded, buzzing, famous, and fun. *Stadsgården 6.* ☎ *641 70 90. www. eriks.se. Entrées 195–495 SEK. Prix fixe menus 475–595 SEK. Mon–Fri 11.30am–1am, Sat 1pm–1am. AE, DC, MC, V. T-bana Slussen. Map p 112.*

★★ **F12** NORRMALM *MODERN SWEDISH* Part of the empire that includes Grill (p 116), Restaurangen (p 119), and Kungsholmen (p 117), F12 is light greens and yellows. The clientele is a mix of the rich and fashionable who choose dishes divided on the menu into Traditional or Innovative. *Fredsgatan 12.* ☎ *24 80 52. www.fredsgatan12. com. Entrées 295–495 SEK. Set menu 1,095 SEK. AE, DC, MC, V. Lunch Mon–Fri, dinner Mon–Sat. T-bana T-Centralen.*

★ **kids Fem Små Hus** GAMLA STAN *TRADITIONAL SWEDISH* Definitely at the old-fashioned end of Stockholm's eateries, Fem Små Hus ('five small houses') still packs people into its romantic, vaulted cellars. It may be popular with tourists, but I love it because it's so cozy and such a slice of old Sweden. And its Swedish food is honestly good. *Nygrand 10.* ☎ *10 87 75. www.fem smahus.se. Entrées 260–325 SEK. Prix fixe menus 415–575 SEK. AE, DC, MC, V. Dinner daily. T-bana Gamla Stan. Map p 112.*

★★★ **Franzén Lindeberg** GAMLA STAN *CONTEMPORARY* In the former Mistral, this small elegant venue concentrates on seasonal, and where possible, organic ingredients. The cooking is adventurous in its two set menus. Try langoustines poached in butter and coconut milk with peas, asparagus, bitter lettuce, and flowers. This is sophisticated, experimental stuff. *Lilla Nyagatan 21.* ☎ *20 85 80. www.franzen-lindeberg.se. Set menus 995 SEK and 1395 SEK. AE, DC, MC, V. Dinner Tues–Sat. T-bana Gamla Stan. Map p 112.*

★★ kids **Frippe** NORRMALM *SWEDISH* With its moody black-and-white photos, long bar with seats, large windows, and proximity to the smaller stage of the Dramaten Theater, this is the perfect pre- or post- theater dining spot. It's good value, too, offering a menu of favorites. *Nybrogatan 6.* ☎ *665 61 42. www.frippe.gastrogate. com. Entrées 136–212 SEK. AE, DC, MC, V. Mon 11.30am–10pm, Tues–Thurs 11.30am–midnight, Fri 11.30am–1am, Sat 1.30pm–1am, Sun 4pm–10pm. T-bana Kungsträdgården. Map p 111.*

★ kids **Grill** NORRMALM *CONTEMPORARY* It's best to decide on your mood and style before booking here. Swedish traditional? American steaks? French courtesan? Grill is a huge old furniture store that's been converted into different areas, making it a multi-themed restaurant with grown-up cooking. I've not exhausted the possibilities yet. Choose your cuisine from Asian to Mediterranean. *Drottninggatan 89.* ☎ *31 45 30. www.grill.se. Entrées 150–310 SEK. AE, DC, MC, V. Lunch Mon–Fri, Sun, dinner Mon–Sat. T-bana Rådmansgatan. Map p 111.*

★★ kids **Halv Grek Plus Turk** ÖSTERMALM *GREEK/ TURKISH* Bright colors, Turkish cushions, blue tiles...you could be anywhere in the Mediterranean. The menu is meze-based, with the classics alongside more unusual concoctions such as seared tuna with sorbet of fried tomato. *Jungfrugatan 33.* ☎ *665 94 22. www.halvgrekplusturk.se. Meze 50–95 SEK. AE, DC, MC, V. Dinner daily. T-bana Stadion. Map p 111.*

★★ **Hotellet** ÖSTERMALM *CONTEMPORARY* This chic venue was a success the moment it opened in 2003. The menu offers all kinds of meat, fish, vegetables, and side

Black and white photographs at Frippe.

orders so you can mix and match. It's also one of the great bars of Stockholm where the cocktails are as beautiful as the bar staff and customers. I advise dressing up not down. *Linnégatan 18.* ☎ *442 89 00. www.hotellet.info Entrées 145–220 SEK. AE, MC, V. Dinner Mon–Sat. T-bana Östermalmstorg. Map p 111.*

★★★ kids **Koh Phangan** SÖDER-MALM *THAI* This brightly decorated, buzzing restaurant stretching back into small spaces of bamboo booths and huts among pools of water also serves some of the best Thai food outside Thailand. Be prepared to queue with a drink until your name is called. *Skånegatan 57.* ☎ *642 68 65. www.kohphangan.se. Entrées 195–265 SEK. AE, DC, MC, V. Dinner Mon–Sat. T-bana Medborgarplatsen. Map p 112.*

★★ kids **Kungsholmen** KUNGS-HOLMEN *CONTEMPORARY* Part of the successful F12 group (p 115), the restaurant has a lovely waterfront, complete with summer pontoon. It's based around seven globally inspired open kitchens—choose from Cuban, Chinese, French, or Swedish. It's large (seats 200), loud, crowded, open late, and fun, but not the place for a romantic tête-à-tête. *Norr Mälarstrand.* ☎ *50 52 44 50. www.kungsholmen.com. Entrées 135–325 SEK. AE, DC, MC, V. Dinner daily. T-bana Rådhuset. Map p 111.*

★★★ **Leijontornet** NORRMALM GAMLA STAN *MODERN SWEDISH* Young chef Gustav Otterberg earned his first Michelin star in 2008 and his cooking just gets better. Championing new Swedish cuisine means taking classic themes and giving them new twists and ingredients. I ordered the saddle of lamb and lamb mince with beetroot, creamed nettles, smoked ox marrow in bread and bee pollen. Believe me, it works and also looks beautiful. The culinary

French bordello style at Grill.

fireworks take place in the medieval cellar where the original fortifications can be seen under the glass floor. Top wine list. *Lilla Nygatan 5.* ☎ *506 400 80. www.leijontornet.se. Menus 695 (3 courses) and 1050 (5 courses). AE, DC, MC, V. Dinner Mon–Sat. T-bana Gamla Stan. Map p 112.*

★★★ kids **Lisa Elmqvist/ Gerdas Fisk** ÖSTERMALM *SWEDISH/FISH* The empire of Lisa Elmqvist is spreading. This first venue, now with nearby Gerdas, is in the food hall and famous for its classic fish dishes; Lisa på Torget is just outside in the square and Lisa på Udden is by the water in leafy Djurgården (Biskopsvägen 7, ☎ 660 94 75, www.lisapaudden.se). *Östermalms Saluhall.* ☎ *55 34 04 00. www.lisaelmqvist.se. Entrées 140–310 SEK. AE, DC, MC, V. Mon–Thurs 9.30am–6pm, Fri 9.30am–6.30pm, Sat 9.30am–4pm. T-bana Östermalmstorg. Map p 111.*

★★★ **Mathias Dahlgren** NOR-RMALM *FRENCH* What can be said about this Michelin-starred grand restaurant where sublime dishes are

PA & Co is a friendly local bistro.

ordered by the wealthy gourmet? Only, go if you can afford it. Or try the menu in Matbaren, which is less a temple of gastronomy, but still top notch. *Grand Hotel, Södra Blasieholmshamnen 6.* ☎ *679 35 84. www.mdghs.com. Entrées 295–485 SEK. AE, DC, MC, V. Dinner Mon–Sat. Matbaren Lunch Mon–Fri, dinner Mon–Sat. T-bana Kungsträdgården. Map p 111.*

★★★ **Operakallaren** NORRMALM *SWEDISH/FRENCH* The gorgeous, richly decorated dining room is all gilded walls, mirrors, and chandeliers. It's a suitably theatrical setting for some dramatic cooking, beautifully presented. Dishes such as steak tartare with duck liver terrine, mushrooms in champagne jelly, and caviar are complex and skillfully prepared—and that's just a starter. No wonder it's the favorite Stockholm restaurant for stars and celebrities. *Operahuset, Karl XII's Torg.* ☎ *676 58 00. www. operakallaren.se. Entrées 290–490 SEK. Tasting menu (whole table) 990 SEK. AE, DC, MC, V. Dinner Tues–Sat. Closed Jul. T-bana Kungsträdgården. Map p 111.*

★★ kids **PA & Co** ÖSTERMALM *BISTRO* It looks like a bistro in a small French town and delivers the goods. Classics are the order of the day here—veal burgers and traditional sausages chalked up on a blackboard. It's mentioned as *the* place for hip celebrities; the last time we were there it was comfortably full of families and a couple of jolly inebriated locals. *Riddargatan 8.* ☎ *611 08 45. Entrées 135–350 SEK. AE, DC, MC, V. Dinner daily. T-bana Östermalmstorg. Map p 111.*

★ kids **Paus Bar & Kök** VASAS-TADEN *SWEDISH/FRENCH* Rörstrandsgatan is becoming something of a gastronomic target but Paus holds its own with adventurous cooking such as pancetta-wrapped veal with artichoke purée. The décor is white tiles and wooden chairs; the bar is the place for cocktails and meeting up with friends. *Rörstrandsgatan 18.* ☎ *34 44 05. www.restaurangpaus. se. Entrées 250–310 SEK. AE, DC, MC, V. T-bana St Eriksplan. Map p 111.*

★ kids **Pelikan** SÖDERMALM
SWEDISH Go to this beer hall for a
feel of old Stockholm. Wood-paneled,
dark, and popular, this is the place
for traditional meatballs, ice-cold
schnapps, and beer. *Blekingegatan
40.* ☎ 55 60 90 90. *www.pelikan.se.
Entrées 140–225 SEK. AE, MC, V.
T-bana Skanstull. Map p 112.*

★★★ **Pontus!** NORRMALM *MOD-
ERN SWEDISH* his is the latest venture from the local hero, Pontus
Frithiof after he closed Pontus in the
Greenhouse. Go past the champagne
and oyster bar and the bar serving
dim sum and sashimi into the dramatic dining room. The menu is
divided into Harvest (vegetarian),
Catch (fish and seafood), and Season
(seasonal), with most dishes as small,
medium, and large. So you really can
graze your way around this gourmet
venture. *Brunnsgatan 1.* ☎ 545 27
300. *www.pontusfrithiof.com. Entrées
185–325 SEK. AE, DC, MC, V. Lunch
and dinner Mon–Sat. T-bana Hötorget. Map p 111.*

★★★ kids **Pon-
tus' Brasserie
by the Sea**
GAMLA STAN
SEAFOOD On the
waterfront, this
relaxed venue of
star chef Pontus
Frithiof looks out
onto the water and is
the right place for fresh
seafood. I recommend a glass of
wine in the outdoor bar for a real
summer experience. *Tullhus 2,
Skeppsbron.* ☎ 20 20 95. *www.
pontusfrithiof.com. Entrées 230–445
SEK. Seafood platters 375–1395 SEK.
AE, DC, MC, V. Summer Mon–Fri
11.30am–1am, Sat, Sun noon–1am.
Winter Mon–Fri 11.30am–1am, Sat
4pm–1am. T-bana Gamla Stan. Map
p 112.*

★★ **Proviant** ÖSTERMALM
BRASSERIE Mattias Edlund and

Håkan Thor moved from Sweden's
top restaurant, Edsbacka Korg, to
open this brasserie and bar looking
onto the park. On offer are exciting
signature dishes like Swedish venison with pistachio nuts and fried
shitake accompanied by pear and
celeriac brulée. *Sturegatan 19.*
☎ 22 60 50. *www.proviant.se.
Entrées 270–295 SEK. AE, DC, MC, V.
Lunch and dinner Mon–Thurs, Fri
11.30am–midnight. T-bana Östermalmstorg. Map p 111.*

★★ **Restaurang 1900** NOR-
RMALM *SWEDISH* Known for his
TV appearances, chef Niklas Ekstedt
moved to central Stockholm to open
his latest restaurant. It's a simple
room with light wood furniture; the
menu is divided into classic and
modern and the cooking concentrates on Swedish ingredients, some
of them less well known, as well as
using Oriental spicing. *Regeringsgatan 66.* ☎ 20 60 10. *www.r1900.
se. Entrées 165–265 SEK. AE, DC,
MC, V. Lunch Mon–Fri,
Dinner Mon–Sat. T-bana
Kungsträdgården. Map
p 111.*

★★ **Restaurangen**
NORRMALM *SWEDISH*
Opened in 1998, this is
the place for 'grazing'.
You order small dishes
under flavors such as
garlic (fish soup with aioli),
olive (Provençale scallops
and ratatouille), and so on. Prices
are by the number of dishes
ordered. Portions are small, but it's
fun. *Oxtorgsgatan 14.* ☎ 22 09 52.
*www.restaurangentm.com. 3 Dishes
300 SEK, 5 dishes 400 SEK, 7 dishes
500 SEK. AE, DC, MC, V. Lunch
Mon–Fri, dinner Mon–Sat. T-bana
Hötorget. Map p 111.*

★★ **Restaurangen Prinsen**
ÖSTERMALM *BRASSERIE* This
charming, busy, small brasserie with

its old-fashioned decor opened in 1897 since when it's been serving the classics to a satisfied literary crowd, mixed with tired shoppers. *Mäster Samuelsgatan 4.* ☎ *08 611 13 11. www.restaurangprinsen.se. Entrées 189–365 SEK. AE, DC, MC, V. Mon–Fri 11.30am–11.30pm, Sat 1pm–11.30pm, Sun 5pm–10.30pm. T-bana Östermalmstorg. Map p 111.*

★★ **Riche** ÖSTERMALM *SWEDISH/ EUROPEAN* Bustling, beautiful, and full of beautiful people (or those who think they are), Riche is fun with its modern décor and buzzing atmosphere. The cooking is fine, but it's the scene you're here for. *Birger Jarlsgatan 4.* ☎ *545 035 60. www.riche.se. Entrées 135–345 SEK. AE, DC, MC, V. Mon 11.30am– midnight, Tues–Fri 11.30am–2am; Sat noon–2am. T-bana Östermalmstorg. Map p 111.*

★★ **Rolfs Kök** NORRMALM *INTERNATIONAL/BRASSERIE* Famous for its wall-hung chairs, this trendy, minimalist-designed bar/restaurant has a great atmosphere and modern cooking, done with a flourish in the

Rich pleasures at Riche.

open kitchen. It's a favorite for lunch. *Tegnérgatan 41.* ☎ *08 10 16 96. www.rolfskok.se. Entrées 185–325 SEK. AE, DC, MC, V. Mon–Fri 11.30am–1am, Sat, Sun 5pm–1am. T-bana Rådmansgatan. Map p 111.*

★★ **Le Rouge** GAMLA STAN *CONTEMPORARY* In the former Pontus in the Greenhouse and Kallaren Diana, there's more than a touch of the Moulin Rouge here with all the red velvet seating, drapes, and Old Master style art. There's a large dining room, bar, and outside terrace, and two entrances. *Brunnsgrand 2–4.* ☎ *505 244 30. www.lerouge.se. Entrées 295–455 SEK. AE, DC, MC, V. T-bana Gamla Stan. Map p 112.*

★★ kids **Lo Scudetto** SÖDERMALM *ITALIAN* It took me a while to find Lo Scudetto the first time, but it was well worth the effort because this restaurant serves some of the best Italian food in town and is far better than you'd imagine from the simple décor. It's candlelit, with photos of Swedish football stars adorning the walls, relaxed and always crowded, so book. *Åsögatan 163.* ☎ *08 640 42 15. www.loscudetto.se. Entrées 215–255 SEK. AE, MC, V. Dinner Mon–Sat. T-bana Medborgarplatsen. Map p 112.*

★ **Sturehof** NORRMALM *SWEDISH/FRENCH* Looking at the beautiful people who frequent this popular spot, it's hard to imagine that this was a beer hall 100 years ago. But, despite its thoroughly modern clientele, the menu sticks to the classics, both Swedish and French, like steak with Café de Paris butter. *Stureplan 2.* ☎ *440 57 30. www.sturehof.com. Entrées 125–415 SEK. AE, DC, MC, V. Mon–Fri 11am–2am, Sat noon–2am, Sun 1pm–2am. T-bana Östermalmstorg. Map p 111.*

The world meets at Sturehof.

★★★ **Teater Grillen** ÖSTERMALM
SWEDISH/FRENCH Beside the Dramaten theater, this restaurant just has to be theatrical. And it is, with a silver trolley doing the rounds when the famous salt-baked entrecôte steak is ordered (which it frequently is). Otherwise go for the classics. The clientele is a mix of media and business, with theater types in abundance. Expensive but a good evening's entertainment. *Nybrogatan 3.* ☎ *545 035 62. www.riche.se. Entrées 165–495 SEK. AE, DC, MC, V. Lunch Mon–Fri, dinner Mon–Sat. T-bana Kungsträdgården. Map p 111.*

★★ kids **Tranan** VASASTADEN
SWEDISH With its no-nonsense décor, red-and-white check tablecloths, and honest dishes from moules to classic Biff Rydberg, this deservedly popular restaurant gets very crowded. In addition, there's a heaving cellar bar with DJs pumping out late-night music. *Karlbergsvagen 14.* ☎ *527 2 81 00. www.tranan.se. Entrées 145–295 SEK. AE, DC, MC, V. Mon–Fri 11.30am–1am, Sat, Sun 5pm–1am. T-bana Odenplan. Map p 111.*

★★ **Ulla Winbladh** DJURGÅRDEN
SWEDISH Romantic and old-fashioned is just what you expect—and get—in this pretty venue named after a friend of the famous composer Carl Michael Bellman. New chefs have upped the ante, but not upset the menu of Swedish classics with French flourishes. Eat outside in summer. *Rosendalsvägen 8.* ☎ *534 897 01. www.ullawinbladh.se. Entrées 235–334 SEK. AE, DC, MC, V. Mon 11.30am–10pm, Tues–Fri 11.30am–11pm, Sat noon–11pm, Sun noon–10pm. Bus 47. Map p 111.*

★★ **Vassa Eggen** ÖSTERMALM
FRENCH The 'Sharp Edge' is just that—chic, stylish, and elegant, attracting the movers and shakers of Stockholm. Like many of the city's

Lunch or Dinner?

Restaurants in Stockholm are expensive, and alcohol, which is heavily taxed, adds greatly to the bill. It's a sophisticated city with elegant tastes. But don't be put off by that; the Swedes have the balance of good food, stylish interiors, and a smart but friendly ambience just right, which makes dining in Stockholm a real pleasure. And don't worry if many restaurants seem to be out of your price range; most, even the top ones, offer special deals at lunchtime, for example a main dish that sometimes includes extras or much lower prices for the same dish you get in the evenings.

Stylish Vassa Eggen.

restaurants, it has a casual feel, and in the evening the bar gets seriously full of late-night clubbers, albeit of an extremely elegant kind. *Birger Jarlsgatan 29.* ☎ *08 21 61 69. www.vassaeggen.com. Entrées 275–345 SEK. Prix fixe menu 865 SEK. AE, DC, MC, V. Lunch Mon–Fri, dinner Mon–Sat. Closed July. T-bana Hötorget. Map p 111.*

★★★ **Wedholms Fisk** ÖSTER-MALM *SEAFOOD* This elegant well-established institution started by the revered Bengt Wedholm in 1985 is now under the care of Nils Molinder

and the approach has lightened. But you still get some of the best fish and seafood cooking in Sweden on a menu that's arranged by fish type, and then ways of cooking. In summer book a table outside and sit and watch the waterside scene just over the road. *Nybrokajen 17.* ☎ *08 611 78 74. www.melanders.se. Entrées 265–545 SEK. Tasting menu 795 SEK. AE, DC, MC, V. Lunch Mon–Fri, dinner Mon–Sat. T-bana Kungstradgården/Östermalmstorg. Map p 111.* ●

Nightlife Best Bets

Best for Beer Fiends
★★ Akkurat, *Hornsgatan 18 (p 127)*

Best for Design Freaks and Foodies
★★ Brasserie Godot, *Grev Ture-gatam 36 (p 127)*

Best for a Drink with a View
★★★ Gondolen, *Stadsgården 6, (p 127)*; and ★★ Och Himlen Dartill, *Götgatan 78 (p 128)*

Best Nightclub
★★★ Berns Salonger, *Berzelli Park 9 (p 129)*

Best for a Voodoo Moment
★★★ Marie Laveau, *Hornsgatan 66 (p 129)*

Best Smart Gay Bar
★★★ Leijonbaren, *Lilla Nygatan 5 (p 130)*

Best for Jazz Legends
★★★ Fasching Jazzclub, *Kungs-gatan 63 (p 131)*

Best for Design Freaks and Foodies
★★ Anglais, *Humlegårdsgatan 23 (p 127)*

Best for Rocking the Night Away
★★ Debaser Medis, *Medbor-garplatsen 8 (p 131)*

Best for Jazz Brunch
★★★ Mosebacke, *Mosebacke Torg 3 (p 132)*

Beer heaven at Akkurat.

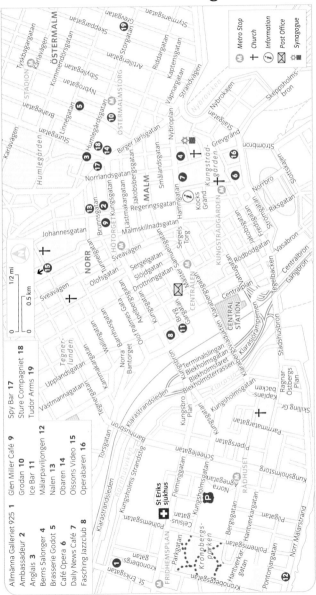

Allmänna Galleriet 925 **1**
Ambassadeur **2**
Anglais **3**
Berns Salonger **4**
Brasserie Godot **5**
Café Opera **6**
Daily News Café **7**
Fasching JazzClub **8**
Glen Miller Café **9**
Grodan **10**
Ice Bar **11**
Mälarpaviljongen **12**
Nalen **13**
Obaren **14**
Olssons Video **15**
Operabaren **16**
Spy Bar **17**
Sture Compagniet **18**
Tudor Arms **19**

Metro Stop
Church
Information
Post Office
Synagogue

South Stockholm Nightlife

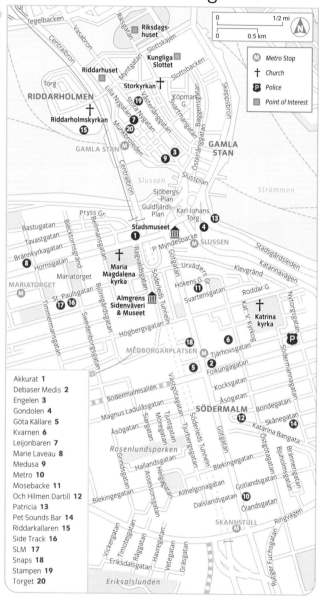

0	1/2 mi
0	0.5 km

M Metro Stop
† Church
P Police
■ Point of Interest

Akkurat **1**
Debaser Medis **2**
Engelen **3**
Gondolen **4**
Göta Källare **5**
Kvarnen **6**
Leijonbaren **7**
Marie Laveau **8**
Medusa **9**
Metro **10**
Mosebacke **11**
Och Hilmen Dartill **12**
Patricia **13**
Pet Sounds Bar **14**
Riddarkällaren **15**
Side Track **16**
SLM **17**
Snaps **18**
Stampen **19**
Torget **20**

Stockholm Nightlife A to Z

Chic drinking at Grodan.

Bars & Pubs

★★ **Akkurat** SÖDERMALM For an impressive beer list, drink at this wooden floored and paneled pub (which also has a good whisky bar) with 28 beers on tap, more than 600 bottles, and 44 whiskies. Sunday evening live music helps the Leffes go down. *Hornsgatan 18.* ☎ *644 00 15. www.akkurat.se. T-bana Maria-torget/Slussen. Map p 126.*

★★ **Allmänna Galleriet 925** KUNGSHOLMEN This bar/restaurant/lounge is housed in an old silver workshop. It's difficult to find and is industrial in feel inside so it was bound to be a hit. *Kronobergs-gatan 37.* ☎ *41 06 81 00. www.ag 925.se. T-bana Fridhemsplan. Map p 125.*

★★ **Anglais** NORRMALM One of Stockholm's chicest hotel bars is a great place for a relaxing drink with a view out to the street. DJs spin music Tuesday to Saturdays. The separate 7th-floor Terrace Bar has extensive views. *Humlegårdsgatan 23.* ☎ *517 340 00. www.scandic hotels.se. T-bana Östermalmstorg. Map p 125.*

★★★ **Brasserie Godot** ÖSTER-MALM The startling white brasserie serves steak and fries and offers one of Stockholm's chicest bars for the young and/or fashionable. Seriously good drinks list. *Grev Turegatan 36.* ☎ *660 06 14. www. godot.se. T-bana Östermalmstorg. Map p 125.*

★★★ **Gondolen** SÖDERMALM Sipping a drink and looking at the view should be on everybody's list. But you'll have to work hard to get your drink at this hugely popular venue. *Stadsgården 6.* ☎ *641 70 90. www.eriks.se. T-bana Slussen. Map p 126.*

★★★ **Grodan** ÖSTERMALM Despite heavy competition from newer venues, Grodan stays top of the nightlife league. The restaurant/bar and nightclub offer different

Drinks at the Windmill.

decors while bar staff are pleased to mix you your own particular cocktail. *Grev Turegatan 16.* ☎ *679 61 00. www.grodan.se. T-bana Östermalmstorg. Map p 125.*

★★ **Ice Bar** NORRMALM In the Nordic Sea Hotel, this is, literally, the coolest place in town to drink. Don a fur-lined coat and boots before sampling vodka, served in ice glasses. Be warned, it's expensive. *Vasaplan.* ☎ *505 630 00. www.nordichotels.se. T-bana T-Centralen. Map p 125.*

★ **Kvarnen** SÖDERMALM It looks traditional from the outside—just like the former beer hall it was before the 'Windmill' began its present life. Today it's a popular late-night pub with a couple of bars and 'Hell' in the basement for dancing and live entertainment. Fun and friendly. *Tjarhovsgatan 4.* ☎ *643 03 80. www.kvarnen.com. Entrance around 130 SEK for shows only. T-bana Medborgarplatsen. Map p 126.*

★★ **Och Himlen Dartill** SÖDERMALM The view from the 25th floor gives Gondolen a run for its money. The décor is so cool it almost hurts. And, the cocktails? Very good. Also a jaw-droppingly expensive restaurant. *Götgatan 78.*

☎ *660 60 65. www.restaurang himlen.se. T-bana Medborgarplatsen. Map p 126.*

★★★ **Operabaren** NORRMALM This is an unusually peaceful place for a drink in splendid Jugendstil surroundings. The old-fashioned waiters are charming; the atmosphere club-like. *Operahuset, Karl XII's Torg.* ☎ *676 58 00. www.operakallaren.se. T-bana Kungsträdgården. Map p 125.*

★ **Snaps** SÖDERMALM Huge bar with summer outdoor terrace and dining area for all-day eating and drinking. There's also a dance club and basement bar that get going after 11pm. *Götgatan 48.* ☎ *640 28 68. www.snaps.se. Entrance 100 SEK after 11pm. T-bana Medborgarplatsen. Map p 126.*

★ **Tudor Arms** ÖSTERMALM Stockholm's oldest British pub founded in 1969 is the place where homesick Brits gather in the wood-beamed room for fish 'n' chips, a pint of bitter, and a game on the huge TV

Berns Salonger opened in 1863.

The slick Metró.

screen. *Grevgatan 31.* ☎ *660 27 12. T-bana Östermalmstorg. Map p 125.*

Dance & Nightclubs

★★ **Ambassadeur** NORRMALM This nightclub has three different rooms, Ambassadeur White, Black, and Gold, which you can recognize by the décor in...white, black, and gold. It's very trendy and has top-class international stars on Friday and Saturday nights. *Kungsgatan 18.* ☎ *24 47 00. www.stureplanns gruppen.se. Prices vary. T-bana Kungsträdgården. Map p 125.*

★★★ **Berns Salonger** NOR-RMALM One of Stockholm's insti-tutions since it first opened in 1863, this elegant club is in two rooms (more relaxed upstairs, garage downstairs in LE) with the likes of Snoop Dogg for the seriously trendy. In theory, it's members only, so turn up early looking good. *Berzelii Park 9.* ☎ *556 322 22. www. berns.se. Tickets 570–795 SEK. T-bana Kungsträdgården. Map p 125.*

★★ **Café Opera** NORRMALM You're in, quite simply, the smartest nightclub in town, which fills up with beautiful young things. If you have the money, the best thing to do is dine at Operakalleren (see p 118) then party on here until 3am.

Operahuset, Kungsträdgården. ☎ *676 58 07. www.cafeopera.se. Admission 180 SEK after 10pm. T-bana Kungsträdgården. Map p 125.*

★★ **Daily News Café** NOR-RMALM Several dance floors spread over the building, unpreten-tious atmosphere, central location, open late, and 1970s disco from the relaxed DJs make this a winner. Sum-mer sees the popular terrace fill up. *Kungsträdgården.* ☎ *21 56 55. T-bana Kungsträdgården. Map p 125.*

★★★ **Marie Laveau** SÖDERMALM This trendy nightspot, named after the New Orleans voodoo Queen, is a bar and club with DJs spinning the best on Bangers 'n' Mash nights. Also a good restaurant if you want to spin out the evening yourself. *Hornsgatan 66.* ☎ *66 88 500. www. marielaveau.se. Entrance fee varies for different shows. T-bana Slussen. Map p 126.*

★★ **Metró** SÖDERMALM The black and red décor and a slick Södermalm crowd who come for the DJs spinning in two bars guarantee its success. Minimum age of 23 is strictly applied. *Götgatan 93.* ☎ *673 38 00. T-bana Medborgarplatsen. Map p 126.*

★★ **Obaren** ÖSTERMALM Above the restaurant Sturehof, DJs and live acts (at least two a week) mix just about everything to an equally mixed crowd, who come here for the music as much as the vibe and keep going to 2am. *Stureplan 2.* ☎ *440 57 30. www.sturehof.com. T-bana Östermalmstorg. Map p 125.*

★★ **Olssons Video** VASASTADEN What do you do with an old shoe shop? In Stockholm, you turn it into a party venue. It's small and very crowded, the décor dominated by a fish tank, and the clientele dance informally to the bar's music mix on Wednesday and to club nights on Saturday. The cocktails are legendary. *Odengatan 41.* ☎ *673 38 00. www.storstad.se. Entrance varies. T-bana Odenplan. Map p 125.*

★ **Spy Bar** NORRMALM Stockholm's best-known bar and club is in a luxurious converted 2nd-floor apartment. It's part of the group owning the adjacent The Lab and Laroy. Expensive once you're past the velvet rope and bouncers. Music ranges from funk to soul. *Birger Jarlsgatan 20.* ☎ *54 50 37 04. T-bana Östermalmstorg. Map p 125.*

★★ **Sture Compagniet** ÖSTER-MALM One of Stockholm's top

Spy Bar for funk and soul.

clubs and difficult to get into, it's large, brash, vibrant, and full of a thoroughly cool crowd. Only go if you're dressed right and feeling brash yourself. Three floors include a restaurant and Hell's Kitchen in the basement. *Sturegatan 4.* ☎ *545 076 01. www.stureplannsgruppen.se. Entry: Thurs 100 SEK, Fri, Sat 140 SEK. T-bana Östermalmstorg. Map p 125.*

Gay & Lesbian Bars/Clubs

★★★ **Leijonbaren** GAMLA STAN One of the smartest bars is in the gay-friendly Victory hotel. This is a great place to chill out in its smart décor with a summer terrace bar and DJs most nights. *Lilla Nygatan 5.* ☎ *50 64 00 80. www.leijonbaren.se. T-bana Gamla Stan. Map p 126.*

★★★ **Mälarpaviljongen** KUNG-SHOLMEN An outdoor bar/restaurant on the waterfront with a new jetty and great view. During the day it's mixed, at night it's gay. Summer only. *Norr Mälarstrand 64.* ☎ *650 87 01. www.malarpaviljongen.se. T-bana Råadhuset/ Fridhemsplan. Map p 125.*

★★★ **Patricia** SÖDERMALM Built in Middlesbrough, England, in 1938, Winston Churchill spent time on this boat (hence an eponymous room) and it became the English royals' private yacht. Now, it has restaurants, live music, and DJs. But it's best known for Sunday gay nights, famous throughout the international gay community. *Stadsgårdskajen 152.* ☎ *743 05 70. www.patricia.st. T-bana Slussen. Map p 126.*

★★ **Riddarkallaren** RIDDARHOL-MEN The restaurant has good views but this big venue (four bars, three dance floors, a terrace, and free Internet surfing) is about gay club nights. Saturday Lino nights (10pm–4am) are devoted to a mixed-age, mixed crowd. For Thursdays, check out www.neoslounge.com. *Södra Riddarholmshannen 19.* ☎ 411 69 76. *www.linoclub.com. Entry 100 SEK. T-bana Gamla Stan. Map p 126.*

★ **Side Track** SÖDERMALM   Good food and great atmosphere at this casual basement venue. It's popular, informal, and fun for the mainly male crowd. *Wollmar Yxkullsgatan 7.* ☎ 641 16 88. *www.sidetrack.nu. T-bana Mariatorget. Map p 126.*

★★ **SLM** SÖDERMALM   This male-only venue is a warren of small dark rooms. The website lays it out: this is the place for leather, rubber, uniform, and fetishes. Dress as you feel. *Wollmar Yxkullsgatan 18.* ☎ 643 31 00.*www.slm.a.se. Membership cards 1 year 350 SEK, 1 month 100 SEK. Or valid ECMC membership. T-bana Mariatorget. Map p 126.*

★★★ **Torget** GAMLA STAN   The gay bar most visitors have heard of hasn't been spoilt by its popularity. This is an excellent venue with good food and an international audience. *Malartorget 13.* ☎ 20 55 60. *www.torget baren.com. T-bana Gamla Stan. Map p 126.*

Jazz Clubs
★★★ **Fasching Jazzclub** NORRMALM   This is a jazz club that does deserve the 'legendary' label— the photographs on the walls show you the great names that have performed here. Concerts and jazz sessions every night and a knowledgeable crowd of all ages come for the mix of music from funk to mainstream jazz, Friday Latin Club, and Soul on Saturdays. *Kungsgatan 63.* ☎ 21 62 67. *www.fasching. se. Tickets* ☎ 53 48 29 60. *Tickets*

110–150 SEK. T-bana T-Centralen. Map p 125.

★ **Glen Miller Café** NORRMALM   Tiny and cramped, this friendly pub hosts a variety of jazz acts. It's decorated with black-and-white photos on tobacco-colored walls and has simple wooden chairs and tables. Free admission but you're asked to contribute something. *Brunnsgatan 21a.* ☎ 10 03 22. *www.glenmiller cafe. com. T-bana Hötorget. Map p 125.*

★★★ **Stampen** GAMLA STAN   This jazz club founded in 1968 is so small you really get up close to the musicians. Two floors: trad jazz and R&B upstairs (and an older audience); rockabilly and country for the younger downstairs. Cluttered interior and grainy old photos. *Stora Nygatan 5.* ☎ 20 57 93. *www. stampen.se. Mon–Thurs free, Fri, Sat 120 SEK (2 bands). T bana Gamla Stan. Map p 126.*

Music Clubs
★★ **Debaser Medis** SÖDERMALM   Tops for live rock, Debaser and its four other venues attract a young crowd for nightly concerts of country, rock, pop, hip-hop, and reggae. It's huge with bars, dance floors, cinema, gallery, and restaurant. *Medborgarplatsen 8.* ☎ 694 79 00. *www.debaser.nu. Admission varies. T-bana Medborgarplatsen. Map p 126.*

Engelen rocks in Gamla Stan.

★ **Engelen** GAMLA STAN   The old-fashioned look fits in well to Gamla Stan. But push open the door and you're met with up-to-date bands playing nightly. The downstairs cellar takes up where the upstairs leaves off with old favorites

How To Get In

Stockholm has one of Europe's liveliest bar scenes but some of it is members only (which can be quite flexible). Otherwise you're faced with long queues and an undefined dress code that you can only pick up on by looking at the beautiful people in the queue—and by then it's too late to change. So if you're going out, dress carefully and turn up before 10pm to avoid the late-night crowds and get past the doormen. The most challenging clubs are around Stureplan, which is Stockholm nightlife central. Many of them charge for the cloakroom—which can be up to 150 SEK per person, so be prepared for unexpected extras.

and new music providing the atmosphere. *Kornhamnstorg 59.* ☎ *50 55 60 90. www.engelenkolingen.se. Entrance after 8pm: Mon–Thurs 50 SEK, Fri, Sat 80 SEK, cloakroom 15 SEK. T-bana Gamla Stan. Map p 126.*

★ **Göta Källare** SÖDERMALM Two dance floors and five bars fill up quickly at this huge venue that offers R&B, hip-hop, funky, and progressive house. *Folkungagatan 45.* ☎ *57 86 79 00. www.gotakallare. com. Tickets 100–250 SEK. T-bana Medborgarplatsen. Map p 126.*

★★ **Medusa** GAMLASTAN Small bar upstairs open all week for the tourists; heavy rock in the basement in the vaults on Fridays and Saturdays for hard-core fans. *Kornhamnstorg 61.* ☎ *21 87 00. www.medusa bar.com. Admission to basement club 60 SEK after 11pm. T-bana Gamla Stan. Map p 126.*

★★★ **Mosebacke** SÖDERMALM Right at the heart of Stockholm's historic entertainment center, many of

Sweden's best have played here. Friday serves funky jazz and soul, Saturdays are club sounds, DJs spin at weekends, and there's a Jazz brunch (165 SEK) at weekends. *Mosebacke Torg 3.* ☎ *556 098 90. www.mose backe.se. Tickets free–250 SEK. T-bana Slussen. Map p 126.*

★★★ **Nalen** NORRMALM Renovation turned Stockholm's original top jazz venue into a place with a range of music, from Harlem gospel singers to the latest Swedish folk singer. The large venue has three stages, a restaurant, rock club, and studio. *Regeringsgatan 74.* ☎ *50 52 92 00. www.nalen.com. Tickets free–350 SEK. T-bana Hötorget. Map p 125.*

★★ **Pet Sounds Bar** SÖDERMALM It started in the rock store opposite; now you can get indierock in the basement below the restaurant. *Skanegatan 80.* ☎ *643 82 25. www.petsoundsbar.se. Admission prices vary. T-bana Medborgarplatsen. Map p 126.*

Stockholm Arts & Entertainment

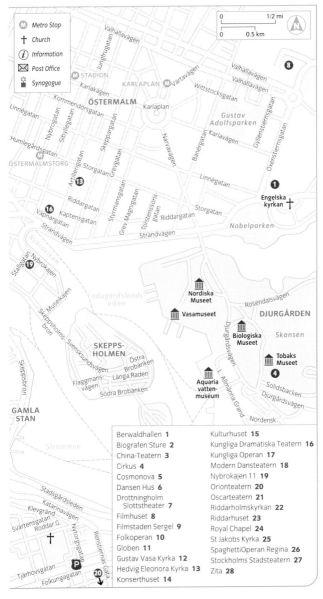

Legend:
- (M) Metro Stop
- † Church
- (i) Information
- ✉ Post Office
- 🕎 Synagogue

Berwaldhallen **1**
Biografen Sture **2**
China-Teatern **3**
Cirkus **4**
Cosmonova **5**
Dansen Hus **6**
Drottningholm
  Slottstheater **7**
Filmhuset **8**
Filmstaden Sergel **9**
Folkoperan **10**
Globen **11**
Gustav Vasa Kyrka **12**
Hedvig Eleonora Kyrka **13**
Konserthuset **14**
Kulturhuset **15**
Kungliga Dramatiska Teatern **16**
Kungliga Operan **17**
Modern Dansteatern **18**
Nybrokajen 11 **19**
Orionteatern **20**
Oscarteatern **21**
Riddarholmskyrkan **22**
Riddarhuset **23**
Royal Chapel **24**
St Jakobs Kyrka **25**
SpaghettiOperan Regina **26**
Stockholms Stadsteatern **27**
Zita **28**

Arts & Entertainment Best Bets

The fabulous Kungliga Opera house.

Best **Modern Music Premièrs**
★★ Berwaldhallen, *Dag Hammarskjoldsväg 3 (p 135)*

Best **Classical Music in an Architectural Masterpiece**
★★ Konserthuset, *Hötorget (p 135)*; and ★★ Riddarhuset, *Riddarhustorget 10 (p 135)*

Best **Contemporary Dance**
★★ Dansens Hus, *Barnhusgatan 12–14 (p 135)*

Best **Opera in a Regal Setting**
★★★ Kungliga Operan, *Gustav Adolfs Torg (p 135)*

Best for **an Ingmar Bergman Moment**
★★ Filmhuset, *Borvagen (p 138)*

Best **Baroque Stage Design**
★★★ Drottningholm Slottstheater, *Drottningholm Palace, (p 139)*

Best **Complete Evening's Entertainment**
★★ SpaghettiOperan Regina, *Drottninggatan 71A (p 139)*

Best for **Romeo & Juliet**
★★ Kungliga Operan, *Gustav Adolfs Torg (p 135)*

Best for **Bach & Buxtehude**
★★ St Jacobs Kyrka, *Jakobs Torg 5 (p 139)*

Buying Tickets

You'll find information on special events in the official *What's On Stockholm* guide, free at most hotels and tourist information centers. For the latest concert, theater, and event listings pick up a copy of the *På stan*, the Thursday supplement of newspaper *Dagens Nyheter*, at newsstands (Swedish only). Useful websites include www.alltomstockholm.se and www.stockholmtown.com. Buy tickets at the venues themselves, via their websites, or at the Stockholm Tourist Office. Or book via Ticnet, ☎ 077 170 70 70, www.ticnet.se. The season runs mainly from September to May or June, so if you come expecting theater, music, and dance in the summer, you'll probably be disappointed.

Arts & Entertainment A to Z

Classical Music & Concert Venues

★★ Berwaldhallen ÖSTERMALM
This modernist concert hall is the home of the Swedish Radio Symphony Orchestra and the Radio Choir, founded in 1967. The Orchestra is particularly known for commissioning new Swedish music. *Dag Hammarskjoldsväg 3.* ☎ *784 18 00. www.berwaldhallen.se. Tickets 100–1250 SEK. T-bana Karlaplan. Map p 136.*

★★ Konserthuset NORRMALM
Konserthuse, an architectural masterpiece, was built in 1926 for the Royal Stockholm Philharmonic Orchestra, which commissions modern works. It also puts on concerts of the classics, and hosts international orchestras, dance companies, and jazz. *Hötorget.* ☎ *50 66 77 88. www.konserthuset.se. Tickets 80–1350 SEK. T bana Hötorget. Map p 136.*

★ Nybrokajen 11 NORRMALM
Originally the home of the Royal Academy of Music, it now houses the Swedish Concert Institute, which performs mainly chamber music. The smaller venue, Stallet, is for world music. *Nybrokajen 11.* ☎ *407 17 00. www.nybrokajen11. Tickets 150–295 SEK. T-bana: Kungsträdgården/ Östermalmstorg. Map p 136.*

★★★ Riddarhuset GAMLA STAN
The magnificent House of the Nobility hosts the occasional opera and music by the Stockholm Sinfonietta. The rare performances are worth attending for first-class music in a magnificent venue. See p 61, bullet ❾. *Riddarhustorget 10. www. riddarhuset.se. Tickets 220–290 SEK. T bana Gamla Stan. Map p 136.*

Dance & Opera

★★★ Dansens Hus NORRMALM
The major venue for Swedish contemporary dance and performance artists offers an exciting program on its two stages, from performances by the Swedish touring Cullberg Ballet to international guests Akram Khan, Helsinki Dance Company, and DV8 Physical Theatre. *Barnhusgatan 12–14.* ☎ *508 990 90. www.dansens hus.se. Tickets 200–270 SEK. T-bana Hötorget/ T-Centralen. Map p 136.*

★★★ Kungliga Operan NORRMALM 'The dancers are not disagreeable and perform accurately; they promise to become quite good in time.' King Gustav III he modestly proud of the company he formed, along with the Royal Opera, in 1773. The company today, one of the four oldest in the world, performs classics and contemporary dance. *Gustav Adolfs Torg. Box office* ☎ *791 44 00. www.operan.se. Tickets 40–690 SEK. T-bana Kungsträdgården. Map p 136.*

★ Moderna Dansteatern VÄSTBERGA The main venue on Skeppsholmen is being refurbished and reopens in 2010. For this experimental dance company, you'll now have to go to different venues, with the main one at Telefonplan. *Telefonplan.* ☎ *611 32 33. www. modernadansteatern.se. Check website for all details. T-bana Telefonplan. Map p 136.*

★★ kids Orionteatern SÖDERMALM Founded in 1983 in an old factory, this avant-garde theater works with international companies from the Peking Opera in Shanghai to Theatre de Complicité in London and Le Cirque Invisible from Paris. *Katarina Bang 77. Info:* ☎ *649 29*

Ingmar Bergman

Ernst Ingmar Bergman, born in Östermalm in 1918, was one of the most influential film-makers of modern cinema. But the 9-times Academy-nominated playwright, director, and producer was also important in the theater and the opera, which was his first love. His first unpaid job was at the opera and in 1991 he returned for a last opera production of *Bacchanalia*. From 1963–1966 he was Director of the Dramatiska Teatern, creating more than 100 theatrical productions. But he is best known for the great cinematic classics, *Smiles of the Summer Night* (1955), *The Seventh Seal* (1957), *Wild Strawberries* (1957), and near the end of his career, the magnificent *Fanny and Alexander* (1982). He died in 2007 and is buried on the island of Fårö.

70. Tickets ☎ 643 88 89. *www. orionteatern.se. Tickets 50–110 SEK. T-bana Skanstull. Map p 136.*

Film

★★ Biografen Sture ÖSTER-MALM   Opened in 1915, Sture shows arthouse films from the Swedish Film Institute daily at 4.30pm and weekends at 2.30pm and 4.30pm. Tickets are 45 SEK, but yearly membership only costs 80 SEK so it may be worth buying if you're planning to visit more than once. Commercial films are also shown here. *Birger Jarlsgatan 41.* ☎ *85 48. www.biosture.se. Tickets for commercial films (non Film Institute) 90 SEK. T-bana Östermalmstorg. Map p 136.*

★★ kids Cosmonova FRESCATI Sweden's only IMAX cinema shows movies on a 760 square meter dome-shaped screen. 3-D options include getting up close to Egyptian mummies and entering the natural world. *Naturhistoriska Riksmuseet. Frescativagen 40.* ☎ *519 540 00. www. nrm.se. 85 SEK adults, 50 SEK children 5–18 years. See p 56. T-bana Universitetet; bus 40, 540. Map p 136.*

★★ Filmhuset GÄRDET   Housing the Swedish Film Institute, the Film House screens arthouse films, often English with Swedish subtitles all week. Tickets 45 SEK; annual membership 80 SEK. *Borvägen 1–5.* ☎ *665 11 00. www.sfi.se. T-bana Karlaplan. Map p 136.*

★ kids Filmstaden Sergel GARDET   Foreign subtitled films are shown in some of the 14 screens in this huge complex. *Hötorget.* ☎ *56 26 00 00. www.sf.se. Tickets 60–100 SEK. T- bana Hötorget. Map p 136.*

★★ Zita ÖSTERMALM   You're likely to find a film by Ken Loach, a Japanese cartoon, or the latest Swedish art film in this movie theater where you can quench your thirst at the bar. *Birger Jarlsgatan 37.* ☎ *23 20 20. www.zita.se. T-bana Östermalmstorg. Map p 136.*

Music in Churches

★ Gustav Vasa Kyrka VASAS-TADEN   Stop by for lunchtime organ concerts on Thursdays at noon and regular summer concerts on Wednesdays. *Odenplan.* ☎ *508 886 00. www. gustafvasa.nu. Tickets 50–150 SEK. T-bana Odenplan. Map p 136.*

★ Hedvig Eleonora Kyrka

ÖSTERMALM   Organ music Monday, Wednesday, and Friday at 12.15pm. From May to November the church bells are played to a psalm tune, daily 9am, noon, 3pm, 6pm, 9pm. *Storgatan 2.* ☎ *663 04 30. www.hedvig eleonora.se. Lunchtime music tickets 40 SEK. T-bana Östermalmstorg. Map p 136.*

★★ Riddarholmskyrkan

GAMLA STAN   Enjoy summer concerts of classic and Gregorian music, chamber music, instrument solos and singing. No advance booking. *Birger Jarls Torg.* ☎ *402 61 30. 30 SEK. Jun–mid-Aug, Sat, Sun at 1pm. www. kungahuset.se. T-bana Gamla Stan. Map p 136.*

★ Royal Chapel

GAMLA STAN   Organ concerts are held on Fridays by the Court and the City Hall Organists. *Kungliga Slottet Gamla Stan.* ☎ *402 61 30. www.royalcourt. se. T-bana Gamla Stan. Map p 136.*

★ St Jakob's Kyrka

ÖSTERMALM   Every Friday at 5pm the church fills with people on their way home to hear the free organ recital. Also Saturday concerts at 3pm. *Jakobs Torg 5.* ☎ *723 30 38. www.stockholmsdom kyrkoforsamling.se. T-bana Kungsträdgården. Map p 136.*

Opera

★★★ Drottningholm Slottstheater

DROTTNINGHOLM PALACE   Here you can enjoy one of Stockholm's most exclusive festivals, offering Monteverdi, Haydn, and more in the Baroque 18th-century theater of the Royal Family's country home, May to September. All music is performed on period instruments and the original stage equipment is used. *Drottningholm Palace.* ☎ *660 82 25. www.royal court.se. Tickets* ☎ *077 170 70 70; 660 82 25. www.dtm.se. For Drottningholm see p 136. Map p 136.*

★★ Folkoperan

SÖDERMALM   The Folk Opera puts on unconventional operas in a theater where the audience and performers are close together. *Hornsgatan 72.* ☎ *616 07 50. www.folkoperan.se. Tickets 130–420 SEK. T- bana Mariatorget. Map p 136.*

★★★ kids SpaghettiOperan Regina

NORRMALM   Entertainment in abundance here where the guests become part of the performance as the singers perform on the stage and between the tables (so in *Cosi fan Tutte* you're guests at a wedding party). Performances are either specially adapted full operas or *Spaghettiopera* nights where you

Gustav Vasa Kyrka's painted dome.

get highlights. Good food, good opera, all thoroughly enjoyable. *Drottninggatan 71A. ☎ 411 63 20. www.regina-operamathus.com. Tickets 695 SEK for performance, 3-course meal, coffee. No drinks. Luxury package 995 SEK performance, Champagne aperitif, wine, and special 3-course dinner. T-bana T-Centralen. Map p 136.*

Rock & Performance Venues

★★ kids Cirkus DJURGÅRDEN
Built in 1892 for circus troupes, this round building seats 1,650 and puts on a wide variety of shows. *Djurgårdsslätten 43–45. Box office ☎ 660 10 20. www.cirkus.se. Tickets 205–895 SEK. Bus 47. Tram 7. Map p 136.*

★ kids Globen JOHANNESHOV
Stockholm's huge, globe-shaped indoor arena is visible from all over Stockholm. It's the venue for big rock concerts (REM, Coldplay, Bruce Springsteen), one-person shows (Leonard Cohen), and sports such as ice hockey. See p 47. *Globentorget 2. Box office ☎ 077 131 00 00. www.globenarenas.se. Tickets 195–1015 SEK. T-bana Globen. Map p 136.*

Theater

★★ China-Teatern NORRMALM
The China Theater was opened in 1928 with the silent film *Anna Karenina*, starring Greta Garbo (who else?) and John Gilbert, with a 17-man orchestra accompanying the film. Today this large venue puts on concerts (Dr John), has club nights, and also shows such as *The Producers* (many in Swedish). It belongs to Berns Hotel (p 143) which offer various attractive dinners and show packages. *Berzelli Park 9. ☎ 566 323 50. www.chinateatern.se.*

Tickets 250–625 SEK. T-bana Östermalmstorg. Map p 136.

★★ Kulturhuset KUNGSHOLMEN
This huge complex has a library, exhibitions, Internet café, and more. There are two stages, Kilen and Horsalen, and the Klara movie theater. The International Writers' Stage hosts international guests. *Sergels Torg. Box office ☎ 508 31 509. www.kulturhuset.stockholm.se. Tickets 40–220 SEK. T-bana T-Centralen. Map p 136.*

★★★ Kungliga Dramatiska Teatern ÖSTERMALM   The Royal Dramatic Theater is splendidly housed in a flamboyant building. It's the major theater in Stockholm, with the country's best actors performing Shakespeare and Strindberg and more unconventional theater in between. The second stage (Elverket, Linnégatan 69) shows modern performance art. *Nybroplan. Box Office ☎ 667 06 80. www.dramaten.se. Tickets 120–300 SEK. T-bana Östermalmstorg/Kungsträdgården. Map p 136.*

★★ kids Oscarsteatern NORRMALM   Large venue putting on musicals such as *My Fair Lady*. *Kungsgatan 63. Box office ☎ 20 50 00. www.oscarsteatern.se. Tickets 275–565 SEK. T-bana T-Centralen. Map p 136.*

★★ Stockholms Stadsteatern NORRMALM   This is one of Scandinavia's largest theater organizations with six stages and the outdoor Parkteatern program in different venues. Wide range from classics to avant-garde. *Sergels Torg. ☎ 50 62 02 00. Tickets 60–230 SEK. www.stadsteatern.stockholm.se. T-bana T-Centralen. Map p 136.* ●

Stockholm Lodging

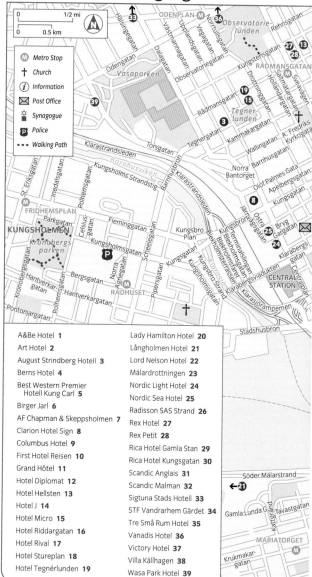

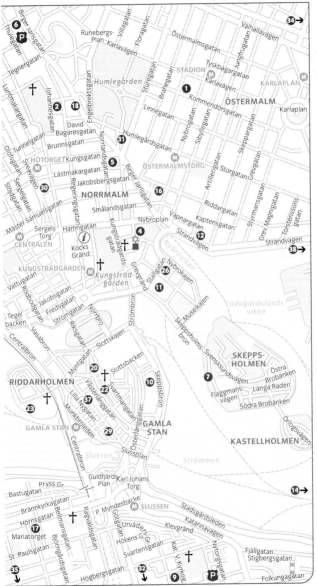

Lodging **Best Bets**

Best for **Star Quality**
★★★ Berns Hotel $$$$ *Näck-strömsgatan 8 (p 143)*

Best for **Winners & Would-Be Award Winners**
★★★ Grand Hôtel $$$$ *Södra Blasieholmshamnen 8 (p 146)*

Best **New Boutique Hotel**
★★★ Hotel Stureplan $$$ *Birger Jarlsgatan 24 (p 148)*

Best for **Cutting-Edge Design**
★★★ Clarion Hotel Sign $$$$ *Östra Järnvagsgatan 35 (p 146)*; and ★★★ Nordic Light $$$$ *Vasaplan 7 (p 149)*

Best **Medieval Location**
★★★ Victory Hotel $$$$ *Lilla Nygatan 5 (p 152)*

Best **Business Hotel**
★★ Best Western Premier Hotell Kung Carl $$$$ *Birger Jarlsgatan 21 (p 143)*

Best for **Antiques**
★★ Lady Hamilton $$$ *Storkyrko-brinken 5 (p 148)*

Best **Floating Option**
★★ AF Chapman & Skeppsholmen $$ *Flaggmansvägen 8 (p 146)*

Best **Ecclesiastical View**
★★★ Columbus Hotel $$$ *Tjärhovsgatan 11 (p 146)*

Best **Sea Views**
★★★ First Hotel Reisen $$$ *Skeppsbron 12 (p 146)*; and ★★★ Radisson SAS Strand $$$$ *Nybrokajen (p 150)*

The Entrance to Berns Hotel.

Best for **Nautical Types**
★★★ Hotel J $$$ *Ellensbiksvägen 1 (p 147)*; and ★★ Mälardrottningen $$$ *Vasaplan 7 (p 149)*

Best for **Families**
★★ Långholmen Hotel $$ *Lång-holmsmuren 20 (p 149)*

Best for **Lovers**
★★★ Hotel Hellsten $$$ *Lunt-makargatan 68 (p 147)*

Best for **Swedish Design**
★★ Birger Jarl $$$$ *Tulegatan 8 (p 143)*

Best **Budget Hotels**
★ A&Be Hotel $$ *Turegatan 50 (p 143)*; and ★ Rex Petit $$ *Lunt-makargatan 73 (p 150)*

Stockholm Lodging **A to Z**

★ **kids** **A&Be Hotel** ÖSTERMALM
Good location, good value, what more could you ask? Small, conventionally decorated rooms all have cable TV; there's useful access to a washing machine. Breakfast is an extra 50 SEK per person. *Grev Turegatan 50.* ☎ *660 21 00.* www.abehotel.com. *12 units. Doubles 740–990 SEK. MC, V. T-bana Stadion. Map p 144.*

★ **kids** **Art Hotel** NORRMALM
Right in the center, but in a quiet street just a stroll away from smart Stureplan, this friendly hotel has small but well-equipped bedrooms and a terrace outside the breakfast room. *Johannesgatan 12.* ☎ *402 37 60.* www.arthotel.se. *31 units. Doubles 1,200 SEK w/breakfast. AE, DC, MC, V. T-bana Hötorget. Map p 144.*

★★ **August Strindberg Hotell** NORRMALM   Just around the corner from August Strindberg's former home, the eponymous hotel has small rooms prettily decorated in pale pastels. The open fire is welcoming in the dining room in winter, and there's a garden for summer breakfasts. *Tegnérgatan 38.* ☎ *35 50 06.* www.hotellstrindberg.se. *27 units. Doubles 1,095–1,795 SEK w/breakfast. AE, MC, V. T-bana Rådmansgatan. Map p 144.*

★★★ **Berns Hotel** NORRMALM
This is where the stars stay and is as chic as you'd expect in a restrained elegant style. All rooms are very well appointed; rates follow room size and the more expensive ones have balconies. If you can, go for the Clock Suite that looks out over Berzelli Park. Entry to the health club of the sister Grand Hôtel (p 146) is included in the room rate of all Berns' rooms. *Nåckströmsgatan 8.* ☎ *56 63 22 00.* www.berns.se. *65*

units. Doubles 2,950–5,250 SEK w/breakfast. Clock Suite 10,500 SEK. AE, DC, MC, V. T-bana Kungsträdgården/Östermalmstorg. Map p 144.*

★★ **Best Western Premier Hotell Kung Carl** NORRMALM
This may be a conference hotel (although old tiled stoves and balconies in the conference rooms are a big hit), but it's just as good for holiday guests with individually decorated rooms in bold colors, a great location, and a warm welcome. *Birger Jarlsgatan 21.* ☎ *463 50 00.* www.kungcarl.se. *134 units. Doubles 1,550–3,130 SEK w/breakfast. AE, DC, MC, V. T-bana Hötorget/Östermalmstorg. Map p 144.*

★★ **Birger Jarl** VASASTADEN
The hotel looks conventional, but inside Swedish designers have produced individual and exciting

Don't sail away on AF Chapman.

rooms. They reflect the Nordic seasons so you can choose a room that echoes the warm lakes of the Swedish summer, or the white ice of winter. Each one is beautifully done, in an abundance of natural materials. There's also a gym and sauna. *Tulegatan 8.* ☎ *674 18 00. www. birgerjarl.se. 235 units. Doubles 2,350 SEK w/breakfast. AE, DC, MC, V. T-bana Rådmansgatan. Map p 144.*

★ **kids** **AF Chapman & Skeppsholmen** SKEPPSHOLMEN This hostel must have one of the best locations anywhere. It's on a fully rigged ship moored off Skeppsholmen, so you'll be rocked quietly to sleep—although there is a land hostel as well. The boat has a bar serving breakfast and drinks and snacks later on. *Flaggmansvägen 8.* ☎ *463 22 66. www.stfchapman.com. 70 units. Doubles land: 260 SEK, ship 310 SEK. AE, MC, V. T-bana Kungsträdgården. Map 144.*

★★★ **Clarion Hotel Sign** NORRMALM One of Stockholm's most recent (and largest) hotels (opened February 2008), the striking granite-and-glass structure looks over Norra Bantorget. Each floor celebrates a different iconic Scandinavian or Nordic designer so if you fancy a room furnished with Arne Jacobson's Egg, you can book it. Room sizes vary; bathrooms are good. The Aquavit Grill and Raw Bar adds a touch of Manhattan and the rooftop spa keeps you fit. *Östra Järnvägsgatan 35.* ☎ *676 98 00. www. clarionsign.com. 558 units. Doubles 2,650–6,950 SEK w/breakfast. AE, DC, MC, V. T-bana T-Centralen. Map p 144.*

★★ **kids** **Columbus Hotel** SÖDERMALM The entrance through a courtyard and small lobby doesn't prepare you for the delightful rooms, classically decorated, in this series of townhouses built in 1780. The lovely two-roomed Lorenz Sifvert Suite comes with its own lobby and looks directly at Katarina Kyrka (p 75, bullet ❸). In summer, you can take your breakfast out to the courtyard. *Tjärhovsgatan 11.* ☎ *50 31 12 00. www.columbus.se. 40 units. Doubles 1,595–2,295 SEK w/breakfast. AE, DC, MC, V. T-bana Medborgplatsen. Map p 144.*

★★ **First Hotel Reisen** GAMLA STAN Right on the water, there's been a hotel here since 1819. Rooms in this old building differ, with bare brick walls, interesting shapes, and great views (book one looking over the sea). Some also have private saunas, Jacuzzis, and balconies, although the hotel does have a spa with pool and sauna. *Skeppsbron 12* ☎ *22 32 60. www. firsthotels.com/reisen. 144 units. Doubles 1,590–2,850 SEK w/breakfast. AE, DC, MC, V. T-bana Gamla Stan. Map p 144.*

★★★ **Grand Hôtel** BLASIEHOLMEN The Grand is a hotel that deserves all the superlatives, with a superb location, gorgeous decorations, plus the Princess Lilian Suite, northern Europe's largest with its

Classic Style at the Columbus Hotel.

Plush room at the Hotel Hellsten.

own movie theater, gym, and sauna (70,000 SEK a night). Nobel Laureates are traditionally guests here after the main Awards ceremony. Chef Matthias Dahlgren produces first-class dining (p 117); service should satisfy the most demanding guest. Breakfast is 245 SEK per person. *Södra Blasieholmshamnen 8.* ☎ *679 35 00. www.grandhotel.se. 374 units. Doubles 2,200–6,900 SEK. AE, DC, MC, V. T-bana Kungsträdgården. Map p 144.*

★★ **Hotel Diplomat** ÖSTERMALM Still owned by the Malmström family, the 1914 Art Nouveau building is decorated in classic style and manages to be both comfortable and comforting. The outdoor terrace of T/Bar is a local meeting place and great for people watching in the summer. *Strandvägen 7C.* ☎ *459 68 00. www.diplomathotel.com. 130 units. Doubles 2,595–5,995 SEK. AE, DC, MC, V. T-bana Östermalmstorg. Map 144.*

★★★ **Hotel Hellsten** VASASTADEN   If you feel even a touch theatrical, this dramatic hotel in an 1898 building will appeal. The dark colored walls, velvet drapes, original tiled stove, and chandeliers in my large room resembled a stage set.

Black-and-white photographs on the walls are mostly taken by the owner, Per Hellsten. Bathrooms are superb with slate-lined walls and heated floors and the bar is full of colonial artifacts and candles. *Luntmakargatan 68.* ☎ *661 86 00. www. hellsten.se. 78 units. Doubles 1,090–2,390 SEK. AE, DC, MC, V. T-bana Rådmansgatan. Map p 144.*

★★★ **Hotel J** NACKA STRAND You could pitch up here in your boat, moor in the hotel's private harbor, and swap your bunk for a deliciously designed bedroom. You'll still feel nautical with the blue-and-white furnishings and scrubbed wooden floors. The J stands for the American's Cup J boats. The restaurant is on the pier. *Ellensbiksvägen 1.* ☎ *0800 37 46 83 57. www.hotelj. com. 45 units. Doubles 1,995–3,495 SEK w/breakfast. AE, DC, MC, V. Taxi. Map p 144.*

★ **Hotel Micro** VASASTADEN It's advertised as an alternative to a hostel with small cabins decorated in blues and reds, with bunk beds, male and female bathrooms, but no windows. You check in at the Hotel Tegnérlunden (p 148, it's in their basement) and the company also owns the upmarket Birger Jarl Hotel

Stunning new boutique Hotel Stureplan.

(p 143). No breakfast, no frills, just good value. *Tegnérlunden 8.* ☎ *54 54 55 69. www.hotelmicro.se. 23 units. Rooms 545 SEK weekends, 745 SEK weekdays. AE, DC, MC, V. T-bana Rådmansgatan. Map p 144.*

★★ **Hotel Riddargatan** ÖSTERMALM   Rooms are pleasantly decorated at this centrally located hotel, which prides itself on its warm welcome and service. Four suites offer a larger alternative. The breakfast room has an open fireplace for cold winter days. Good bar. *Riddargatan 14.* ☎ *55 57 30 00. www.profilhotels. se. 78 units. Doubles 1,225–2,625 SEK. AE, DC, MC, V. T-bana Östermalmstorg. Map p 144.*

★★★ **Hotel Stureplan** ÖSTERMALM   This new boutique hotel has spacious, high-ceilinged rooms, classically and elegantly decorated; smaller, pretty loft rooms have skylights. Bedrooms on the first floor open onto a shared library and drawing room—perfect for a large family or business stay. The Bollinger Champagne Bar is challenging the Stureplan bars in popularity and an excellent breakfast is served in the dining room, which opens onto a garden; service is charming. *Birger Jarlsgatan 24.* ☎ *440 66 00. www.hotelstureplan.se. 102 units. Doubles 1,350–4,850 SEK w/breakfast. AE, DC, MC, V. T-bana Östermalmstorg. Map p 144.*

★★ **Hotel Tegnérlunden** NORRMALM   This hotel looks out onto the green Tegnérlunden park and has comfortable rooms simply designed. The two suites on the 5th and 6th floors are spacious with wooden floors and bright furnishings and you're served breakfast in a rooftop dining room. Staff are particularly friendly and welcoming. *Tegnérlunden 8.* ☎ *54 54 55 50. www.hoteltegnerlunden.se. 102 units. Doubles 990–1,850 SEK w/breakfast. AE, DC, MC, V. T-bana Rådmansgatan. Map p 144.*

★★ **Lady Hamilton Hotel** GAMLA STAN   Owned by the Bengtsson family along with the Lord Nelson (p 149) and the Victory (p 152), the Lady Hamilton is stuffed full of antiques and has traditional paintings from the Dalarna region on the walls. The rooms are named after regional flowers; Bistro Emma is open all day. It's ideal for single women—who find special lady kits in their rooms—as well as families.

Storkyrkobrinken 5. ☎ *50 64 01 00.* *www.ladyhamiltonhotel.se.* 34 units. Doubles 2,050–3,250 SEK w/breakfast. AE, DC, MC, V. T-bana Gamla Stan. Map p 144.

★★ Långholmen Hotel LÅNG-HOLMEN Former prisons make good hotels, if you don't mind small rooms with windows high up in the walls; thick walls and doors keep the noise down. The cells here have been well renovated with bunk beds and good bathrooms. The restaurant serves ambitious food while there's a friendly bar and an outside terrace. *Långholmsmuren 20.* ☎ *720 85 00. www.langholmen.com.* 102 units. Doubles 1,370–1,740 SEK. AE, DC, MC, V. T-bana Hornstull. Map p 144.

★★ kids Lord Nelson Hotel GAMLA STAN Opened in 1974 and the first of the Bengtsson family's three hotels, this 17th-century building is long and narrow (6m wide). Like all the hotels in the group, you're greeted by assorted naval artifacts and here, a portrait of Nelson. Each floor is named after a deck and each room after a ship (a model of which adds to the room's décor). A small rooftop terrace gives

a bird's eye view of Gamla Stan. It tends to appeal to naval types. *Västerlånggatan 22.* ☎ *50 64 01 20. www.lordnelsonhotel.se.* 29 units. Doubles 1,750–2,380 SEK w/breakfast. AE, DC, MC, V. T-bana Gamla Stan. Map p 144.

★★ Mälardrottningen GAMLA STAN Landlubbers should steer clear of this hotel on a luxury motor yacht on Riddarholmen. The yacht was built for American socialite, Barbara Hutton's 18th birthday, so cabins are very well appointed, with en-suite bathrooms, and some have a lake view. *Riddarholmen.* ☎ *545 187 80. www.malardrottningen.se.* 60 units. Doubles 1,300–2,350 SEK w/breakfast. AE, MC, V. T-bana Gamla Stan/T Centralen. Map p 144.

★★★ Nordic Light VASASTADEN Light is this lifestyle hotel's striking feature, with a lobby that changes color according to the time of day and individual lighting systems in the 'Mood' bedrooms. You can call a light therapist and masseuse to your room to combat the winter darkness. With a chic bar and lounge, I recommend you dress appropriately; the staff look as if they've stepped out of a magazine, but

Langholmen Hotel was once a prison.

Breakfast at the Radisson SAS Strand.

are delightful with it. *Vasaplan 7.*
☎ *50 56 30 00.* www.nordiclight
hotel.se/en. *175 units. Doubles*
1,970–3,500 SEK w/breakfast.
AE, DC, MC, V. T-bana T-Centralen.
Map p 144.

★★ **Nordic Sea Hotel** NOR-
RMALM Less trendy than its smart
cousin, Nordic Light, it nonetheless
boasts the ultra-chic Absolut Icebar.
Bedrooms are blue and white; bathrooms are good sized and it's as
central as you can get, right next to
the Arlanda Express from the airport. *Vasaplan 4.* ☎ *50 56 30 00.*
ww.nordicseahotel.se/en. *367 units.*
Doubles 1,490–2,900 SEK w/break-
fast. AE, DC, MC, V. T-bana T Cen-
tralen. Map p 144.

★★★ **Radisson SAS Strand**
Hotel BLASIEHOLMEN This large
hotel has a wonderful position looking straight onto boats and the sea.
The open, airy lobby, comfortable
lounge, and boldly colored dining
room and bar that you see as you
walk in act as a welcoming meeting
place. Rooms are relatively small but
suites have good lounges. It's all
very well decorated and the staff
are delightfully friendly and professional. The outside terrace is great
for watching the world go by.
Nybrokajen 9. ☎ *50 66 40 00.*

www.strand.stockholm.radissonsas.
com. *152 units. Doubles 1,695–3,295*
SEK w/breakfast. AE, DC, MC, V. T-
bana Östermalmstorg. Map p 144.

★★ **kids** **Rex Hotel** VASASTADEN
The Rex is the sister to the Hotel
Hellsten (p 147) right opposite. It's
less flamboyant, but has lovely
rooms, all with old pine floors and
tastefully decorated in good colors,
around a splendid grand staircase.
The owner of the 1866 building
recently opened a budget hotel, Rex
Petit, in the basement. *Luntmakar-*
gatan 73. ☎ *16 00 40.* www.rex
hotel.se. *55 units. Doubles 990–*
2,290 SEK w/breakfast. AE, DC, MC, V.
T-bana Rådmansgatan. Map p 144.

★ **Rex Petit** VASASTADEN The
basement of the Rex Hotel was converted in 2008 into 20 cabin-style
rooms, making small and window-
less but attractive rooms at a very
attractive price. Breakfast is in the
Hotel Rex's dining room upstairs.
Luntmakargatan 73. ☎ *16 00 40.*
www.rexhotel.se. *20 units. Doubles*
590–1,190 SEK w/breakfast. AE, DC,
MC, V. T-bana Rådmansgatan.
Map p 144.

★★ **Rica Hotel Gamla Stan**
GAMLA STAN Located in the oldest part of the city, this 17th-century

building is decorated in classic style, with antiques in the bedrooms, which are small but cozy. *Lilla Nygatan 5.* ☎ *723 72 59. www.rica. se. 51 units. Doubles 1,245–2,575 SEK. AE, DC, MC, V. T-bana Gamla Stan. Map p 144.*

★★ Rica Hotel Kungsgatan

NORRMALM Located above the PUB department store, and looking onto the outdoor market in Hötorget square, the hotel has large, high-ceilinged rooms. A perfect location for those needing retail therapy. *Kungsgatan 47.* ☎ *723 72 20. www.rica.se. 271 units. Doubles 995–2,475 SEK. AE, DC, MC, V. T-bana Hötorget. Map p 144.*

★★ Hotel Rival SÖDERMALM

You can't get trendier than this boutique hotel, opened in 2003 by Benny Andersson of Abba fame. Good-sized rooms come in a variety of decors, from the distinctly jazzy colored to the svelte and sexy de luxe style. Some have balconies and all have access to a large film library (free). There's a striking foyer with bar and bistro, separate café, and bakery (p 20, bullet ❹). *Mariatorget 3.* ☎ *545 789 00. www.rival.se. 99 units. Doubles 1,490–3,190 SEK w/breakfast (weekends), no breakfast on weekdays. AE, DC, MC, V. T-bana Mariatorget. Map p 144.*

★★★ Scandic Anglais NOR-

RMALM The Anglais is cool and chic and you get totally swept up by it as you step into the white lobby with its red wire mousse sculpture. Rooms are equally contemporary, some with good views. The bar is the place to see and be seen. The Anglais is particularly environmentally friendly and, as with all Scandic hotels, kids go free. *Humlegårdsgatan 23.* ☎ *51 73 40 00. www. scandichotels.com. 233 units. Doubles 1,500–2,250 w/breakfast. AE, DC, MC, V. T-bana Östermalmstorg. Map p 144.*

★★ Scandic Malman SÖDER-

MALM All Scandic hotels are good value, and this one is no exception. It has well-decorated, light and airy rooms, and a recently refurbished restaurant. Breakfast sets you up for the day and kids go free in the rooms. *Götgatan 49–51.* ☎ *51 73 47 00. www.scandichotels.com. 332 units. Doubles 941–2,690 SEK w/breakfast. AE, DC, MC, V. T-bana Medborgplatsen. Map p 144.*

★★★ 🅺🅸🅳🆂 Sigtuna Stads Hotell

SIGTUNA This is where Stockholmers come to escape the city. This hotel is a large white building, with different sized bedrooms, decorated in pretty pale shades and natural

The Victory Hotel in Gamla Stan.

materials. The dining room is large and gracious and looks out over the sea. The restaurant is well known for top dining, and breakfast was one of the best I've ever had. A sauna keeps you warm on chilly days. Various weekend packages will tempt. *Stora Nygatan 3, Sigtuna.* ☎ *592 501 00. www.sigtunastadshotell.se. 26 units. Doubles 2,190–2,590 SEK w/breakfast. AE, DC, MC, V. Directions see p 144.*

★ **STF Vandrarhem Gärdet**
GÄRDET   The hostel opened in July 2008 and is part of the centrally run hostel association. Rooms are brightly decorated, have showers and TVs, and it's only a short hop into central Stockholm. *Sandhamns-gatan 65.* ☎ *463 22 99. www.stf turist.se/gardet. 120 units. Doubles from 340 SEL per person. AE, MC, V. T-bana Gärdet. Map p 144.*

★ **Tre Små Rum Hotel** SÖDER-MALM   The three rooms have been increased to seven, sharing shower rooms. Rooms are small, but it's friendly and welcoming and the owner Jakob von Arndt is never far away. *Högbergsgatan 81.* ☎ *641 23 71. www.tresmarum.se. 7 units. Doubles 795 SEK w/breakfast. MC, V. T-bana Mariatorget. Map p 144.*

★ **Vanadis Hotel** VASASTADEN
The hotel was originally converted from the changing rooms of the open-air pool in leafy Vanadis park. Small rooms vary between those with or without showers, windows, etc. so check when you book. The pool is currently being converted into a leisure complex. Takeaway breakfast. *Sveavägen 142.* ☎ *30 12 11. www.vanadishotel.com. 67 units.*

Doubles 499–1,099 SEK w/breakfast. AE, DC, MC, V. T-bana Rådmans-gatan. Map p 144.

★★★ **Victory Hotel** GAMLA STAN
This is the top hotel in the small family-owned group that also owns the Lord Nelson (p 149) and Lady Hamilton (p 148). Like the others, nautical decoration is the main point here, so seafaring Brits will feel at home. A superb restaurant, Leijontornet (p 117), gay-friendly bar and summer terrace keep guests returning. *Lilla Nygatan 5.* ☎ *50 64 00 00. www.victoryhotel.se. 45 units. Doubles 2,450–7,550 SEK w/breakfast. AE, DC, MC, V. T-bana Gamla Stan. Map p 144.*

★★★ **Villa Källhagen** DJURGÅR-DEN   Perfectly positioned beside the Djurgården canal, rooms have views over the water or onto green spaces. The freshly decorated rooms come in different color schemes, echoing the seasons. There's a good restaurant and you can take your breakfast on the terrace. *Djurgårdsbrunnsvägen 10.* ☎ *665 03 00. www.kallhagen.se. 36 units. Doubles 1,200–4,000 SEK. AE, DC, MC, V. Bus 69. Map p 144.*

★★ **Wasa Park Hotel** VASASTAN
This old-fashioned, charmingly decorated hotel in an early 19th-century house keeps prices down by locating bathrooms just outside the rooms, which are decorated in blue and white. A simple continental breakfast is included. *St Eriksplan 1.* ☎ *545 453 00. www.wasapark hotel.se. 15 units. Doubles 750–950 SEK. MC, V. T-bana St Eriksplan. Map p 144.* ●

Sigtuna

❶ The main street
❷ Radhus
❸ Tant Bruns Kaffestuga
❹ Tant Grån
❺ Lundströmska Gården
❻ Sigtuna Museum
❼ RC Chocolat
❽ St Maria
❾ Runic stones
❿ Sigtunaskolan Humanistiska Laroverk
⓫ Dinner

Few visitors make it to Sigtuna, which is a great shame because this former Viking settlement is Sweden's oldest existing town. It's only an hour from Stockholm and just half an hour from the airport so I recommend you do as I did and plan a visit either at the beginning or end of your holiday. I went to Sigtuna on a Saturday evening, spent the night there, and flew back home on Sunday.

❶ ★★★ 🄺🄸🄳🅂 **The main street.** It all began when Eric the Victorious settled here in 980AD to fulfill his ambition of building a Christian center in what was a Viking-led country. Pick up information at the well-stocked tourist office housed in the 18th-century house known as the Dragon. Then start along the main street that follows Eric's original city plan of 8-square-meter plots for each of Eric's followers—and a much larger one for Eric himself at the end of the street. *Tourist Office,*

Stora Gatan 33. 📞 *59 48 06 52.* *www.sigtuna.se/turism. Jun–Aug Mon–Sat 10am–6pm, Sun 11am–5pm, Sept–May Mon–Fri 10am–5pm, Sat, Sun noon–4pm.*

❷ ★ **Radhus.** Is Sigtuna's Town Hall the smallest in Europe? It's a compact, wooden building in a spacious square, and was built in 1744. Inside, the main Council Chamber is a gem with portraits of kings, old chairs, and a gleaming crystal chandelier. Outside, open shutters conceal a hook for a key, left there over

Practical Matters—Sigtuna

Take the Pendeltäg train (www.sl.se) or the Uppsala train (www.tim-trafik.se) from T-Centralen to Märsta (about 30 mins). From Märsta, take bus no. 570 to Hällsboskolan to Sigtuna bus station (about 30 mins), and then it's a 3-minute walk to the main street. From/to Arlanda, book a taxi or get the no. 803 bus that leaves hourly and takes about 30 minutes to the airport.

the centuries for any drunken citizen who was fearful of the wrath of his family. He could take the key, open a cell, lock himself in, and sleep it off to return home sober in the morning. It's a delightful story, though it's hard to imagine how that fooled anyone. ⏱ *20 mins. Jun–Aug noon–4pm.*

3 ★★ **kids Tant Bruns Kaffestuga.** 16th-century Aunt Brown's Café is in the oldest wooden house in town. Inside it's cozy, and the open fire in winter makes it the place for a cup of hot chocolate when the streets outside are covered in snow. In summer, grab a bench in the small garden and sit back under the old trees. They serve coffee, snacks, and not-to-be-missed homemade pies; I recommend the blueberry version. *Laurentii Gränd 3.* ☎ *592 509 34. $.*

4 ★★ **Tant Grän.** Storagatan is lined with shops selling books, crafts, gifts, and design items, but you can't miss Aunt Green. Her cat sits in the window surrounded by covetable antiques and some good contemporary design pieces. The gallery is particularly strong on modern glass and forged ironwork items such as candlesticks. ⏱ *45 mins. Storagatan 35.* ☎ *592 519 77. MC, V.*

5 ★★ **kids Lundströmska Gården.** In 1873 C A Lundström bought this house, enlarged it, and added a store at the front. Opened as a museum in 1958, it shows the life of a middle-class family—and life was clearly good to the Lundströms. Past the shop, full of tempting items that are sadly not on sale, you step straight into the heart of the house, the kitchen with its large fireplace and oven. The family was wealthy

Sigtuna's main street.

The Lundstrom's drawing room.

enough to have a separate drawing and living room and an upper floor, reached by a narrow staircase, of small bedrooms. The house is full of period furniture, but where's the bathroom? ⏱ *30 mins. Stora Gatan 39. Admission 10 SEK. Jun–Aug noon–4pm.*

6 ★ **Sigtuna Museum.** The king had his plot at the end of the main street where you now find the museum. Sigtuna might have been small but it was important as revealed by the gold rings, coins (Sigtuna was the first place to mint coins, produced by English workers brought over by King Ulaf in 995), runic inscriptions, and a superb, tiny Viking head. ⏱ *30 mins. Stora Gatan 55. ☎ 59 78 38 70. www.sigtunamuseum.se. Admission 20 SEK adults, under-19s free. Jun–Aug noon–4pm; Sep–May Tue–Sun noon–4pm.*

7 ★★ **RC Chocolat.** Customers flock here for its sandwiches, which you can eat in or take away for a picnic; but its real purpose is as an excellent chocolate shop, so stock up on gifts to take home. *Stora Gatan 49. ☎ 594 803 85. $.*

8 ★ **St Maria.** The 13th-century church of St Maria was built by the Dominicans who brought the art of brick-making here and made this Sweden's first brick building. It was a large abbey with separate buildings for the monks but, in 1540, the country's conversion to Lutheranism brought destruction to the abbey

Sigtuna's Annual Events

The annual **Viking Fair** (end June–end July) takes place in the town's very own Viking camp. Jewelers, bakers, fighters, and weavers live and work here for a month, just as their ancestors did. At the annual **Market Fair**, held over the last weekend in August, you meet Sigtuna's three best-known residents: Aunt Green, Aunt Brown, and Aunt Lavender. They first appeared in a children's book in 1918, written by Elsa Maartman Beskow (1874–1953), one of the founders of children's literature in Sweden. Buy the English version here if you have children; it'll keep them occupied all day. Sigtuna's **Christmas Market** takes place on the four Sundays before Christmas Eve filling the streets with stalls selling traditional handicrafts. Copious glasses of grogg help the dancing, singing, and general merriment.

and the church is all that is left. Nearby the atmospheric ruins of the churches of St Lars, St Per, and St Olof are reminders of the time when Sigtuna produced most of Sweden's bishops and archbishops. ⏱ *30 mins.*

9 ★★ **Runic stones.** Sigtuna may be small but it has more runic stones than anywhere else in the world: more than 150 have been found. Carved with crosses and fantastic beasts, these huge stones are memorials to worthy dead men (although some were put up by the living) as a sure ticket into the next world. ⏱ *30 mins.*

10 ★ **Sigtunaskolan Humanistiska Laroverk.** Sweden's top private school stands on the hills above Sigtuna. The present King was educated at this boarding school, the largest in Sweden, where the teaching is based on humanist principles. Beside it, the Sigtunastiftelsen is a private cultural institution with its origins in Christian Humanist ethics, founded in 1917 when education and temperance were strong principles in Sweden. It's a peaceful place to walk around, offering a real retreat from life. ⏱ *30 mins.*

Runic stone, Sigtuna.

11 ★★★ **Dinner.** Sigtuna is home to two restaurants that attract diners from all over Sweden. You can eat excellent seafood in the small boathouse, **Båthuset Krog & Bar** (☎ 592 567 80, www.bathuset. com, $$$), or push another boat out at the critically acclaimed **1909 Sigtuna Stads Hotell** (p 151) where superbly cooked food is served in very pleasant surroundings (Stora Nygatan 3, ☎ 592 501 00, www. sigtunastadshotell.se, $$$).

Vikings limbering up for a fight in the town square.

Fjäderholmarna

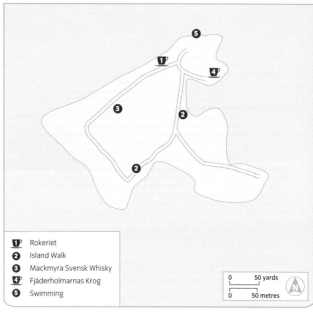

1 Rokeriet
2 Island Walk
3 Mackmyra Svensk Whisky
4 Fjäderholmarnas Krog
5 Swimming

0	50 yards
0	50 metres

Four islands make up Fjäderholmarna, although Stora Fjäderholmen is the one visitors go to. It's a pretty island, with enough to keep you there for a half or whole day. In 1995, it became part of the National City Park, taking the city's green lung out into the waters of the archipelago. As it's a mere 25 minutes by boat from Stockholm, it can be busy on summer weekends. Half the fun is of course taking the boat out there. START: **Nybroplan for the boat to the island.**

---

1 ★ kids **Rokeriet.** With fish dishes from its own smokery (mussels, gravadlax, and of course herrings) and a perfect position out on the waterside, this restaurant is a natural stop during the summer (open end of April to September). But it's also a great place for a coffee before taking the less than arduous circular island stroll.
☎ *716 50 88. www.rokeriet.nu. $$.*

2 ★★ kids **Island Walk.** A path takes you right around the island but it's worth taking the path to the west and south to avoid the crowds. The stroll goes past Workshop Row and Handicrafts Terrace, where wood-turners and ceramicists work and sell their goods. Attractions are few and so you may find yourself taking an inordinate amount of interest in the charming small Allmogebåtar (**Boat Museum**

Practical Matters—Fjäderholmarna

From Nybroplan, **Strömma Kanalbolaget** ferries run end Apr–mid-May, mid-Aug–end Sep hourly 10am–8pm, 9.30pm, 10.30pm, 11.30pm. Mid-May–mid-Aug every half hour 10am–8.30pm, 9.30pm, 10.30pm, 11.30pm. One way 70 SEK; return 95 SEK. Free with Stockholm Card. Tickets from the booth or online. www.strommakanalbolaget.se. **Fjäderholmslinjen** (www.fjaderholmslinjen.se) runs daily May–Sep from Slussen 10am–11pm, leaving from Slussen: return fare is 95 SEK. Return times for both are a half hour later than outward journey. Information on the island: www.fjaderholmarna.se.

☎ 070 477 98 51)—a couple of boathouses where they restore historic sailing boats. ⏱ *45 mins.*

❸ ★★ Mackmyra Svensk Whisky. No, this is not a mistake; since 2001 this distillery has been producing Swedish whisky with Swedish ingredients and stored in

Catch the steam ferry boat to Fjäderholmarna.

Swedish oak barrels. The main distillery is in Gastrikland but you can see the museum and warehouse with the old equipment and barrels and taste and buy it here—and believe me Swedish whisky makes a great talking point. It's also very good. ⏱ *1 hr guided tour and warehouse; 2 hrs tasting.* ☎ *06 25 80. www.mackmyra.se. Museum free; guided tour museum and warehouse 125 SEK; tasting 400 SEK.*

❹ ★★ Fjäderholmarnas Krog. As you will see, a lot of eating and drinking is done on the island and many people come from Stockholm just for a meal at this lovely waterside location. Go for the Baltic herring, or halibut with horseradish, and if you can, get a seat on the seaside terrace. *Stora Fjäderholmen.* ☎ *718 33 55. www.fjaderholmarnaskrog.se. $$$.*

❺ ★★ Swimming. Take your swimming gear and spend a sunny afternoon diving off the rocks into the clear waters of the Baltic. It's sheer bliss—and surprisingly not too cold.

The Best Day Trips & Excursions

Vaxholm

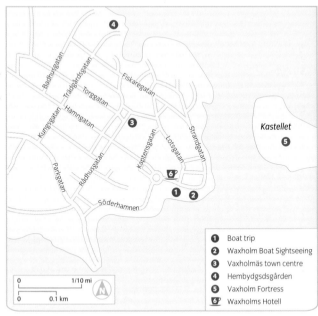

Kastellet

❶	Boat trip
❷	Waxholm Boat Sightseeing
❸	Vaxholmäs town centre
❹	Hembydgsdsgården
❺	Vaxholm Fortress
❻	Waxholms Hotell

0   1/10 mi

0   0.1 km

This small island, known as the Gateway to the Archipelago, is a popular half- or full-day trip. Vaxholm is 17km northeast of Stockholm by road. But it's more fun to arrive in traditional style—by boat. It can be very busy in summer, so avoid the weekends if you can. If you want to stay, book ahead and take waterproofs with you because it can rain heavily. START: **Strömkajen or Strandvägen for the boat trip.**

❶ ★★ kids **Boat trip.** The best way to get to Vaxholm is by a short 1-hour boat journey. The trip takes you past the southern end of Djurgården, and then past Fjäderholmana (see p 158) and on to this island, which is the capital of the archipelago. For information, see box p 161. ⏲ *1 hr.*

❷ ★ **Waxholm Boat Sightseeing.** A 50-minute tour around Vaxholm on a small sightseeing boat gives you the sea view of the island

and its castle. ⏲ *50 mins. Waxholm Sightseeing.* ☎ *0708 747 585. www.waxholmsightseeing.se. Tickets 100 SEK. Tours run end Jun–mid-Aug 9.10am–17.40pm, mid–end Aug Sat, Sun.*

❸ ★ **Vaxholmäs town center.** The island has been inhabited since the 16th century when King Gustav Vasa, victorious against Denmark in the 1540s, founded a defensive city here. The fortress, built between 1548 and the 1560s, needed a

Practical Matters—Vaxholm

Waxholmsbolaget runs boats from Strömkajen (☎ 679 58 30, www.waxholmsbolaget.se), and operates throughout the archipelago, offering special island-hopping fares valid for several days. **Strömma Kanalbolaget** leaves from Strandvägen (☎ 58 71 40 00, www.strommakanalbolaget.com), operating the steamship S/S Stockholm, built in 1931. Fast ferries from **Cindarellabåtarna** (☎ 58 71 40 00, www.cinderellabatarna.com) run between the islands. Prices are around 90 SEK single to 200 SEK return depending on the company. Or take the T-bana to Tekniska Högskolan, and then bus no. 670 to Vaxholm (about 1 hr). The **Tourist Office** is in the old Radhuset (Town Hall) (☎ 541 314 80, www.vaxholm.se). There are B&Bs on the island (book via the tourist office) and one hotel, Waxholms Hotell, Hamngatan 2 (☎ 54 13 01 50. www.waxholmshotell.se).

civilian population to serve as watchmen. Gustav Vasa had to coerce the poor and beggars here and then offered farmers free fishing rights, tax-free status, and land. Today's crowds come more voluntarily to this little town, where galleries and shops sell souvenirs and nautical what-nots. Vaxholm's Kyrka, designed in the 1760s by C F Adelcrantz, has models of boats to placate God and the sea. The church holds summer concerts. *30 mins.*

④ ★★ **Hembygdsgården.** The Homestead Museum, only open on summer weekends, is tiny and easy to miss because it's part of the café/restaurant at Norrhamnen. Go inside for a very real idea of the simple life of 100 years ago. *15 mins. Tradgårdsgatan 19.* ☎ *541 319 80.*

⑤ ★★ **kids** **Vaxholm Fortress.** In the early days the strategically built fortress provided an effective defense against the Poles in 1598, the Danes in 1612, and the Russians in 1719, all

A local shop sells nautical themed goods.

Herrings & History

Vaxholm was known for Baltic herrings, which its workforce caught in their spare time when not building Gustav Vasa's castle in the 16th century. On the first Saturday in August, locals row old boats carrying 1kg (½ pound) of herrings all around Vaxholm, commemorating the days when the first fisherman landed his catch and sold all his herrings. There's little left today of the herring tradition except for the Baltic herring sandwiches sold in boxes on Thursdays to Sundays at Trädsgården. Take them away for a picnic on a headland looking out to sea.

trying to reach the rich city of Stockholm. After Sweden lost Finland to the Russians in 1809, the country was dragged into the Napoleonic wars and conflict with England. Once again, Vaxholm Fortress became important, and was rebuilt between 1833 and 1863. But during those 30 years, defenses changed and, when a Swedish naval ship fired three cannonballs directly at the citadel as a test, all of them embarrassingly went straight through the walls. Luckily the fortress was not needed after that. The Museum shows how fighting has changed from the 16th century to today. It can be a bit spooky, with models suddenly moving as you approach, but children love it. Today you reach the island citadel by a ferry

that goes every 15 minutes, but if the ferry is on a leisurely timetable, the café provides refreshment. *1 hr.* ☎ *541 718 90. www.vaxholms fastning.se. Admission 50 SEK adults, under-19s free. Free with Stockholm Card. Jun noon–4pm, Jul, Aug 11am–5pm, Sep first two weekends 11am–5pm.*

⑥ **Waxholms Hotell.** Built in 1901, this vaguely Art Nouveau hotel was designed in 1899 by Erik Lallerstedt, a well-known Swedish architect (1864–1955). It's the best place on the island to eat, specializing in freshly caught fish. The Baltic herring buffet is pure indulgence (see box above). *$$.* ●

Inside the fortress.

The
Savvy Traveler

Before You Go

Government Tourist Offices
In the US: Visit Sweden (not open to the public), PO Box 4649, Grand Central Station, New York, NY 10163-4649 (☎ 212/885 9700).
In the UK: Sweden House, 5 Upper Montagu St, London W1H 2AG (☎ 020-7870 5600).

The Best Times to Go
May to **September** is the most popular time to visit Stockholm because the weather is glorious. The city gets very crowded with tourists in late June to August, while the Stockholmers themselves generally leave town for their summer cottages. Most of the theaters and concert halls shut in July and August and some restaurants also close. However, many other attractions, particularly those with outdoor features, only open fully during this time and operate restricted opening times during the rest of the year. Due to the country's high latitude, it stays light long into the summer nights, with the skies only getting dusky from around midnight to 3am in June. At Midsummer, hotels are often full in Stockholm, so book in advance. The low season is from **November to March**. During the coldest times in winter, the sea can freeze over. Conversely, cultural life is very lively at this time. **December** is a magical month in Stockholm, with Christmas markets, beautifully decorated shop windows, clear light, and the whiteness of snow and ice providing a wonderful reflective quality.

Festivals & Special Events
SPRING. One of the high points of the artistic calendar is the **Stockholm Art Fair**, the leading Nordic/Scandinavian art event at the Royal Academy of Arts (www.market-art.se) in February/March. It's followed by the all-important **Stockholm Spring Exhibition,** when Liljevalchs Konsthall (p 35) on Djurgården showcases new artists.

On April 30, the bonfires on **Walpurgis** night traditionally gave the Swedes protection from wicked witches. Today it's seen as a celebration of winter giving way to spring. Two places where you can ensure you're also under the spell are on Evert Taubes Terras on Riddarholmen (p 61) or Skansen where the sky is lit up with bonfires (p 46).

Första Maj (May Day) is a day for the workers to protest, as it is throughout the world. Trotting is a huge sport in Sweden, so everyone turns out for **Elitloppet**, the major European Elite Race at Solvalla, Sweden's biggest harness race track, northwest of Stockholm (☎ 635 90 00, www.solvalla.se). At the end of the month, the largest women-only bicycle race (**Tjejtrampet**) takes place when the 48km course sees thousands of women cyclists pedaling away from Gärdet (www.tjejtrampet.com).

SUMMER. The **Parkteatern** (Park Theater) is a wide-ranging free festival in outdoor venues from workshops on folk dancing to serious plays. Daily at parks throughout the city June to August (☎ 506 20 284, www.stadsteatern.stockholm.se). One of the top European Baroque, Renaissance, and **Early Music Festival** in the first week in June is held in the old buildings of Gamla Stan, such as the German Church and the Royal Armory. Wonderful surroundings to hear a European assortment of medieval lutes, madrigals, and Baroque ensembles (Tyska Brinken 13, Gamla Stan ☎ 070 460 03 90, www.semf.se).

Skärgårdsbatens Dag (Archipelago Boat Day) sees classic steamboats assembling at Strömkajen for a trip to Vaxholm. Here they're greeted with bands and a market before returning (☎ 662 89 02).

Sweden's **National Day** on June 6 celebrates the election of Gustav Vasa as King of Sweden in 1523. Since 1916, the Royal Family, dressed in traditional blue and yellow costumes, has gathered at Skansen to present flags to various organizations. The other great public summer celebration is **Midsommarafton** (Midsummer Eve) on the Friday closest to Midsummer Day, June 24.

The **Stockholm Jazz Festival** in July is one of Europe's biggest. It takes place on Skeppsholmen with some jam sessions at other venues (☎ 505 331 70, tickets: www.stockholmjazz.com).

Stockholm is a particularly gay-friendly city, and so its **Pride** celebration is the biggest in Scandinavia. For one week in July/August, parades, parties, entertainment, exhibitions, films, and more take place in Tantolunden Park on Södermalm and around the city (www.stockholmpride.org).

In a country further south, the idea of the **Midnattsloppet** (Midnight Race) would be impossible, but in mid-August in the land of the midnight sun this huge event sees 16,000 people run 10km around Södermalm. The many spectators turn it into an all-night party (☎ 649 71 71, www.midnattsloppet.com). In the last week in August, the Swedes celebrate the **Crayfish Season** in restaurants, which serve overflowing plates of crayfish and aquavit.

FALL. **Lidingöloppet** is the world's largest cross-country race with categories for amateurs and professionals. It's held on the last weekend in September around Lidingö (☎ 765 26 15, www.lidingoloppet.se). Tennis fans congregate at Norra Djurgården in October for the **Stockholm Open Tennis** tournament (☎ 450 26 25, www.stockholmopen.se).

In mid-November the 10-day **Stockholm Film Festival** shows experimental films and ones by young filmmakers (☎ 677 50 00, www.filmfestivalen.se).

WINTER. The end of November/beginning of December sees the enormously popular **Stockholm International Horse Show** at Globen (☎ 077 131 00 00, www.stockholmhorseshow.com).

The **Christmas Markets** run from early to end December. Skansen is particularly popular (see p 46); also Gamla Stan and Sigtuna (p 47).

On **Nobeldagen** (Nobel Day, Dec 10), the year's Nobel Prize laureates attend a ceremony in their honor at Konserthuset followed by a banquet at Stadshuset (p 8), along with the Royal Family and extremely distinguished guests. (Nobel Foundation ☎ 663 09 20, www.nobel.se). Mid-December is relieved by **Luciadagen** (Lucia Day), one of Sweden's best-known festivals. The 'Queen of Light' and her attendants process through the streets before going to Skansen for fireworks.

Christmas is celebrated on Christmas Eve. It's a private, family time with a huge smörgåsbord followed by present giving from someone dressed up as Santa Claus. Many restaurants offer Christmas smörgåsbord during the month. The official holiday lasts December 24–26.

Nyarsafton (New Year's Eve) is a public occasion when, since 1895, crowds have gathered at Skansen. Throughout the city, the streets are full; the restaurants are booked and the clubs keep going till dawn.

In January, skate off any festive excess in the annual 77km **Viking Run** from Uppsala via Sigtuna to Stockholm. But it depends on the weather and the ice (2008 was cancelled). The route and date are decided only about two weeks before the event. Check it out on ☎ 556 312 45, www.vikingarannet.com.

The Weather

Stockholm has real seasons and all have their attractions, although with its proximity to the sea, the city is not as cold as you might expect. May to September is when Stockholm really comes alive with summer events and outdoor living encouraged by the long daylight hours. Around Midsummer it hardly gets dark at all. At this time Stockholm empties because its inhabitants go on holiday. Winter lasts from November to March with very short days and temperatures that can vary from just above freezing to well below zero. Snow is not predictable but when it does snow there is a glorious lightness to the city. Days are often crisp and sunny and the city takes on a fairytale quality. Rainfall also varies with the heaviest falls in the summer.

Useful Websites

- **www.stockholmtown.com**: The official visitor's guide to Stockholm with comprehensive information on events, hotels, restaurants, shops, attractions, and more. Also offers a useful online hotel booking service.

- **www.sweden.se**: Sweden's official website administered by different organizations, including the Swedish Institute, trade organizations, and Visit Sweden, with information, blogs, and news.

- **www.stockholm.se**: the City of Stockholm's official website with news, services, and history.

- **www.sl.se**: The official site for Stockholm's transport system.

- **www.cityguide.se**: Commercial site with all attractions and hotel booking service.

- **www.swedenbooking.com**: Website to book trains throughout Scandinavia.

- **www.nobelprize.org**: Official site of the Nobel Prizes, with full information.

- **www.scandinaiandesign.com**: Nordic products and designers, information on museums, events, etc.

Cellphones

World phones—or GSM (Global System for Mobiles)—work in Sweden (and most of the world). If your cellphone is on a GSM system, and you have a world-capable multiband phone, you can make and receive calls from Sweden. Call your wireless operator and ask for 'international roaming' to be activated.

TEMPERATURE AND RAINFALL IN STOCKHOLM

	JAN	FEB	MAR	APR	MAY	JUNE
Daily Temp. (°C)	−1	−2	2	7	12	16
Daily Temp. (°F)	30	30	45	45	64	61
Rainfall (Inches)	1.5	1.06	1.02	1.18	1.18	1.7

	JULY	AUG	SEPT	OCT	NOV	DEC
Daily Temp. (°C)	19	18	14	8	3	0
Daily Temp. (°F)	66	64	57	46	37	32
Rainfall (Inches)	2.8	2.6	2.6	1.9	2.08	1.18

For calls within the Stockholm area, dial the area code 08 before the local number.

Car Rentals

Driving in Stockholm isn't necessary because the public transport system is good and taxis, if expensive, are plentiful. Hiring a car is relatively expensive; all the major chains have desks at Stockholm Arland airport and offices in the city. It is advisable to book your car before you leave home. **Auto Europe** (☎ 0800-89 9893/00-800-223-5555-5, www. autoeurope.com), **Avis** (☎ 797 99 70, www.avis.com), **Budget** www. budget.com), **Europcar** (☎ 555 984 00, www.europcar.com) **Hertz** (☎ 797 99 00, www.hertz.com), A big reasonable Swedish company is **Mabi Hyrbilar** (☎ 591 144 99, www.mabirent.se). **Statoil** hires cars from large petrol stations (☎ 020 25 25 25, www.statoil.se/biluthyrn). You have to return to the same hire point.

Getting **There**

By Plane

The major airport is **Arlanda** Airport (information ☎ 797 60 00, flight information ☎ 797 61 00, www. arlanda.se) about 40km from the city center. As Sweden is the center of the Baltic region, the airport is an important transit destination, well served from all over the world with direct daily flights to and from most major European and American cities.

The major airline flying into Sweden is **SAS** (Scandinavian Airlines System) which offers the most routes and competitive prices. In USA ☎ 1-800-221 2350; dialing from abroad to the USA ☎ +1 201 896 3600. In the UK ☎ 0871 521 2772; dialing from abroad to the UK ☎ +44 208 990 7159. Or: www.fly sas.com.

From the airport the quickest way into the center is by the **Arlanda Express** Train (☎ 588 890 00, www. arlandaexpress.com). Trains run regularly (4–6 times an hour at peak times) leaving Arlanda from 5am to 1.05am, taking 20 minutes to Central Station. Single fare weekends 240 SEK adults (up to four children aged 0-17 years old free with fare-paying passenger). Unaccompanied 8-25 years old 110 SEK.

Return is 420 SEK (adult). Same conditions for children apply. Buy tickets from the Information Center, the ticket machine, or on-board (50 SEK extra).

Flygbussarna airport buses (☎ 600 10 00, www.flygbussarna.se) leave every 15 minutes from bus stop 11 at Arlanda and from Cityterminalen from 4am–10pm daily. The journey takes 50–55 minutes; single fare is 110 SEK for adults, up to four children aged 0-16 years old free with fare-paying passenger, 199 SEK return. Saturday two adults traveling together 149 SEK (single). Buy your ticket from the Tourist Center or online.

Taxis operate from Arlanda; the fixed fare is 450 SEK, marked on the side, but check first as some companies operate their own rates. The best company is Flygtaxi (☎ 020 97 97 97, www.flygtaxi.se).

Bromma Airport (☎ 797 68 00, www.lfv.se) is 8km west of the city center and used by **Malmö Aviation** from London via Malmö and some other airlines.

Get into the city center on **Flygbussarna** airport buses. From Bromma Mon–Fri 7.30am–10.10pm, Sat 10.15am–4.10pm, Sun 11.30–

7.45pm. The journey takes about 20 mins to Cityterminalen; single fare is 79 SEK, return is 150 SEK, up to two children aged 0–16 years travel free with fare paying adult.

By Car

From Denmark you can use the stunning Öresund toll bridge between Copenhagen and Malmo. The bridge connects with the **E4**, the 550km motorway to Stockholm. There are car ferries from Denmark (Frederikshavn) and Germany (Kiel) to Gothenburg connecting with the **E3** to Stockholm (450 km).

By Ferry

You can get to Stockholm easily by ferry from Helsinki (Finland) on **Silja Line** (☎ 330 59 90, www.tallinksilja. se) and **Viking Line** (☎ 452 40 00, www.vikingline.se).

Silja Line ferries dock at Värtahamnen, northeast of the city center. Take a taxi or the Silja Line bus connection to Cityterminalen; or it's a 5 minute walk to T-bana Gärdet.

Viking Line docks at the Viking terminal on Södermalm. Take a taxi from here, or it's a 10 minute walk to Slussen. Viking Line buses run from Slussen to Cityterminalen.

Tallink from Tallinn (Estonia) (☎ 440 59 90, www.tallinksilja.se) operates from the Frihamnen terminal, northeast of the city center near the Silja Line Terminal. Taxis and its own bus service operate between the terminal and Cityterminalen.

By Train

National (**SJ**, ☎ 07 71 75 75 75, www.sj.se) and international trains arrive at **Central Station,** Vasagatan, Norrmalm. Book tickets ☎ 498 20 33 80) or online at www.swedenbooking.com.

Getting **Around**

By Tunnelbana (T-bana Subway)

The **T-bana** (run by Statens Lokaltrafik (SL), ☎ 600 10 00, www. sl.se) is the easiest, cheapest, and best way around the city. Three metro lines are marked by color, red, green, and blue on maps and station signs. All run through T-Centralen. Buying a single ticket doesn't make sense (they cost 20–60 SEK. Instead buy a multi-ticket (16 trips 180 SEK) or a travel card. 24 hours: 100 SEK, 3 days 200 SEK, 7 days 260 SEK, 30 days 690 SEK. The **Stockholm Card** includes unlimited travel on public transport as well as other advantages (p 11).

By Bus

Running from 5am to midnight, buses are operated by **Statens Lokaltrafik (SL)** (☎ 600 10 00, www.sl.se) with the T-Bana. Same ticket prices and areas apply as the T-bana. Pre-paid tickets are stamped by the driver or show your travel pass.

By Taxi

Order by telephone, online, or hail taxis in the street. Taxi ranks are found near railway and bus stations. The initial charge is 30 SEK with an additional 80–130 SEK for journeys in the central area. 'Black taxis' are unauthorized, so beware of using them. Use **Taxi Kurir** (☎ 30 00 00, www.taxikurir.se); **Taxi Stockholm** (☎ 15 00 00; www.taxistockholm. se/english); **Taxi 020** (☎ 020 30 30 30, www.taxi020.se).

By Tram

In the summer, tourists take the number 7, which goes past many of the main sights from Norrmalmstorg to Djurgården.

By Car

It really is not worth driving in Stockholm, but if you do it is relatively straightforward. Rush hours are busy 7.30am–9.30am, noon–1pm, and 3.30pm–6pm. The speed limit is 50km/h (31mph), reduced in some areas (near schools and hospitals) to 30km/h (19mph). On roads in and out of the city the limit is 70 km/h (43 mph); on motorways it is 90km/h (55mph). Police use hand-held radar equipment on highways and can impose on the spot fines. The blood-alcohol limit is so low it in effect means no alcohol at all. The penalties of being caught drunk-driving are extremely high.

By Ferry

Many ferry companies operate around Stockholm and into the Archipelago.

Cinderella Båtarna ☎ 58 71 40 00, www.cinderallebatarna. Boats from Nybrokajen on Strandvägen to the inner Archipelago islands such as Grinda, Moja, and Vaxholm.

Strömma Kanalbolaget ☎ 58 71 40 00, www.stromma kanalbolaget.com. Boats leave from Stadshusbron to Birka and Drottning-holm (p 41), and from Strandvägen to Fjäderholmarna (p 158), Vaxholm (p 160), and Sandhamn.

Waxholmsbolaget ☎ 679 58 30, www.waxholmsbolaget.com. Operates most of the traffic in the Archipelago. Boats go from Strömkajen. It also operates the year-round ferry service Slussen–Skeppsholm–Allmänna Gränd. From May to August the boat stops at the Vasamuseet on Djurgården.

By Local Train

You can go into the suburbs and nearby towns by the SL commuter trains, using the same tickets as on the T-bana. The main commuter station is Central Station.

By Bicycle

The city runs **Stockholm City Bikes** with specially designed city-friendly bikes. With over 50 stands all over the city, you get and return one with a card bought from the Tourist Information Center or from the website. Use is restricted to three hours and then you need to hire another one. The season runs from April to October. A 3-day card is 125 SEK; a season ticket is 250 SEK (www.stockholmcitybikes.se). Or hire a bike from Djurgårdsbrons Sjocafé (p 63, bullet **❶**).

On Foot

The best way around Stockholm is by foot. But there are pedestrian traffic rules. Do not cross a road against a red light, although you do have the right of way on zebra crossings without traffic lights. Do not walk in the lanes that are for cyclists (they normally run beside the pavement walking lanes and are marked with the sign of a bicycle) or you may get run into by an irate local.

Fast **Facts**

ACCOMMODATION   Most of Stockholm's hotels are expensive, but there are bargains, particularly in the hostels most of which have high standards. The Swedish capital is a big conference city, and so occupancy is high between May and November, and lower in July. Rates vary according to time of year and are generally cheaper at the weekends. Book through **SVB**'s excellent booking service, in person at the Tourist Office (small fee, p 173), by telephone ☎ 50 82 85 08, or online www.stockholmtown.com. **Destination Stockholm** ☎ 663 00 80, www.destination-stockholm.com offers good rates and packages at the upper end of the scale.

Bed and Breakfast Agencies offer a wide choice at good prices. **Stockholm Guesthouse** www.stockholmguesthouse.com; **Bed and Breakfast Service Stockholm** www.bedbreakfast.a.se, and **Gästrummet (The Guestroom)** www.gastrummet.com.

ATMS/CASHPOINTS Maestro, Cirrus, and Visa cards are readily accepted at all ATMs, which are all over the city from department stores to banks. There are two kinds: Bankomat (the joint system of the business banks) and Uttag (belonging to Swedbank).

Exchange currency either at banks or bureaux de change. **Forex** (www.forex.se) and **X-change** (www.x-change.se) are throughout the city.

BUSINESS HOURS Banks are open Mon–Fri 9am–3pm; some open until 6pm one night a week. Most offices are open Mon–Fri 8.30am–5pm but can close at 3pm in the summer. Most shops open 10am–6pm on weekdays. Smaller shops usually open from 11am–2pm on Saturdays and may have even more restricted hours during the summer. Department stores usually open 10am–7pm on weekdays and 10am or 11am–5pm or 6pm at weekends. Restaurants operate odd times. They are usually open by 11am if they serve lunch; otherwise they open around 5pm. Closing time is around midnight, though they often stay open later particularly if they have a bar. Many restaurants close in July.

DENTAL EMERGENCIES For severe toothache and other emergency dental problems, go to **St Eriks Ögonsjukh,** Fleminggatan, Kungsholmen ☎ 672 31 00, open 7.45am–8.30pm or after 8.30pm to the **Emergency Dental Clinic** (same address) ☎ 32 01 00.

DOCTORS Dial ☎ 112 for an ambulance. For healthcare information (24-hr) ☎ 32 01 00.

ELECTRICITY Along with most of Europe, Sweden has 220-volt AC, 50Hz current and uses two-pin continental plugs. US 110V equipment requires a current transformer.

EMBASSIES **U.S. Embassy,** Dag Hammarskjöldsväg 31, Östermalm (☎ 783 53 00, http://stockholm.usembassy.gov); **Canadian Embassy,** Tegelbacken 4, Norrmalm (☎ 453 30 00, www.canadaemb.se); **UK Embassy,** Skarpögatan 6–8, Östermalm (☎ 671 90 00, www.britishembassy.se); **Australian Embassy**, Sergels Torg 12, Norrmalm (☎ 613 29 00, www.sweden.embassy.gov.au); **New Zealand Embassy**, Nybrogatan 34 Norrmalm, (☎ 660 04 60); **Irish Embassy**, Östermalmsgatan 97, Östermalm (☎ 661 80 05).

EMERGENCIES For ambulance or medical emergencies, fire and police, dial ☎ 112. Central 24-hr emergency services at: **St Görans Sjikhus**, Sanktgöransplan 1, Kungsholmen ☎ 58 70 10 00 (privately owned); **Södersjukhuset**, Ringvagen 52, Södermalm ☎ 616 10 00.

GAY & LESBIAN TRAVELERS Sweden is known as one of Europe's most liberal countries. **RFSL—The Swedish Federation for Lesbian, Gay, Bisexual, and Transgender Rights,** Sveavägen 59 (☎ 501 62 900, www.rfsl.se/stockholm), the national organization for gay and lesbian rights in Stockholm, has a bookshop, restaurant, and club and gives good advice about bars, etc.

The free monthly magazine QX gives useful information on gay venues and produces a map in May.

HOLIDAYS Include January 1 (New Year's Day), January 6 (Feast of the Epiphany), March/April (Good Friday and Easter Monday), 6th Thurs after Easter (Ascension Day), May 1 (May Day), May/June (Whit Monday), June 6 (Swedish National Day), Midsummer Eve (end June), December 25 (Christmas Day), and December 26 (Boxing Day).

INSURANCE Check your existing insurance policies before you buy travel insurance to cover trip cancellation, lost luggage, medical expenses, or car rental insurance. For travel overseas, most US health plans (including Medicare and Medicaid) do not provide coverage, and the ones that do often require payment for services upfront. EU citizens pay a fee for all medical treatment, but must show an EHIC card (UK: www.ehic.org.uk; Ireland: www.ehic.ie).

INTERNET Internet access is plentiful and many hotels and hostels offer free WiFi in your room and in the public areas and also a computer you can use. Otherwise many 7-Elevens, newspaper stands, and grocery stores have Internet access. Try **Sidewalk Express** (www.sidewalkexpress. se) for its many terminals, including City Terminalen. Also **Café Access**, Basement, Kulturhuset, Sergels Torn, Norrmalm ☎ 20 52 10, www.kultur huset.stockholm.se, or **CP & KS Ganes Internet Café**, Lützeg 9 ☎ 709 72 76 27. The main city library, **Stadsbiblioteket**, Sveagen 73 ☎ 508 311 00, offers limited, timed Internet access.

LOST PROPERTY For objects lost on public transport, contact **SL** (Klara Ostra Kyrkogata 4, Norrmalm ☎ 610 00 00). For objects lost on long-distance trains, contact **SJ**

(Central Station, Vasagatan, Norrmalm ☎ 762 25 02).

Call credit card companies the minute you discover your wallet has been lost or stolen and file a report at the nearest police station. **American Express** cardholders and traveler's check holders ☎ 429 54 29; **Diners Club** holders ☎ 14 68 78; **MasterCard** holders ☎ 020 79 13 24; **Visa** holders ☎ 020 79 31 46.

LIQUOR LAWS Most restaurants, pubs, and bars in Sweden are licensed to serve liquor, wine, and beer. Some places are licensed only for wine and beer. Purchases of wine, liquor, and imported beer are available only through the government-controlled monopoly *Systembolaget*. Branch stores, spread throughout the country, are usually open Monday through Friday from 9am to 6pm. The minimum age for buying alcoholic beverages in Swedish restaurants is 18, from Systembolaget you must be 18 to buy beer, but 20 to buy any other alcohol.

MAIL & POSTAGE The main post office is **Posten**, Central Station, Vasagatan, Norrmalm ☎ 020 23 22 21, www.posten.se. For stamps and main services, use the postal kiosks in grocery stores, and **Pressbyrån** kiosks and tourist information offices.

MONEY Sweden voted against joining the European Monetary Union. The Swedish krona (SEK or kr) is divided into 50 öre,100 öre, 1 SEK, 5 SEK, 10 SEK, and notes of 20 SEK, 50 SEK, 100 SEK, 500 SEK and 1,000 SEK. At the time of going to press, the exchange was approximately 1 SEK = $0.15, £0.08, and €0.10. For up-to-the-minute exchange rates between the SEK and other currencies, check the currency converter website **www.xe.com/ucc**.

PASSPORTS No visas are required for US, Canadian, Australian, and

New Zealand visitors to Sweden providing your stay does not exceed 90 days. If your passport is lost or stolen, contact your country's embassy or consulate immediately. See 'Embassies' above. Make a copy of your passport's critical pages and keep it separate from your passport.

PHARMACIES Pharmacies *(apotek)* are identified by a green and white J-shaped sign. They can dispense medicines for minor ailments without a prescription and normally open Mon–Fri 8.30am–6pm. Some open on Saturday. For a 24-hr pharmacy, go to **Apoteket CW Scheele,** Klarabergs-gatan 64, Norrmalm ☎ 458 81 30, www.apoteket.se. For general information, ☎ 0771 450 450.

POLICE The national police emergency number is ☎ 112.

SAFETY Stockholm is a very safe city, but as everywhere, tourists should beware of petty crime in tourist areas and major attractions such as museums, restaurants, hotels, trains, train stations, airports, subways, and ATMs.

SENIOR TRAVELERS Senior Travelers can get discounts on travel and admission to attractions. Carry your ID or passport for verification of your age.

SMOKING A law banning smoking in public places where food and drink is served was passed in 2005. Smoking is forbidden in most public places, including all T-bana stations and bus stop shelters

TAXES The sales tax ('moms' in Swedish) for most items is 25%; but it's 12% on food and hotel bills, and 6% tax on books, movie and concert tickets, and all transport. Non-EU residents are entitled to a reimbursement of the sales tax they have paid. Look for shops offering 'Tax Free' or 'Global Refund' shopping. Forms, obtained from the store where you made your purchase, must be stamped at Customs upon departure. For more information see www.globalrefund.com.

TELEPHONES For national telephone information, ☎ 118 118. For international telephone information, ☎ 118 119. For the national and international operator ☎ 90 200. There are few public telephone kiosks as most people have mobiles. Kiosks are operated by card only, which you buy at newspaper kiosks and in shops. **To make a call within Stockholm, dial 08 before the local number.** To make an international call, dial ☎ 00, the country code, the area code (without the initial 0), and then the local number.

TIPPING The service charge is nearly always included in the bill but if you have had good service, then leave 5–10%. Round up the bill at bars and to taxi drivers.

TOILETS Public toilets are abundant and kept scrupulously clean. The 'toalett' (small green booths) cost 5 SEK.

TOURIST INFORMATION **Stockholm Tourist Centre,** Sverigehuset (Sweden House), Hamngatan 27, Norrmalm, ☎ 50 82 85 08, www.stockholm.town.se, is the main tourist office. It is large, well stocked, and very busy. Get the free monthly magazine *What's On Stockholm* here. You can also book hotels, buy the Stockholm Card, theater and concert tickets, and change money at the Forex exchange bureau. It is open Mon–Fri 9am–7pm, Sat 10am–5pm, Sun 10am–4pm. T-bana Kungsträdgården.

TRAVELERS WITH DISABILITIES Stockholm is a particularly friendly city for disabled travelers with wide pavements and ramps at kerbs for wheelchairs. By Swedish law all public areas must be accessible for both visually and physically disabled people, putting Stockholm way ahead of most other cities. The Tunnelbana has lifts and most buses 'kneel' at bus stops. More information at **De Handikappades Riksförbund**,

Katrinebergsvagen 6, Liljeholmen
☎ 685 80 00, www.dhr.se.

Stockholm: **A Brief History**

550AD–MID-11TH CENTURY The Vikings dominate Sweden.

1008 King Olof Skötkonung converts to Christianity.

1229 Birger Jarl becomes king after deposing Erik Erikssen.

1252 Birger Jarl founds Stockholm with his Tre Kronor fortress on Gamla Stan. The town becomes an important trading center, part of the German Hanseatic League that traded in the Baltic.

1397 Sweden, Norway, and Denmark sign the Kalmar Union, forming a Nordic alliance to challenge the Hanseatic League. It eventually includes Finland, Iceland, and Greenland, becoming the largest kingdom in Europe.

1471 Sten Sture the Elder defeats the Danish King Kristian at the battle of Brunkeberg in Stockholm.

1520 Sten Sture the Younger is killed by the Danish King Christian II who then kills 80 Swedish noblemen at the 'Stockholm Bloodbath'.

1520 Gustav Vasa who had escaped the Bloodbath ousts the Danish King from Sweden.

1523 Gustav Vasa is named King on June 6 (Sweden's National Day). Sweden enters a period of greater prosperity under a hereditary monarchy.

1633–54 Queen Kristina comes to the throne at the age of 6. Her

reign is marked by an emphasis on science and philosophy.

17TH CENTURY The major European Thirty Years War results in the Swedes getting land in northern Germany, parts of Norway, and Danish provinces, and Sweden becomes the most powerful nation in northern Europe.

1697 The Tre Kronor fortress is destroyed by fire.

1709 A devastating defeat at Poltava in Russia marks the end of Sweden as a European great power.

MID-18TH CENTURY Stockholm's population grows to 70,000. Key figures in Sweden's cultural life include Carl von Linné (aka Linnaeus 1707–1778), the philosopher Emanuel Swedenborg (1688–1772), Anders Celsius (1701–1744) inventor of the centigrade temperature scale, and the poet Carl Michael Bellman (1740–1795).

1771–92 Reign of Gustav III, who makes the monarchy absolute after a *coup d'état* in 1772. But in 1792, opposition from the nobles to his absolute power leads to his assassination at a masked ball at the Kungliga Operan in 1792.

1805 His successor, Gustav IV Adolf (1792–1809) is drawn into the Napoleonic Wars on the British side.

1809 Sweden loses Finland in the war against Russia (1808–1809) and the King abdicates.

1810 Parliament chooses one of Napoleon's Marshalls, Jean-Baptiste Bernadotte to become King Karl XIV Johan even though he speaks no Swedish and his wife prefers Paris.

1813 Victory against Napoleon leads to Denmark handing over Norway to Sweden, forming a union, which lasts from 1814 to 1905.

1850–1900 Sweden's farmers and rural workers suffer, but the country's Industrial Revolution brings railways between Stockholm and the rest of the country. Stockholm booms with the steel and safety match industry and the establishment of large industries producing steam engines, cast-iron stoves, and shoes. Lars Magnus Ericsson opens his telephone company in Stockholm in 1876, giving the Swedes the greatest number of phones per capita in Europe.

1860s–1880s Stockholm is transformed by Paris-style town planning. August Strindberg (1849–1912) is an international figure; Artur Hazelius founds the Nordiska Museet and Skansen. The Academy of Stockholm (now the University) is founded in 1878 and in 1896 Alfred Nobel donates his fortune to fund the Nobel Awards.

1900 Despite mass emigration to America (1.5 million leave between the 1850s and 1930s), Sweden's population reaches 5 million with Stockholm at 300,000.

1921 Universal Suffrage for men and women is introduced.

1930s From 1932 to 1972 the Social Democrats rule the country and with the Farmer's Union set about making the welfare state the main plank of Sweden's government.

1939–45 Sweden declares its neutrality in World War II as it had done in World War I. In 1942–3 Raoul Wallenberg, among others, stops the SS deportation of 100,000 Hungarian Jews. Wallenberg is arrested as a spy and disappears, probably dying in a Moscow prison.

1960s Sweden develops its famous Third Way, which combines corporate capitalism with a full-blown welfare state, from cradle to grave.

1970–1990 A booming economy leads to immigration, at its peak in 1969–1970 with over 75,000 people entering Sweden annually. By the mid-1990s, 11% of the population is foreign born. In 1974 the monarch loses all political power.

1982–86 Prime Minister Olof Palme suffers from international economic pressures that begin to attack the Third Way ideal. His assassination in 1986 is a national trauma.

1990s A center-right coalition coincides with a severe recession and a devaluation of the krona. Unemployment is 14% and in 1994 the Social Democrats return to power.

1995 On Jan 1 Sweden joins the European Union.

2000 The Öresund bridge between Denmark and Sweden opens.

2003 Sweden votes to stay outside the single currency zone.

2006 The Social Democrats are defeated by the Alliance—four center-right parties.

Stockholm's **Architecture**

Medieval 12th Century
The city started on Gamla Stan, but there is very little left of the original buildings except the 12th-century defensive wall and later 16th- and 17th-century brick vaults of **Kungliga Slottet** (p 8). The 13th century Royal church and Birger Jarl's Tower remain on Riddarholmen. The renovated Museum of Medieval Stockholm on Norrbro, telling more about this period, will re-open in 2010.

Renaissance, Baroque, and Rococo 16th–18th Century
The golden age of Stockholm's architecture was largely due to one family. Nicodemus Tessin the Elder (1615–1681) designed **Drottningholm Palace** in a wonderfully ornate baroque style; his son Nicodemus Tessin the Younger (1654–1728) designed the **Royal Palace** and other buildings on Gamla Stan (p 59). Gracious buildings such as the Dutch baroque **Riddarhuset** and the magnificent, baroque, 17th century **churches** illustrate Sweden's power as a great nation.

Drottningholm Palace.

Swedish Romanticism and Functionalism (1900s–1930)
Using elements of the late 19th century Jugendstil (best seen in the flamboyant **Kungliga Dramatiska Teatern** of 1908), a Swedish Romantic style appeared, boosted by a rise in nationalist feeling, producing the extraordinary red brick **Stadshuset** of 1923 by Ragnar Östberg (p 8). Buildings such as the **Nordiska museet** (1907) were a Swedish version of Renaissance style (p 13, bullet ❶).

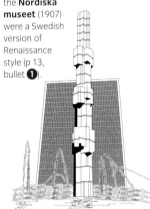

Sergels Torg.

The most famous proponent of the Functionalist style was Gunnar Asplund (p 106) whose great work, the neo-classical **Stadsbiblioteket** (City Library) marked the transition. Functionalism as a part of town planning is seen at **Tessinparken** in Gärdet (p 106, bullet ❺).

Modern Architecture Late 20th and Early 21st Century
The post war period and 1960s saw the destruction of a large part of the city center, replaced by concrete buildings such as the **Kulturhuset** in **Sergels Torg**. They

were luckily stopped before major damage was done to the rest of Stockholm. The building of the **Tunnelbana** in the 1950s led to the development of the suburbs. The most ambitious area is at **Hammarby Sjöstad**, where ecology has taken center stage, resulting in a suburb using recycling and sustainable energy sources.

Stadshuset.

Useful Phrases

Useful Words & Phrases

ENGLISH	SWEDISH	PRONUNCIATION
Hello	Hej	*hay*
How are you?	Hur mår du?	*Hewr mawr dew*
Very well	Mycket bra	*mewkay brah*
Thank you	Tak	*tak*
Pleased to meet you	Trevligt att träffas	*treavlit att traiffas*
Goodbye	Hej då/adjö	*ah-haydaw/ahyour*
Please	Varsågod	*varshawgood*
Yes	Ja	*yah*
No	Nej	*nay*
Excuse me	Ursakta	*ewrshekta*
I would like	Jag skulle vilja	*Yah skewleh vilya*
Do you have . . . ?	Har du/ni...?	*Hahr dew/nee*
What?	Vad?	*Vah*
How much is this?	Hur mycket kostar den har?	*Hewt mewkeh kostar dehn hair*
Do you take credit cards?	Tar du/ni kreditkort?	*Tahr dew/nee kredeetkoort*
Yesterday	Igår	*ee gawr*
Today	Idag	*ee dahg*
Tomorrow	I morgon	*moron*
Good	Bra	*brah*
Enough	Tillråcklig	*tillraikleeg*
Do you speak English?	Talar du/ni engelska?	*Tahlar dew/nee engelska*
Could you speak more slowly please?	Kan du/ni tala långsammare, tack	*kan dew/nee tahla lawngsamareh, tack*
I don't understand	Jag förstår inte	*yah furshtawr inteh*
What time do you open?	Nar öppnar ni?	*Nair urpnar nee*
Call a doctor!	Ring efter en doctor!	*Ring efter ehn doktor*
Do you have any vacancies?	Har ni några lediga rum?	*Hahr nee negra leadiga rewm*
I have a reservation	Jag har beställt rum	*yah hahr bestelt rewm*

Index

See also Accommodations and Restaurant indexes, below.

Index

Accommodations Index

Restaurant Index

Photo **Credits**

day BY day

Frommer's New York City **day BY day**
22 Smart Ways to See the City

Frommer's Barcelona **day BY day**
23 Smart Ways to See the City

Frommer's Shanghai **day BY day**
22 Smart Ways to See the City

Get the best of a city in 1,2 or 3 days

Day by Day Destinations

Europe

Amsterdam
Athens
Barcelona
Berlin
Bordeaux &
  Southwest France
Brussels & Bruges
Budapest
Edinburgh
Dublin
Florence and Tuscany
Lisbon
London
Madrid
Malta & Gozo
Moscow
Paris
Provence & the Riviera

Prague
Rome
Seville
St Petersburg
Stockholm
Valencia
Vienna
Venice

Canada and The Americas

Boston
Cancun & the Yucatan
Chicago
Honolulu & Oahu

Los Angeles
Las Vegas
Maui
Montreal
Napa & Sonama
New York City
San Diego
San Francisco
Seattle
Washington

Rest of the World

Beijing
Hong Kong

Frommer's®
A Branded Imprint of ⓦ**WILEY**

Available wherever books are sold